Lean Six Sigma
Project Execution Guide

The Integrated Enterprise Excellence (IEE) Process Improvement Project Roadmap

Forrest W. Breyfogle III
Founder and CEO
Smarter Solutions, Inc.

Forrest @SmarterSolutions.com
www.SmarterSolutions.com
Austin, TX

Lean Six Sigma Project Execution Guide
The Integrated Enterprise Excellence (IEE) Process Improvement Project Roadmap

Copyright © 2010 by Citius Publishing, Inc. All rights reserved.

Published by Citius Publishing, Inc. Austin, Texas.

Cataloging-in-Publication

Breyfogle, Forrest W., 1946-
    Lean six sigma project execution guide : the
    integrated enterprise excellence (IEE) process
    improvement project roadmap / Forrest W. Breyfogle III.
        p. cm.
    Includes bibliographical references.
    ISBN-13: 978-0-615-34948-0
    ISBN-10: 0-615-34948-X

    1. Project management--Handbooks, manuals, etc.
    2. Six sigma (Quality control standard)--Handbooks,
    manuals, etc.   I. Title.

    HD69.P75B74 2010   658.4'04
                                  QBI10-600018

Printed in the United States of America.

10 9 8 7 6 5 4 3

CONTENTS

PREFACE

The term sigma (σ), in the phrase Six Sigma, is a letter in the Greek alphabet used to describe variability. A sigma quality level metric is an indicator of how often defects are likely to occur. A higher sigma quality level describes a process that is less likely to create defects. A Six Sigma quality level equates to a failure rate of 3.4 defects per million opportunities (dpmo).

The term Lean describes improving operations and the supply chain with an emphasis on the reduction of wasteful activities like waiting, transportation, material hand-offs, inventory, and overproduction. Practitioners often contend as to which comes first, Six Sigma or Lean, or have difficulty integrating the two techniques so that the right activity is done when most appropriate.

Organizations have created Lean Six Sigma programs for executing improvement projects that are to have business financial benefits; however, it is important to note that Lean Six Sigma is not a business system. Lean Six Sigma is a project-based process improvement methodology that organizations have can benefited from; however, silo projects, which do not have business-as-a-whole benefits, need to be avoided.

The *Integrated Enterprise Excellence* (Breyfogle 2008) series of four book-volumes describe the Integrated Enterprise Excellence (IEE) methodology, which structurally integrates and aligns Lean, Six Sigma, and other tools, such as Theory of Constraints (TOC), to business metrics and improvement needs. Within IEE, satellite-level business metrics and 30,000-foot-level operational metrics pull for the most appropriate Six Sigma/Lean tool.

Integrated Enterprise Excellence, Volume II (Breyfogle 2008c) provides a business-system roadmap for integrating predictive scorecards, strategic planning (analytically/innovatively determined), and the creation of improvement projects so that the business as a whole benefits. *Integrated Enterprise Excellence, Volume III* (Breyfogle 2008c) describes a project execution roadmap for continuous improvement, which is an extension of the traditional Define-Measure-Analyze-Improve-Control (DMAIC) roadmap typically encountered in Lean Six Sigma deployments. This book provides in a condensed format the roadmaps for project selection and detailed process improvement project execution for Lean Six Sigma practitioners (e.g., Master Black Belts, Black Belts, and Green Belts) and organizational executives and champions.

Book Objectives

There are many memory-jogger type books, which list the tools of Lean, Six Sigma, and continuous improvement. These books can do a good job explaining tool applications; however, I have not seen a book that links these tools together in a detailed project execution roadmap format. There can be many benefits from the utilization of a document, which offers a consistent roadmap-delivered methodology that can be readily referenced when executing organizational improvement projects. This roadmap-document fulfills this need and also provides a vehicle which expedites the tool-application learning process and improves the efficiency/effectiveness of experienced-practitioner coaching sessions.

In addition to project selection, this workbook provides the following deliverables for a successful process improvement project completion:

- List of deliverables and suggested tools: High-level summary of what is expected in each phase and what tools you may consider.
- Road maps: A detailed step-by-step process of selecting and applying various Six Sigma/Lean tools and techniques to meet all the project deliverables. Shadow boxes indicate there is a drill down sub-process roadmap included on a following page.
- Check sheets: High-level check lists for each project phase which can be used by Black Belts, Green Belts, Champions, and/or executives to ensure that all major phase requirements have been met.
- Tools: A high-level description of many tools where there is reference to Volume III or II of the IEE book series for more details.
- Statistical program execution: Described tool-application techniques are independent of statistical software; however, I did include the syntax for tool execution in Minitab.

Deviations from "Standard" Lean Six Sigma

Sometimes a reader asks why I have drilled down the measure phase into additional categories. The reason I did this is that when I wrote the book *Implementing Six Sigma* in 1999 I positioned tools in the phase where I understood that GE had placed them in their roadmap. However, I thought that many people would have difficulty relating to some of GE's-measure-phase tools as a measurement tool. Because of this, I decided to add additional measure-phase drill downs, which had more descriptive titles.

In the 2nd edition of *Implementing Six Sigma*, I added Lean Considerations as another measure-phase drill down. Some large proponents of Lean tell me that they believe that value stream mapping should be the first thing that is done when executing a project. My thinking is different. In my opinion, a project measurement quantification should be made first and let the measurement improvement need dictate which tool is used to facilitate that improvement. For example, if the 30,000-foot-level metric is lead time then a value stream map could be the most appropriate next tool; however, if the project measurement is defective rate then a Design of Experiment (DOE) might be the best next-step-application tool.

Nomenclature and Service Marks

The first page of each chapter includes a flowchart, which describes the execution steps of a project roadmap phase. Shaded execution steps within these descriptions indicate that additional drill downs are provided on one or more of the following pages.

The Appendix describes referenced book details. The referencing syntax to these other publications (e.g., beginning of book sections) has the example forms: *Integrated Enterprise Excellence, Volume III* (Breyfogle 2008c), where "c" indicates that this is the third listed author publication for the year or *IEE Volume III*, Section 8.2. The syntax for figure or table references in this volume series is that the first number is the chapter number. The Glossary and List of Acronyms and Symbols near the back of this book are a useful reference for the understanding of unfamiliar statistical terms or acronyms/symbols.

Integrated Enterprise Excellence, IEE, satellite-level, 30,000-foot-level, and 50-foot-level are registered marks of Smarter Solutions, Inc. In implementing the program or methods identified in this text, you are authorized to refer to these marks in a manner that is consistent with the standards set forth herein by Smarter Solutions, Inc., but any and all use of the marks shall be inure to the sole benefit of Smarter Solutions, Inc. Business Way of Life and Smarter Solutions are registered service marks of Smarter Solutions, Inc.

Acknowledgments

I want to thank Rick Haynes, Mallary Musgrove, and Dorothy Stewart for their help with this book. Rick provided great inputs to the selection of book content from Smarter Solutions' material and composure of some material that amplified key concepts. Mallary did a great job managing the books publication/distribution process. Dorothy provided great editing in a very timely fashion. I want to also thank my wife, Becki Breyfogle, who has been very supportive of this effort, which involved the sacrifice of family time for this book to become a reality.

Statistical charts were created using Minitab. Flowcharts were created using Igrafx.

About Smarter Solutions, Inc., Contacting the Author

Your comments and improvement suggestions for this book are greatly appreciated. For more information about business measurements and improvement systems, sign up for our newsletter or webinars. Over 100 articles, videos, and information about our training, coaching, and consulting is available on our website.

FORREST W. BREYFOGLE III
Smarter Solutions, Inc. (P. O. Box 202644, Austin, TX 78720)
Forrest@SmarterSolutions.com
www.SmarterSolutions.com
512-918-0280

0   Improvement Project Selection and Execution Roadmap

Reference: *IEE Volume II*, Chapters 6 – 12

The financials of an enterprise are a result of the integration and interaction of its processes, not of individual procedures in isolation. Using a whole-system perspective, one realizes that the output of a system is a function of its weakest link or constraint. If care is not exercised, one can be focusing on a subsystem that, even though improved, does not impact the overall system big-picture output.

0.1   Selecting Projects that Positively Impact the Business as a Whole

In Lean Six Sigma and Lean kaizen event programs, improvement projects are often selected from a list of potential opportunities that were determined from a brainstorming session. This effort might provide some initial gains when starting a deployment; however, this effort typically stalls out, and the process improvement teams are laid off when times get tough. The reason for this downsizing is that often process improvement efforts are not expended in areas where the overall enterprise benefits the most; e.g., sales and marketing when excess production capacity is available.

Process improvement efforts need to focus on the orchestration of efforts so that this work concentrates on overall system optimization, not on individual procedure component improvement. Unfortunately, organizational-chart-functional thinking can result in competing forces for process improvement efforts, where much of this work leads to siloed projects that do not benefit the enterprise as a whole.

With Theory of Constraints (TOC), systems are viewed as a whole, and work activities are directed so that whole-system-performance measures are improved. To illustrate this, consider the following system graphic, which is not unlike water flow through a garden hose: the squeezing of one portion of the hose reduces water flow volume; i.e., step 5 in the figure.

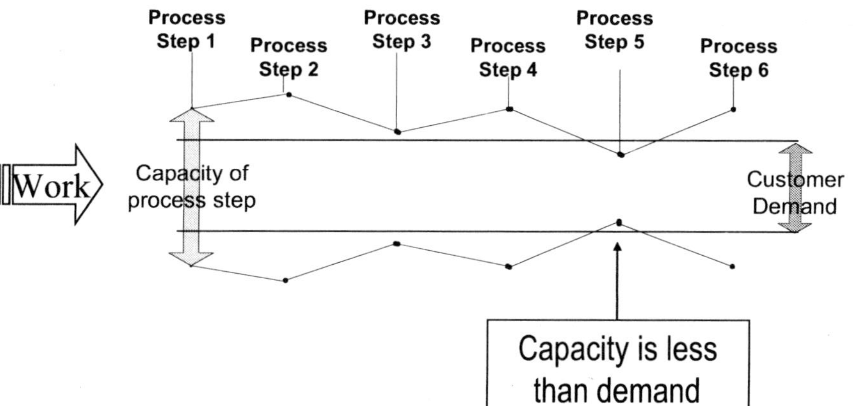

From Figure 10.1 *Integrated Enterprise Excellence, Volume II – Business Deployment: A Leader's Guide for Going Beyond Lean Six Sigma and the Balanced Scorecard*, Forrest W. Breyfogle III, Bridgeway Books, 2008.

Without considering the whole system, we might be spending a great deal of time and effort working on process step 2 because this step is not meeting its localized-created target objectives relative to operating efficiencies, equipment utilization, etc. If we consider the figure to represent a series of departments through which a transaction is processed, where each step has a separate manager who is trying to support a strategy to improve the capacity of the business, without the theory of constraints concept, each department would apply resources to improve its step only. This would create a situation in which only 1/6th of the improvement resources are being applied to the single location that is limiting the system capacity. From this figure, we note that improvements to process step 2 will not significantly impact the overall system and may actually degrade the overall metrics if additional WIP is created from the improvements.

The TOC system chain extends from market demand through the organization chain to suppliers. Let's consider an example when this high-level view of the overall system is not addressed. An organization works at improving internal process efficiencies. Capacity then increases. Excess inventory is then created because there is not sufficient demand. It is then discovered that the constraint is really the sales and marketing process.

Within an organization, there are often constraints that we may or may not consider. Types of constraints include market, resource, material, supplier, financial, and knowledge/competency. We need to look at the rules (i.e., policies) that drive the constraints.

0.2   Project Identification using Theory of Constraints

In this example, I will use terms typically associated with manufacturing; however, the concepts apply equally to transactional processes. In the following graphically described system, raw materials are processed through four component steps to produce a finished product.

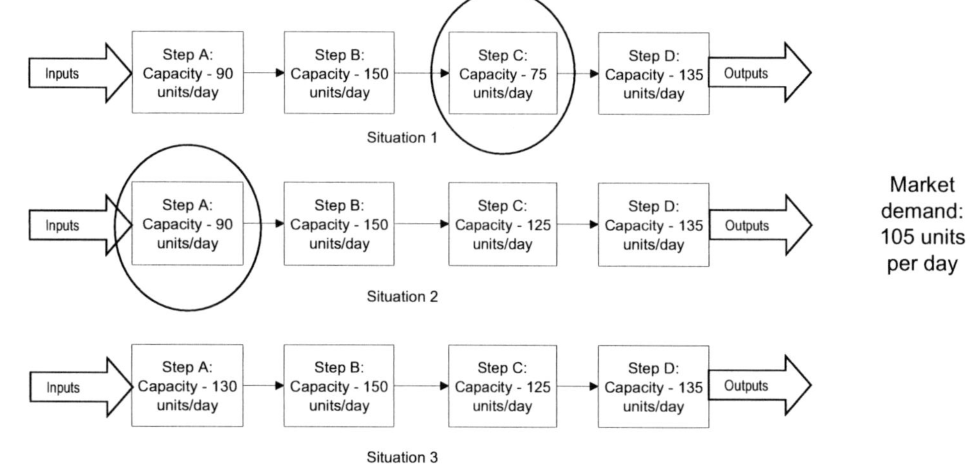

From Figure 10.1 *Integrated Enterprise Excellence, Volume II – Business Deployment: A Leader's Guide for Going Beyond Lean Six Sigma and the Balanced Scorecard,* Forrest W. Breyfogle III, Bridgeway Books, 2008.

Each process step is an overall value stream link. The capacity of each step is described in the figure along with the market demand of 105 units per day. The goal is to make as much money as possible from the process.

From the examination of situation 1 in the figure, it is noted that the capacity of Step C is 75, which is less than the market demand of 105. Even though other steps in our value stream process may not be performing up to their equipment utilization and efficiency goals, focus should be given first to increasing the capacity of Step C. From this enterprise-system analysis, Step C would be an opportunity for a Lean Six Sigma improvement project.

Upon completion of this project for Step C, the process then exhibited the characteristics of situation 2 shown in the figure. An analysis of this situation indicates that the constraint is now at Step A. From this enterprise system analysis, it would now be appropriate for a Lean Six Sigma project to focus on Step A.

Upon completion of a Lean Six Sigma project of Step A, the process then started exhibiting the characteristics of situation 3. An analysis of this situation indicates that all four steps of the process have enough capacity to meet the market demand. The internal system constraints relative to satisfying a market demand of 115 units per day have been removed. The constraint has moved outside the system to the market place. The next Lean Six Sigma project should focus on determining what can be done to increase product demand through improvements in the marketing and sales processes.

This example illustrated the importance of starting by analyzing the big picture to determine where efforts should focus when creating projects. Losing sight of the big picture can lead to the ineffective utilization of resources and the sub-optimization of processes.

0.3 Shortcomings of Traditional Process Improvement Efforts and Resolution

The implementation of traditional Total Quality Management (TQM) and Lean Six Sigma has often been accomplished by dividing the system into processes and then optimizing the quality of each process. This approach is preferable to chasing symptoms; however, new problems can be created if the individual process is not considered in concert with other processes that it affects.

The theory of constraints approach focuses on reducing system bottlenecks as a means to continually improve the performance of the entire system. Rather than viewing the system in terms of discrete processes, TOC addresses the larger systematic picture as a chain or grid of interlinked chains. The performance of the weakest link determines the performance of the whole chain.

TOC considers three dimensions of system performance in the following order: throughput (total sales revenues minus the total variable costs for producing a product or service), inventory (all the money which a company invests in items it sells), and operating expense (money a company spends transforming inventory into throughput). Focus on these dimensions can lead a company to abandon traditional management cost accounting while at the same time causing an improvement in competitive price advantage.

0.4   Application of TOC in an Overall Business System for Project Identification

The IEE system consists of the following 9-steps, as described in *Integrated Enterprise Excellence, Volume III* (Breyfogle 2008b):

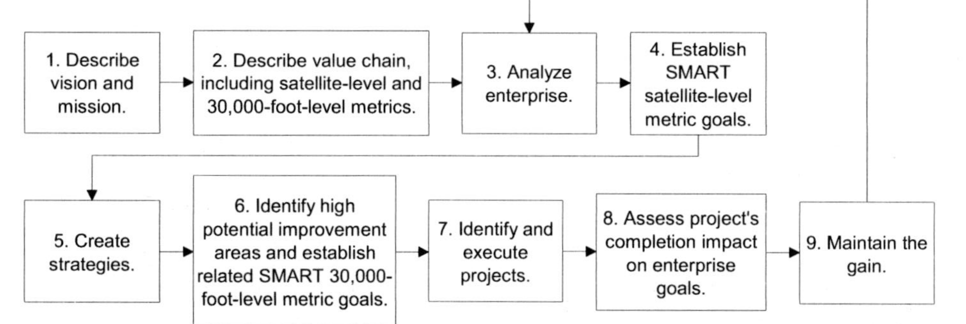

From Figure 4.7 *Integrated Enterprise Excellence, Volume II – Business Deployment: A Leader's Guide for Going Beyond Lean Six Sigma and the Balanced Scorecard,* Forrest W. Breyfogle III, Bridgeway Books, 2008.

TOC would be part of the Integrated Enterprise Excellence "analyze enterprise" (step 3), which would provide input to the following sequence:
1. Determination of realistic business financial goals (step 4).
2. Creation of analytically/innovatively determined targeted strategies (step 5).
3. Identification of potential improvement focused areas (step 6).
4. Recognition of targeted projects so that the business as a whole benefits (step 7).

In IEE, targeted alignment of projects to the overall business needs is conveyed through an Enterprise Improvement Plan (EIP), as illustrated in:

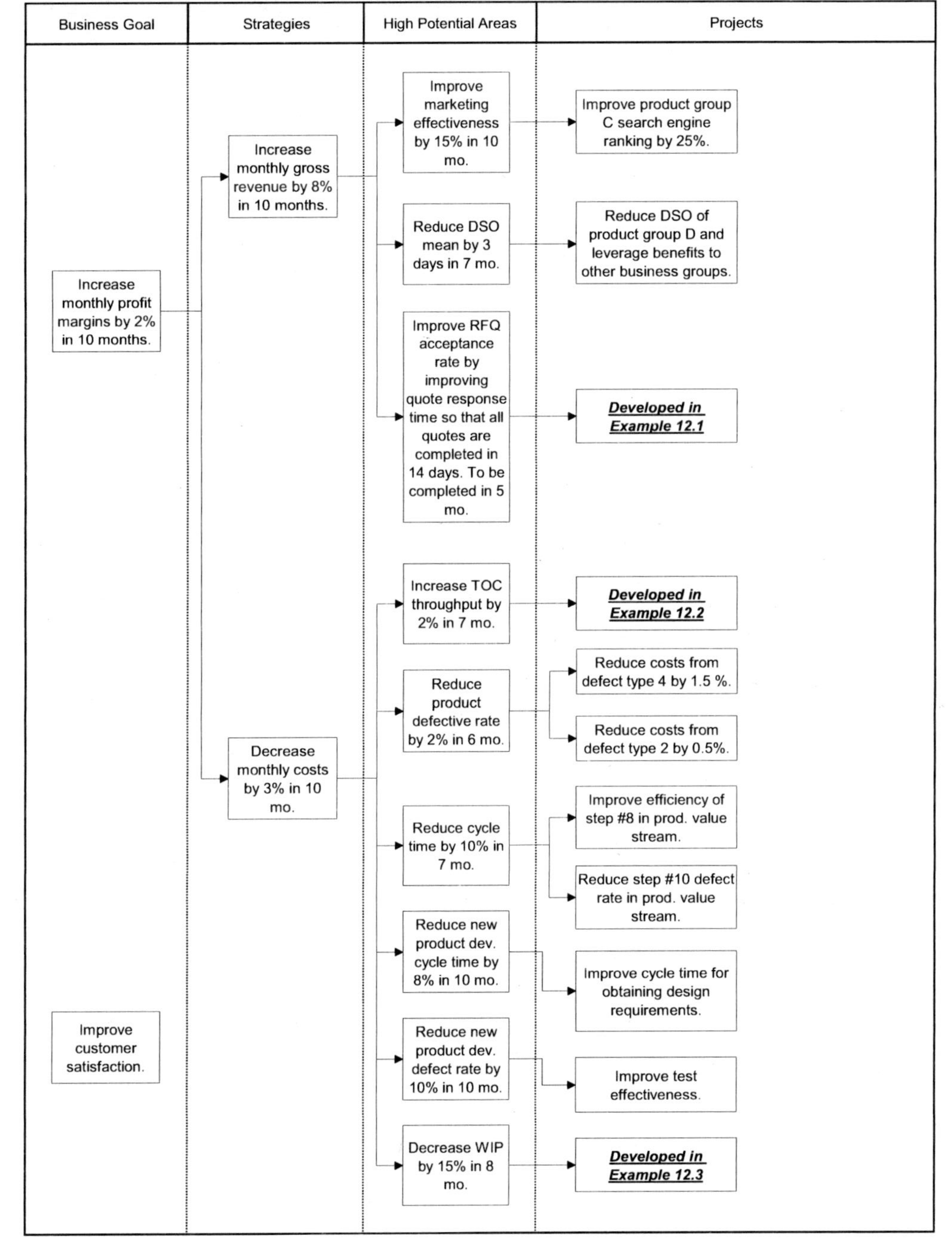

From Figure 12.1 *Integrated Enterprise Excellence, Volume II – Business Deployment: A Leader's Guide for Going Beyond Lean Six Sigma and the Balanced Scorecard,* Forrest W. Breyfogle III, Bridgeway Books, 2008.

The integration of TOC within the Integrated Enterprise Excellence system provides an overall business-management system so that Lean Six Sigma and Lean kaizen events can be targeted to improve the overall enterprise financials.

0.5   Integrating IEE Business System with Project Execution Roadmap

In IEE, the business system for integrating predictive scorecards with analytically/innovatively determined strategies and then executing projects that truly benefit the business as a whole is described in the following graphic, where Project Define-Measure-Analyze-Improve-Control (P-DMAIC) and design projects are linked to the improvement phase of the overall business system E-DMAIC roadmap.

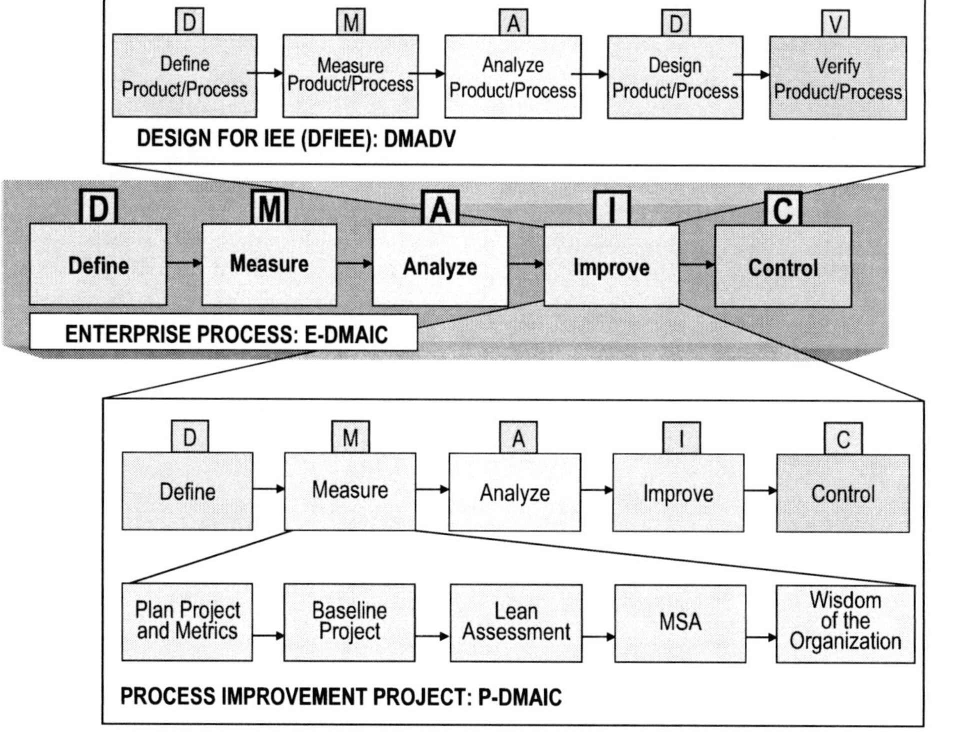

From Figure 4.2 Integrated Enterprise Excellence, Volume II – Business Deployment: A Leader's Guide for Going Beyond Lean Six Sigma and the Balanced Scorecard, Forrest W. Breyfogle III, Bridgeway Books, 2008.

0.6   Improvement Project P-DMAIC Phases, Purposes and Deliverables

Phase		Purpose	Deliverables
Define		To determine the organizational issue and define the scope of the project	Problem statement Team charter, SIPOC Initial financial benefits
M E A S U R E	Plan Project and Metrics	To plan the scope of work with timeline and define additional metrics	Process description Determine additional performance metrics Data collection plan (if needed) Develop project plan with timeline
	Baseline Project	To determine current process performance that provides a baseline to judge the improvement.	Baseline predictability assessment Process capability/performance assessment Updated CODND financial estimate
	Lean Assessment	To evaluate the process using lean tools and philosophy	A lean assessment of the process Applicable lean-tools applications
	Measurement System Analysis	To determine current measurement system performance and validity	Measurement system analysis Identification of measurement system issues A capable measurement system
	Wisdom of the Organization	To include a broad range of inputs from experienced members of the organization describing the current process	Detailed process description (process map) List of low-hanging-fruit problems for immediate improvement A prioritized list of potential problem causes to evaluate in analyze phase
Analyze		To identify and analyze data for improvement opportunities	Data relationships between problem and causes based on evidence Validate input and output process variables Prioritized list of improvement opportunities that are to be evaluated in the improve phase.
Improve		To improve process performance based on data analysis and other assessments	Quantified relationships between process inputs and outputs Quantification of improved process predictability and capability Implemented changes Demonstrated improvement
Control		To control variation sources and maintain the gains realized from improvement actions	Documentation of process changes Control plan with hand off to process owner Final report Communication of results and leveraging opportunities Financial audit of results

1   P-DMAIC: Define Phase

Purpose: To determine the organizational issue and define the scope of the project

Deliverables:

- Problem statement
- Team charter
- SIPOC
- Initial financial benefits

Reference: Chapters 4 & 5 of *Integrated Enterprise Excellence, Volume III* (Breyfogle 2008c)

1.1   Roadmap

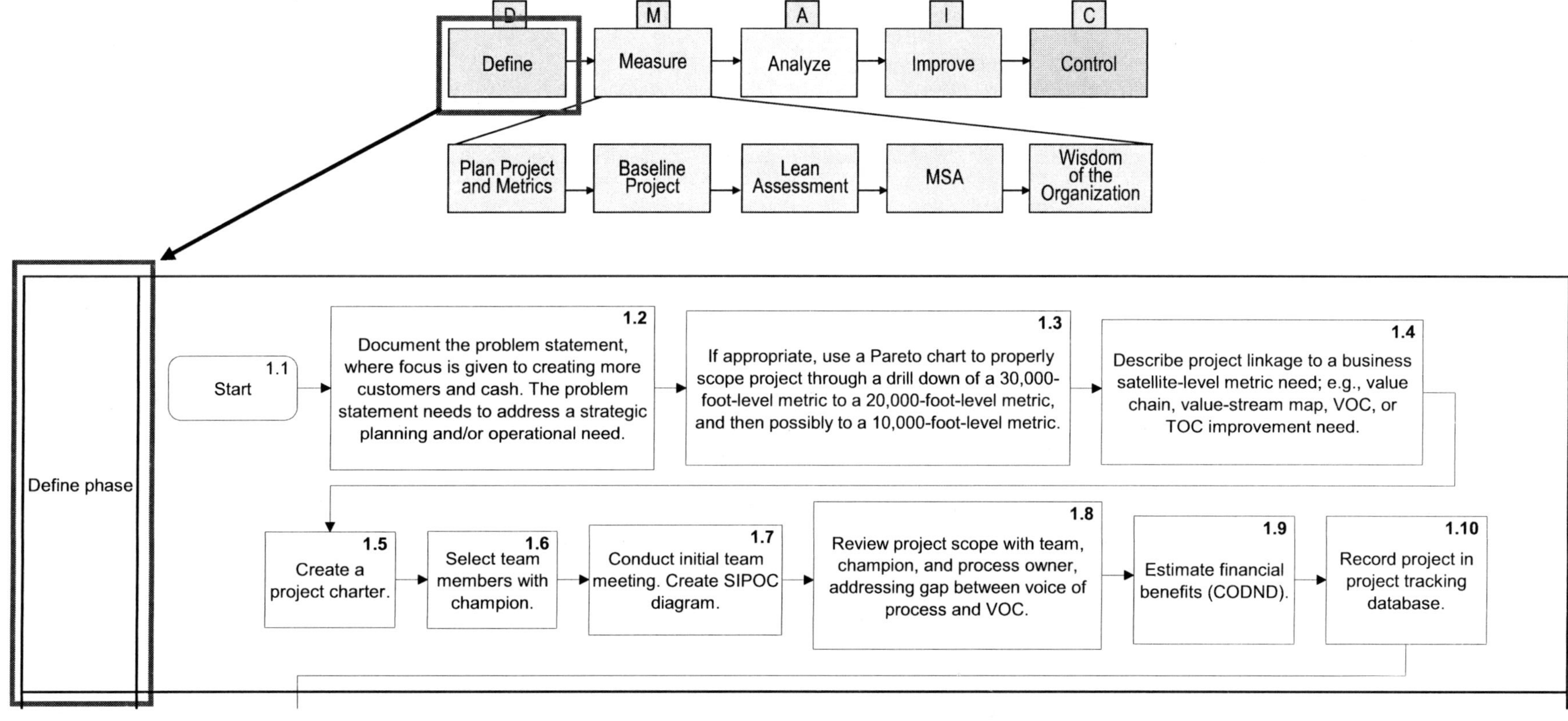

1.2 Check Sheet

Define Phase Check Sheet		
Description	**Questions**	**Yes/No NA**
Tool/Methodology		
Project selection	Is the project aligned with a company goal and current needs?	
	Is this the best project to be working on at this time?	
COPQ/CODND	Was a rough estimate of COPQ/CODND used to determine potential benefits?	
	Is there agreement on how hard/soft financial benefits will be determined?	
Problem Statement	KPOV is defined and quantifiable?	
	KPOV links to customer requirements and business goals?	
	Impact is quantified based on process data?	
	Data source and measurement method are indicated?	
	No stated or predetermined solutions?	
	Outlines scope of the project?	
Project description	Completed a gap analysis of what the customer of the process needs versus what the process is delivering?	
	Completed a goal statement with measurable targets?	
	Created an SIPOC which includes the primary customer and key requirements of the process?	
	Completed a visual representation of what high-level value chain metric is to be improved by the project?	
	Completed an EIP visual representation of how the project aligns with the organization's goals?	
Project charter	Are the roles and goals of the team clear to all members and upper management?	
	Has the team reviewed and accepted the charter?	
	Is the project scoped sufficiently?	
Communication plan	Is there a communication plan for communicating project status and results to appropriate levels of the organization?	
	Has the project been recorded in a S^4/IEE database?	
Team		
Resources	Does the team include cross-functional members/process experts?	
	Are all team members motivated and committed to the project?	
	Is the process owner supportive of the project?	
	Is the champion supportive of the project?	
	Has a kickoff team meeting been held?	
Next Phase		
Approval to proceed	Did the team adequately complete the above steps?	
	What is the detailed plan for the Measure Phase?	
	Are barriers to success identified and planned for?	

1.3 *Problem Statement*

Roadmap Step: 1.2
Reference: *IEE Volume III*, Section 4.7

- Purpose
  - To describe the problem and estimate its impact
- To gain agreement with sponsor, champion, Black Belt, and team on the problem the project will address
- What is it?
  - A two-three sentence problem statement needs to focus on the symptoms and not the possible solution
  - Customer and business impact information should be included along with current nonconformance rate or other baseline information, data sources for problem analysis, and a COPQ/CODND estimate
- Example:
  On-time deliveries of Product ABC ordered from our website for the past 12 months are averaging 70%, as measured from shipping reports. This non-compliances rate results in customer complaints, increased shipping costs and lost sales.
  - Shipping penalties totaled $120,000 in the last six months; lost sales have not yet been quantified but are thought to exceed $1 million per year
  - On-time shipment has dropped from 85% to 70% in the last nine months
    On-time shipment is defined as arriving on the date requested by the customer

  Note: This example illustrates how a 30,000-foot-level operational metric within an IEE enterprise can pull (using a lean term) for the creation of a project.

1.4 *Project Drill-Down*

Roadmap Step: 1.3

- Purpose
  - Provide consideration on narrowing the project scope from the initial problem statement.
  - As the problem statement develops, information may be found that indicates the project focus may need to change to address part of the 30,000-foot-level metric problem. The new project scope may be called a 20,000-foot-level metric.
- What it is
  - For attribute projects, a Pareto chart may be the appropriate tool to identify a subset of the problems that will be the focus of the improvement project.
  - When the goal is to reduce time or cost, Pareto charts of the time or cost by process step may also help focus the improvement efforts.

1.5   Project Linkage

Roadmap Step: 1.4
Reference: *IEE Volume III*, Section 3.6

- Purpose
  - Connects the project goal to a satellite level organizational metric, organizational strategy, and organizational goal.
  - Ensures that the improvement project is targeting a true need of the organization. Projects that are difficult to link to a true organizational need are generally more difficult to complete and may not obtain support for implementation.
- What it is
  - A great tool to diagram the linkage is the Enterprise Improvement Plan (EIP), a tool used in the E-DMAIC.
  - Any linkage to true organizational needs will not only improve the support for the project with the leadership but also with the team members.

1.6   Project Charter

Roadmap Step: 1.5
Reference *: IEE Volume III*, Section 4.9

- Purpose
  - To clearly communicate project goals and team member responsibilities.
  - To create a sense of ownership for the project.
- What it is
  - A contract between the project champion and the Black Belt, the champion representing the sponsor and the Black Belt representing the team.
  - The handoff of the project from the champion to the Black Belt and team.
  - A written document that details the roles, responsibilities, and metrics-expected benefits for the project.
  - A tool to ensure that the project supports the company's strategy.

Template: can be found in *IEE Volume III*, Figure 4.4

1.7   Team Selection

Roadmap Step: 1.6
Reference: *IEE Volume III*, Chapter 5

When initiating teams, it is important to have members who have the appropriate skill sets; e.g., self-facilitation and technical/subject-matter expertise. The teams should have an appropriate number of members and representation. When launching a team, it is important to have a clear purpose, goals, commitment, ground rules, roles, and responsibilities set for the team members. Schedules, support from management, and team empowerment issues must also be addressed.

Team dynamics and performance issues must also be addressed, such as:

1. Team-building techniques that address goals, roles, responsibilities, introductions, and stated/hidden agenda.

2. Team facilitation techniques that include applying coaching, mentoring, and facilitation techniques that guide a team to overcome problems; e.g., overbearing, dominant, or reluctant participants. In addition, the unquestioned acceptances of opinions as facts, feuding, floundering, rush to accomplishment, attribution, digressions, tangents, etc.

3. Measurement of team performance in relationship to goals, objectives, and metrics.

4. Use of team tools such as nominal group technique, force-field analysis, and other similar methodologies.

1.8   Tool: SIPOC

Roadmap Step: 1.7
Reference: *IEE Volume III*, Section 4.3

- Purpose
  - To clearly communicate project scope.
  - The project scope is to improve the process steps or the quality of the inputs.
- What it is
  - The SIPOC (Supplier, Input, Process, Outputs, Customer).
  - A high-level diagram that relates the suppliers to the customers. There are typically only 5 to 7 process steps in a SIPOC diagram.
  - Should relate to the Organizational Value Chain.
  - First step in creating a process view of the business issue being addressed by the project.
  - The inputs and suppliers are only identified in general terms and are just lists that do not align in rows.
  - The outputs and customers are only identified in general terms and are just lists that do not align in rows.
  - Items or information passed between process steps are not listed as inputs or outputs.

$$Y = f(X)$$

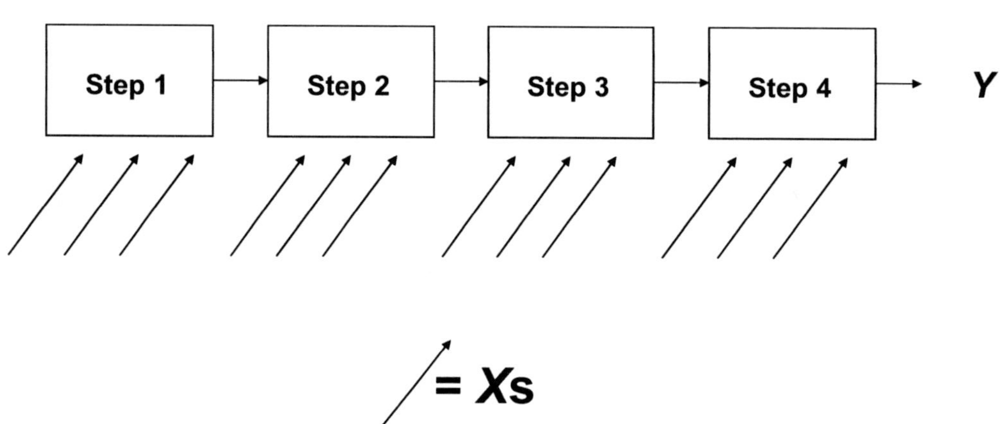

From Figure 2.6 *Integrated Enterprise Excellence, Volume III – Improvement Project Execution: A Management and Black Belt Guide for Going Beyond Lean Six Sigma and the Balanced Scorecard,* Forrest W. Breyfogle III, Bridgeway Books, 2008.

Example

Suppliers	Inputs	Process	Outputs	Customers
AOM system	Flat data files	Receive flat files from system.	Reports	PPMs
QAD system	Orders/invoices	Execute programs to create reports.	Report files	Site Managers
	Inventory	Transmit reports to their destinations.	Data files	Executives
		Process report data to create finshed service reports.		
		Publish the final reports.		

1.9 Communication Plan

Roadmap Step: 1.8

Stakeholders for a project include customers, sponsors, managers, and process operators. A plan needs to be developed for keeping participants and stakeholders involved and/or informed about project status. This is the first effort to understand the needs of the organization and contact all the stakeholders to understand their needs and how they want to keep informed on the team effort. All stakeholders are not necessarily on the team, but most just stay informed.

1.10 Project's Financial Benefits

Roadmap step: 1.9

In traditional Lean Six Sigma, financial considerations for undertaking a project are often expressed in terms of cost of poor quality (COPQ). In IEE, a cost of doing nothing different (CODND) quantification expands the implication of this assessment.

Project benefits are usually classified as hard or soft savings. Hard savings are either above or below the operating profit line. Soft savings have indirect benefits. Above the operating profit line examples are cost reduction and revenue enhancement. Below the operating profit line examples are working capital reductions and cost avoidance.

Categories of hard savings are:

- Revenue Increase (collections, sales, capacity, lead time)
- Labor reduction (salary, wages, overtime, benefits)
- Other Fixed Savings (travel, communications, pagers, cell phones, shipping, utilities)

Soft Savings may be quantified, but the estimation method should follow a common set of rules used throughout the organization.

The decision on hard and soft savings is the most controversial part of an improvement program. One point to keep in mind is that hard savings must be for the entire organization, not for just a single profit/loss center. A common error is to declare a hard savings for a labor reduction in a department when the person is just transferred to another department and the entire organization staffing does not change. This shifting of labor should be considered as a soft savings.

2   P-DMAIC: Measure Phase – Planning and Metrics

Purpose: To plan the scope of work with timeline and define additional metrics
Deliverables:

- Process description
- Determine additional performance metrics
- Data collection plan (if needed)
- Develop project plan with timeline

Reference: Chapters 6 & 7 of *Integrated Enterprise Excellence, Volume III* (Breyfogle 2008c)

2.1   Roadmap

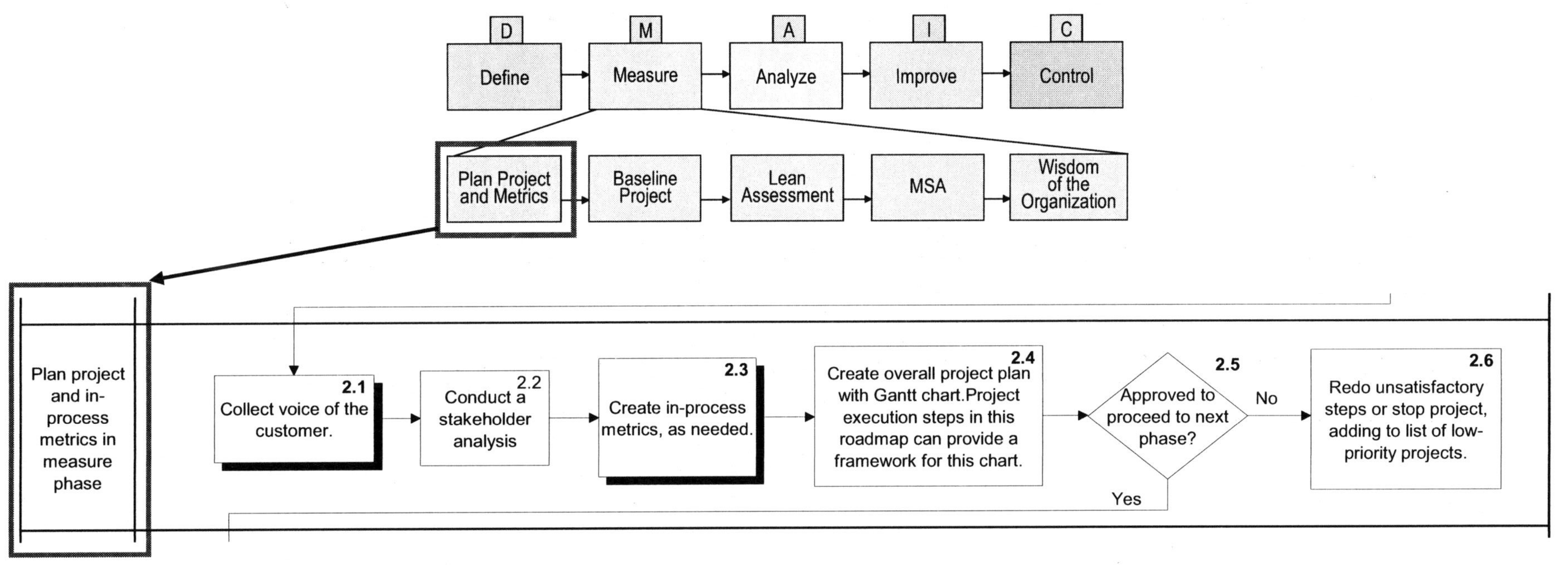

Step 2.1 drill down

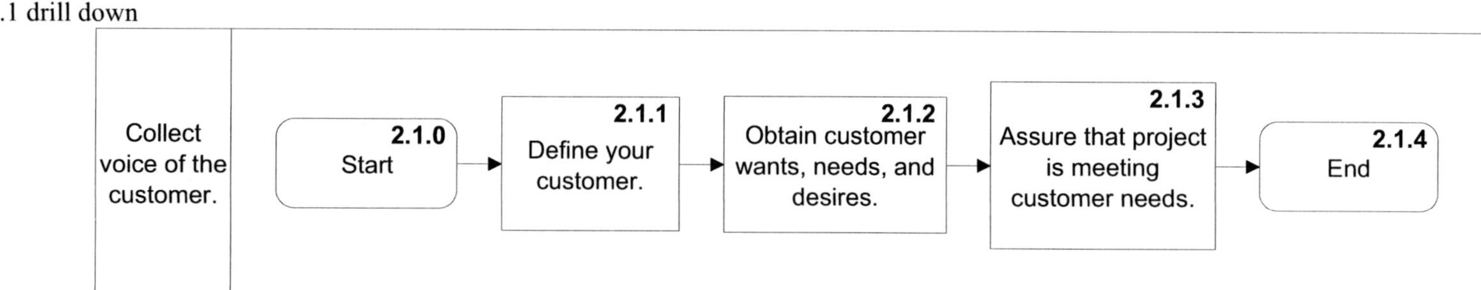

Step 2.3 drill down

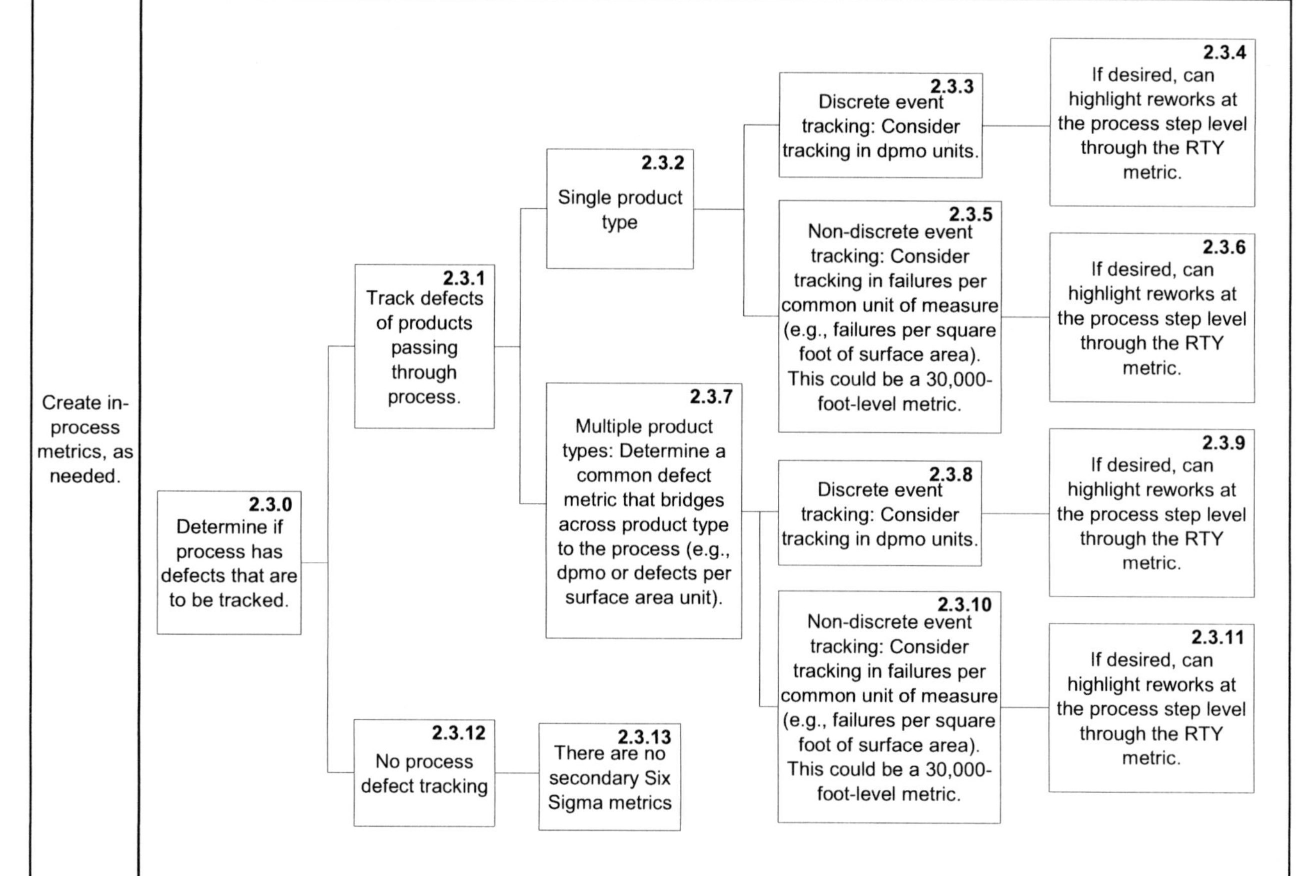

2.2 Check Sheet

Description	Questions	Yes/No NA
Measure Phase: Plan Project and Metrics Check Sheet		
Tool/Methodology		
KPOV	Are the key process output variables clearly defined?	
	Were the most appropriate metrics chosen in order to give insight into the process (continuous vs. attribute)?	
	Were continuous data used when available?	
Secondary Six Sigma metrics	Are any secondary Six Sigma metrics such as DPMO and RTY going to be used?	
Financial metrics	Has there been finalized with Finance how financial benefits will be calculated?	
	Does the project include any cost avoidance, improved efficiency, improved customer satisfaction or other soft money considerations?	
Voice of the customer	Did the team identify key internal and external customers of the project process?	
	Did the team speak with customers of the project process?	
	Has this customer input been included in the project description and scope?	
Project plan	Are project milestones identified?	
	Is the project time line reasonable and acceptable?	
Team		
Resources	Are team members and key stakeholders identified and engaged?	
	Are all team members motivated and committed to the project?	
	Is the process owner committed to the project?	
Next Phase		
Approval to proceed	Did the team adequately complete the above steps?	
	Has the project database been updated and communication plan followed?	
	Is there a detailed plan for baselining the project?	
	Are barriers to success identified and planned for?	
	Is the team tracking with the project schedule?	
	Have schedule revisions been approved?	

2.3　Project Customer Definition and Information Sources

Roadmap Step: 2.1
Reference: *IEE Volume III*, Section 6.4

In a SIPOC, suppliers of a customer focus on what they do in a process; i.e., lead time, cost, and defects. Customers focus on their needs; i.e., delivery, price, and quality. Process output variables provide a voice of the process quantification. Process output specifications are a quantification of the voice of the customer needs. The overlay of specifications on process output distributions quantifies customer do/need gap.

A step-by-step process to obtain project voice of the customer input is:

1. Define your customer.

2. Obtain customer's wants, needs, and desires.

It is important to insure that project is meeting customer needs. Voice of the customer can originate from many sources:

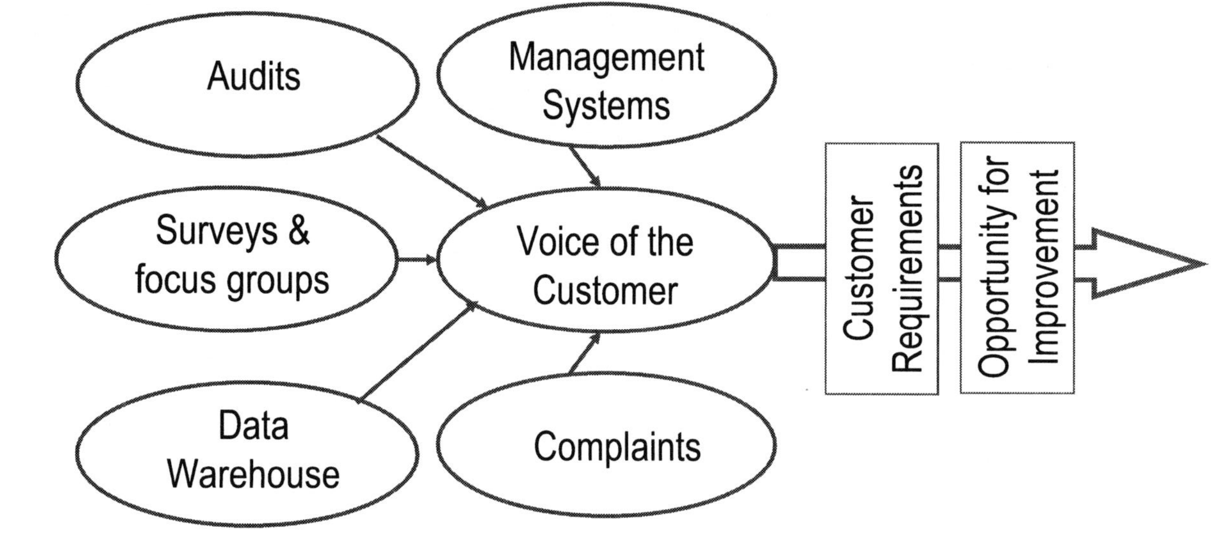

From Figure 6.1 *Integrated Enterprise Excellence, Volume III – Improvement Project Execution: A Management and Black Belt Guide for Going Beyond Lean Six Sigma and the Balanced Scorecard,* Forrest W. Breyfogle III, Bridgeway Books, 2008.

Needs, Wants, and Desires of the customer are best considered using the Kano model. Project metrics are typically considered as wants or one-dimensional quality metrics in this model. The customer voice that relates to the needs or take-for-granted quality issues, when not met, may be more a serious issue than the improvement project focus. Any customer voice which is considered as a desire or attractive quality is generally not considered in the project scope at this point. They may be re-addressed in the improve phase.

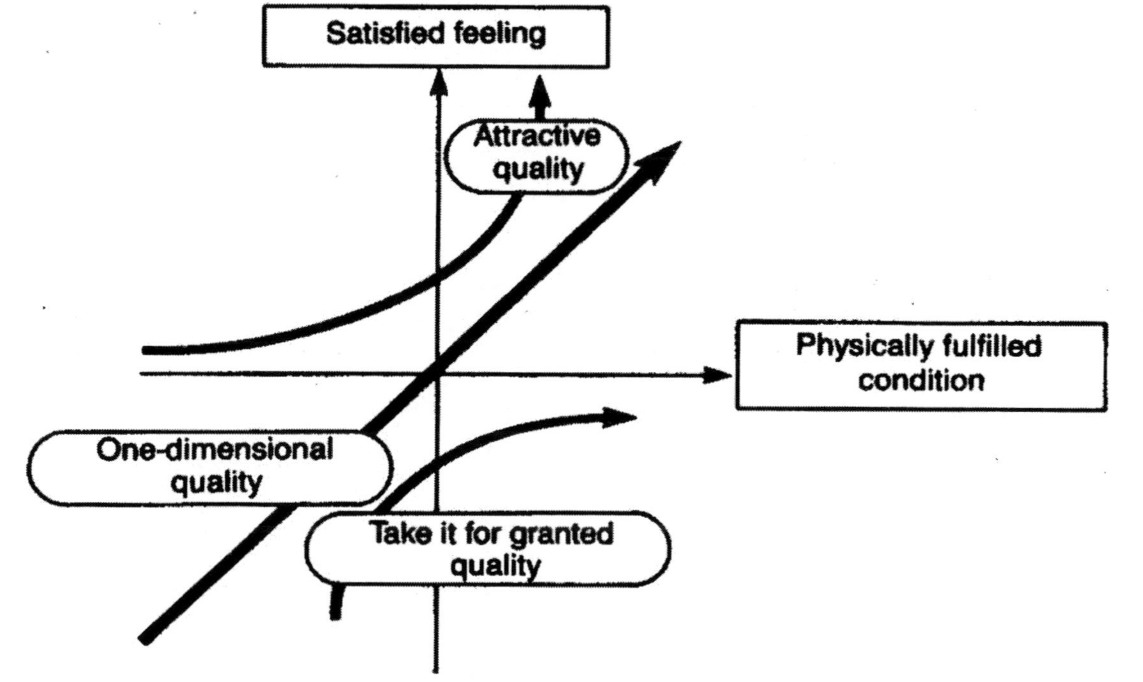

Noriaki Kano's description of customer's feelings

2.4   In-process Metrics (e.g., DPMO)

Roadmap Step: 2.2
Reference: *IEE Volume III*, Sections 6.5 – 6.8

The following two sections describe the calculation defects per million opportunities (DPMO) and rolled throughput yield (RTY). The Six Sigma metric, sigma quality level, is described in Appendix Section B1 of *IEE Volume III* (Breyfogle 2008c).

Six Sigma deployments have traditionally emphasized the quantification of DPMO for all projects. Selecting the proper project metrics is critical to driving the right behavior. Business metrics should make sense, be easy to understand, and be independent of who is compiling the metrics. Organizations that require a DPMO rate or sigma-quality-level metric for every project will find that this metric can often be very subjective. For example, what is a defect when the 30,000-foot-level metric is inventory level? There is none. Whenever there is not a true specification, organizations that make DPMO/sigma-quality-level requirement typically establish a goal in lieu of having a specification; e.g., a DSO defect occurs if an invoice is beyond 10 days late. However, this goal is not the same as a mechanical specification where the parts will not function properly if they are not made within a certain tolerance. A specification needs to be a customer requirement that is not dependent upon the individual who happens to be creating the goal.

However, there are instances when a DPMO metric or RTY is an appropriate in-process project metric such as solder defect rate in a printed circuit board manufacturing process.

2.5   Project Management

Roadmap Step: 2.3
Reference: *IEE Volume III*, Chapter 7

Project management is the management, allocation, and timely use of resources for the purpose of achieving a specific goal. Focus in project management should be given to the efficient utilization of resources and minimization of execution time.

The three pillars of project management are: project objectives, resources, and time. Project management involves the balancing of these pillars. For example, a team could increase resources in order to reduce the time it takes to meet objectives, or the team could extend the time for project completion to reduce resources and still meet objectives. The champion and team need to understand the flexibility that a project has for each pillar.

For example:

	Most Flexible	Moderately Flexible	Least Flexible
Time			X
Resource	X		
Project Objectives		X	

From Table 7.1 *Integrated Enterprise Excellence, Volume III – Improvement Project Execution: A Management and Black Belt Guide for Going Beyond Lean Six Sigma and the Balanced Scorecard,* Forrest W. Breyfogle III, Bridgeway Books, 2008.

A Gantt chart shows the planned and actual start and completion dates/times for a project. Gantt charts are easy to understand and simple to change. Gantt charts can track progress versus goals and checkpoints.   The complexity of the project plan should match the complexity of the project. Quick projects may only have a few milestones being tracked, while complex projects may be managed with project management software.

3 P-DMAIC: Measure Phase – Baseline Project

Purpose: To determine current process performance that provides a baseline to judge the improvement
Deliverables: Baseline predictability assessment, process capability/performance assessment, updated CODND financial estimate
Reference: Chapters 12 – 13 of *Integrated Enterprise Excellence, Volume III* (Breyfogle 2008c)

3.1 Roadmap

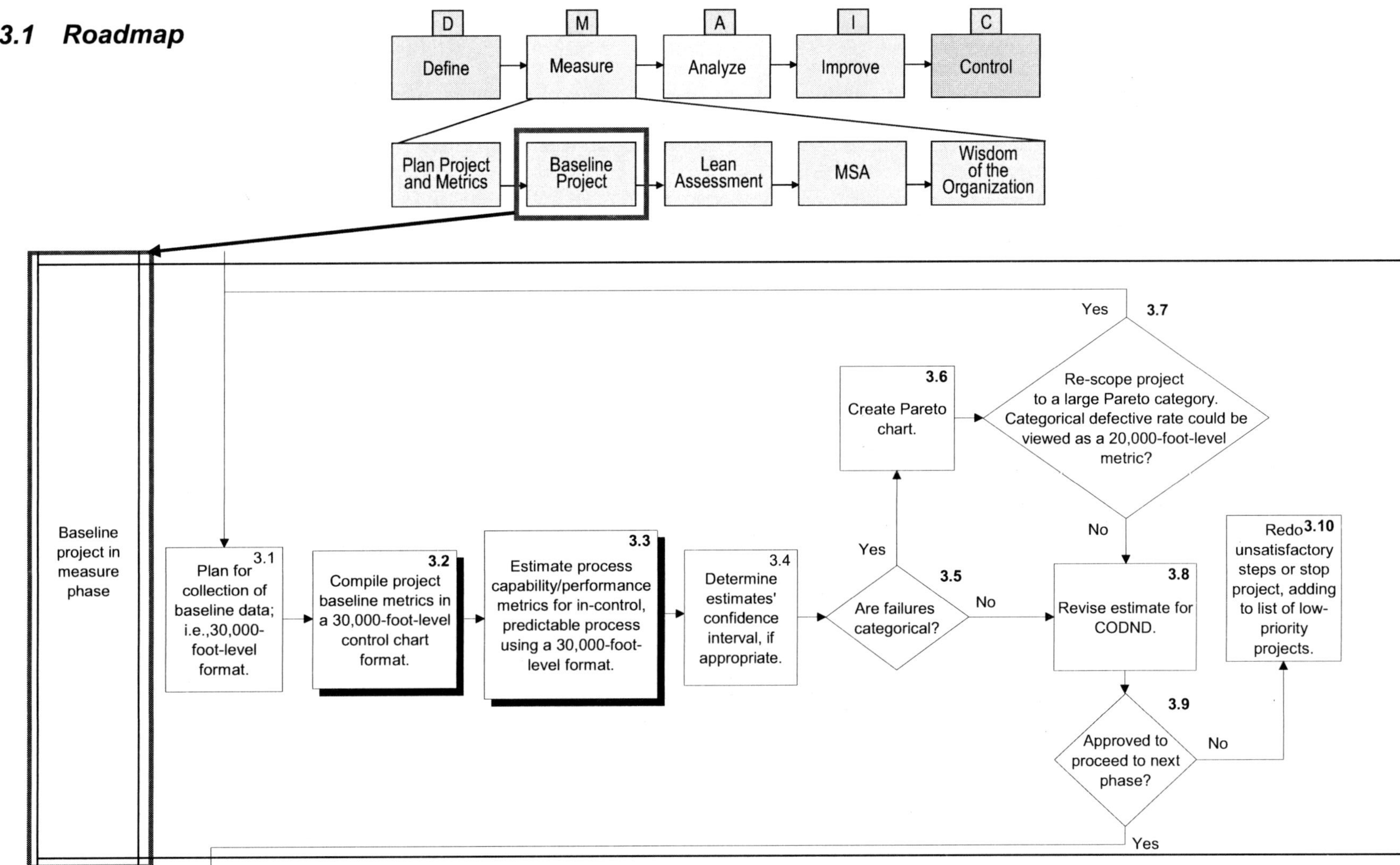

26

Step 3.2 drill down

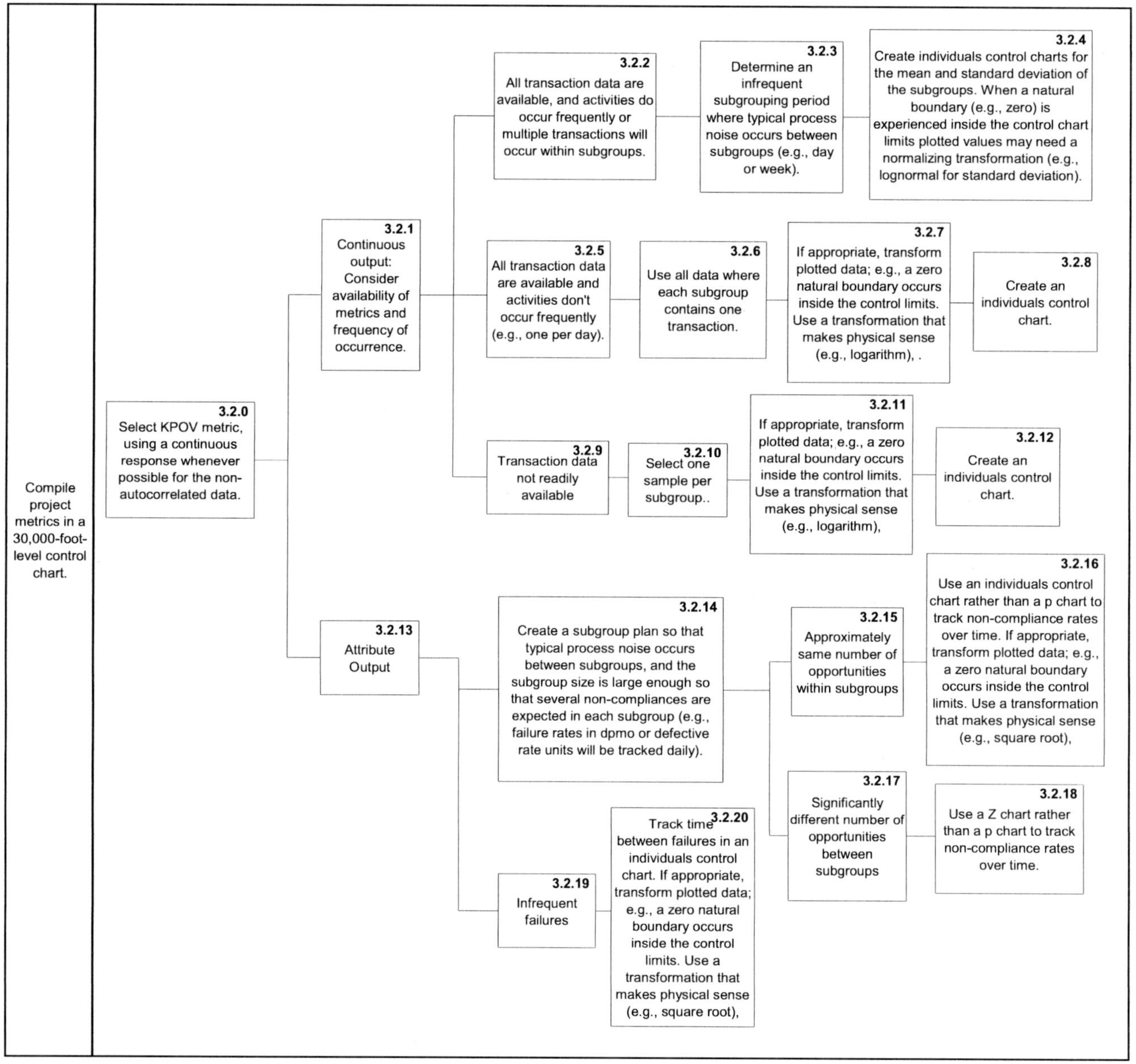

Compile project metrics in a 30,000-foot-level control chart.

3.2.0 Select KPOV metric, using a continuous response whenever possible for the non-autocorrelated data.

3.2.1 Continuous output: Consider availability of metrics and frequency of occurrence.

3.2.2 All transaction data are available, and activities do occur frequently or multiple transactions will occur within subgroups.

3.2.3 Determine an infrequent subgrouping period where typical process noise occurs between subgroups (e.g., day or week).

3.2.4 Create individuals control charts for the mean and standard deviation of the subgroups. When a natural boundary (e.g., zero) is experienced inside the control chart limits plotted values may need a normalizing transformation (e.g., lognormal for standard deviation).

3.2.5 All transaction data are available and activities don't occur frequently (e.g., one per day).

3.2.6 Use all data where each subgroup contains one transaction.

3.2.7 If appropriate, transform plotted data; e.g., a zero natural boundary occurs inside the control limits. Use a transformation that makes physical sense (e.g., logarithm), .

3.2.8 Create an individuals control chart.

3.2.9 Transaction data not readily available

3.2.10 Select one sample per subgroup..

3.2.11 If appropriate, transform plotted data; e.g., a zero natural boundary occurs inside the control limits. Use a transformation that makes physical sense (e.g., logarithm),

3.2.12 Create an individuals control chart.

3.2.13 Attribute Output

3.2.14 Create a subgroup plan so that typical process noise occurs between subgroups, and the subgroup size is large enough so that several non-compliances are expected in each subgroup (e.g., failure rates in dpmo or defective rate units will be tracked daily).

3.2.15 Approximately same number of opportunities within subgroups

3.2.16 Use an individuals control chart rather than a p chart to track non-compliance rates over time. If appropriate, transform plotted data; e.g., a zero natural boundary occurs inside the control limits. Use a transformation that makes physical sense (e.g., square root),

3.2.17 Significantly different number of opportunities between subgroups

3.2.18 Use a Z chart rather than a p chart to track non-compliance rates over time.

3.2.19 Infrequent failures

3.2.20 Track time between failures in an individuals control chart. If appropriate, transform plotted data; e.g., a zero natural boundary occurs inside the control limits. Use a transformation that makes physical sense (e.g., square root),

Step 3.3 Drill down

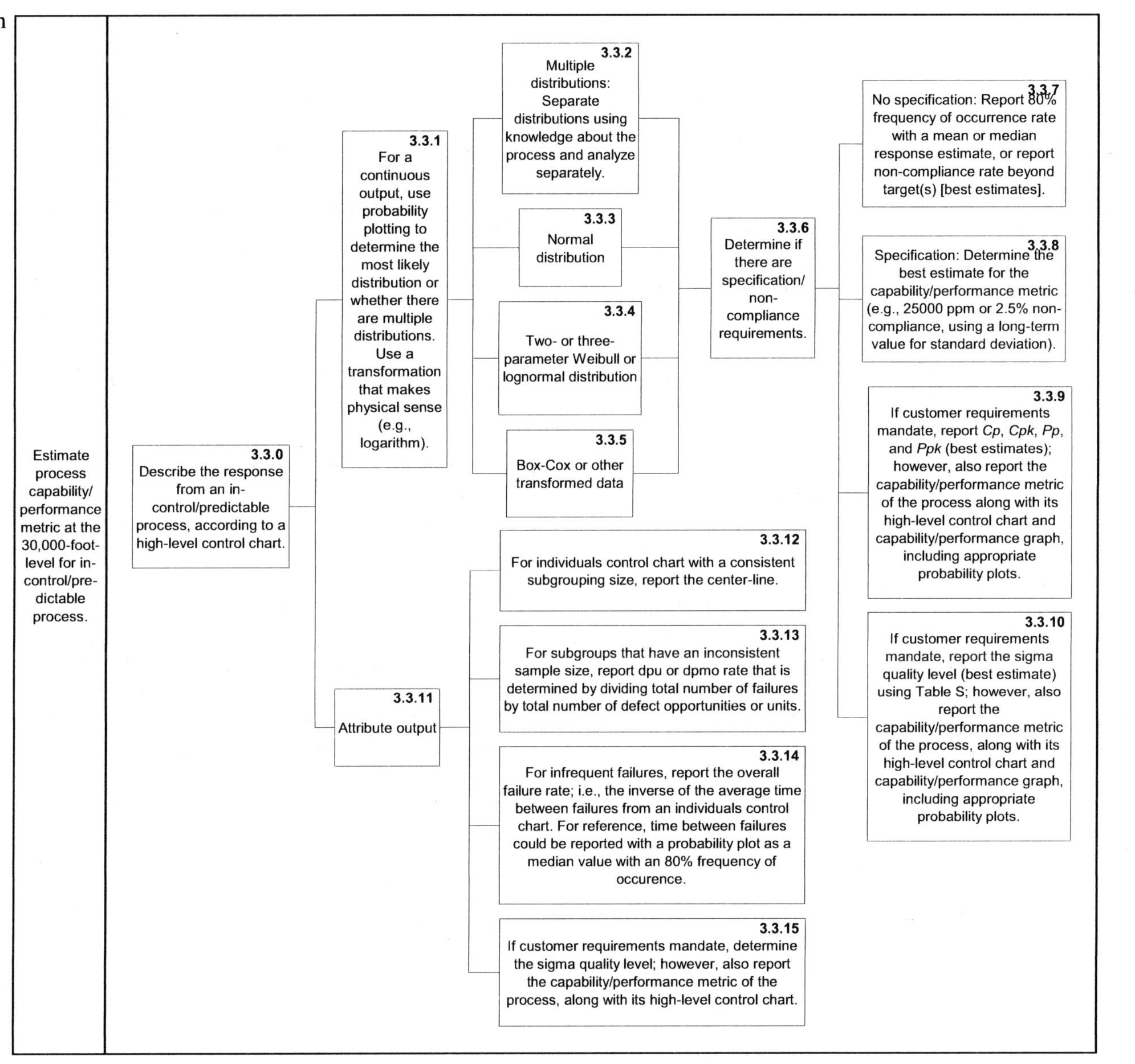

3.2 Check Sheet

Measure Phase: Baseline Project Check Sheet		
Description	**Questions**	**Yes/No NA**
Tool/Methodology		
30,000-foot-level control chart	Were project metrics compliled in a 30,000-foot-level control chart with an infrequent subgrouping/sampling plan so that typical process noise occurs between samples?	
	Was historical data used when initiating the 30,000-foot-level control charts?	
	Is the 30,000-foot-level control chart now being updated regularly?	
	Is the process in control/predictable?	
	Have special-cause issues been resolved?	
Process capability/performance metric	If specification limits exist for continuous data, was the process capability/performance metric estimated as a percentage or ppm of non-compliance?	
	If data are attribute, has the process capability been shown as the centerline of a 30,000-foot-level control chart?	
Probability plot/ dot plot	If data are continuous, were probability plots and/or dot plots used to show process capability?	
	Was the appropriate probability plot used?	
	Are the data normally distributed?	
	If there is more than one distribution, were the data separated for further analysis?	
Pareto chart	If KPOV data are classified by failure type, was a Pareto Chart used to prioritize failure types?	
Data collection	Has the team collected and reviewed the current standard operating procedures?	
	Are the data you are using good and truly representative of the process?	
	Do you know how much data you will need?	
	Is your data collection plan satisfactory to all stakeholders?	
COPQ/CODND	Now that the process capability/performance metric has been determined, given the refined COPQ/CODND estimate, is this still the right project to work on?	
Team		
Resources	Are all team members motivated and committed to the project?	
	Is there a plan for executive management to interface with the team to keep motivation alive and commitment visible?	
	Does process owner understand and agree with baselining?	
Next Phase		
Approval to proceed	Did the team adequately complete the above steps?	
	Has the project database been updated and communication plan followed?	
	Is the team considering Lean Tools?	
	Have barriers to success been identified and resolved?	
	Is the team tracking with the project schedule?	
	Have schedule revisions been approved?	

3.3 Data Collection Planning

Roadmap Step: 3.1

- Purpose
  - This is key effort for every project, starting the baseline step with good data.
  - Some projects have a clear 30,000-foot-level metric identified, but no data exists. The collection of this data should not be skipped.
- What it is
  - Even when it is clear that there is an organization problem that must be improved or corrected, going forward without data entails a significant risk.
  - It is reasonable to work through all the measure phase sections prior to obtaining project metric data. Entering the analyze phase activities without baseline data may lead to improper conclusions.
  - The baseline effort is used not only to understand the scope of the problem, but to identify how far back into history that the process is predictable so that you know what period of time data can be used in the analyze phase activities.

3.4 IEE 30,000-foot-level Scorecards and Project Baselining

Process output tracking needs to lead to the most appropriate action or non-action. This decision-making process can summarized as:
1. Is the process unstable or did something out of the ordinary occur, which requires action or no action?
2. Is the process stable and meeting internal and external customer needs? If so, no action is required.
3. Is the process stable but does not meet internal and external customer needs? If so, process improvement efforts are needed.

Processes that fall into category number three are candidates for the process improvement efforts which this book describes. When a process improvement project is undertaken, the proof that improvement was made is when this project-baseline performance transitions to a new, improved level of performance.

Chapters 10 and 11 of *Integrated Enterprise Excellence, Volume III* (Breyfogle 2008c) describe traditional control charting and process capability practices as a means to create this baseline metric. However, chapters 12 and 13 of the book describe technical issues with many of these traditional approaches in giving direction to the most appropriate action or non-action.

Provided also in chapters 12 and 13 is an alternative Statistical Business Performance Charting (SBPC) methodology which addresses these traditional-report-out issues and provides a systematic reporting methodology that leads to the most appropriate action or non-action. This IEE 30,000-foot-level reporting alternative is not only applicable for project measurement reporting but also enterprise business scorecards.

The IEE scorecard/dashboard metric reporting process is basically a two-step process:
1. Assess process predictability.
2. When the process is considered predictable, formulate a prediction statement for the latest region of stability. The usual reporting format for this statement is:
   a. When there is a specification requirement: nonconformance percentage or parts per million (PPM) nonconforming.
   b. When there are no specification requirements: median response and 80% frequency of occurrence rate

This chapter will describe some of the aspects of this performance-reporting system.

3.5   Tool: 30,000-foot-level Control Chart

Roadmap step: 3.2
Reference: *IEE Volume III*, Chapters 12 & 13
Minitab Syntax:
- Stat>Control Charts
- Stat>Control Charts>Variables Charts for Individuals>Individuals (I chart options – Box Cox, if appropriate)

Application Notes:
- The individuals chart is not robust to non-normality.
- Certain situations are inherently non-normally distributed. For these situations, a data transformation may be appropriate. The probability plotting technique in the next section helps determine whether, and what, transformations can be appropriate.
  - Care must be exercised not to force a distribution that does not make physical sense. A control chart might have special cause instances, which could be masked by such a transformation.
- There are two kinds of Non-Normal data:
  1. Data that exist in another distribution, such as lognormal or Weibull.
  2. Data that are a mixture of multiple distributions or processes.
  - The first is the easiest to deal with. We determine what the distribution really is and then deal with it appropriately.
    - Distribution deterministic specific functions.
    - Transformations and then treat as normal data.
  - The second case, mixed distributions, is more difficult to deal with.
    - One typically realizes this is the case after no transformation or distribution is found to fit your data.
    - Now a way is needed to separate the mixed distributions.

- Three options are available for non-normal data:
  1. Transform the data so that it can be treated as normally distributed data.
  2. Analyze subgroup averages rather than the data.
  3. Analyze the data with tools specific to the data distribution.

  - For control charting, we typically take the transformation option (1) or use subgroup averages (2), because there are limited options for non-normal distribution control charts.

- For capability/performance assessments, you are required to use the data. This is performed using transformed data (1) or with distribution specific tools (3).

- Inherent data transformation applications (using Box Cox Transformation)
  - Cycle or lead time data: use $\lambda = 0$ (lognormal distribution)
  - Percentage data: Use $\lambda = .5$ (square root transformation)
  - Time between events: Poisson distribution, $\lambda = .5$, (square root transform)
  - Mean time to failure data: Weibull, $\lambda = 0$ or $.5$ (log transform or square root)
  - Speed or rate: $\lambda = -1$ (converts to time)

- Subgrouped data
  - Roadmap steps 3.2.2 to 3.2.4
  - The IEE recommendation for subgrouped data involves the plotting of the mean of each subgroup and the standard deviation (or natural log of the standard deviation) with individual charts rather than using the traditional X-bar-R chart because of the variation source used in the estimation of the control limits. Since the 30,000-foot-level project metric is the result of multiple processes and products, the control chart focus should be on longer term variation sources, not on the short term variation sources that are used for X-bar-R charts.
  - This method allows for two independent assessments: one for the between subgroup predictability and one for the within subgroup predictability. This can be a key concept that will focus the improvement efforts on variation sources that relate to the chart showing the significant issues.
  - If the predictability is assessed using this method, you must still return to the original data for the capability/performance assessment.

Tool:

Individuals Chart: A chart of individual values is typically referred to as an *I* chart or a *X* chart. A moving range chart often accompanies these charts; hence, the designation *I-MR* or *XmR* chart. For an individual-measurement control chart, the process average is simply the mean of the *n* data points, which are represented in the following equation as x_i.

$$\bar{x} = \frac{\sum_{i=1}^{n} x_i}{n}$$

Most frequently, adjacent values are used to determine the moving range; however, someone could use a larger duration when making this calculation. The constants shown would need to be adjusted accordingly. When using adjacent values, moving ranges (MRs) are determined from the data using the equations

$$MR_1 = |x_2 - x_1| \qquad MR_2 = |x_3 - x_2| \quad ,\ldots$$

The average moving range ($\overline{MR}$) is the average MR value for the m values described by

$$\overline{MR} = \frac{\sum_{i=1}^{m} MR_i}{m} = \frac{(MR_1) + (MR_2) + (MR_3), \ldots, (MR_m)}{m}$$

The charting parameters for the individuals chart are

$$CL = \bar{x} \qquad UCL = \bar{x} + \frac{3(\overline{MR})}{d_2} = \bar{x} + 2.66(\overline{MR}) \qquad LCL = \bar{x} - \frac{3(\overline{MR})}{d_2} = \bar{x} - 2.66(\overline{MR})$$

where CL = centerline, UCL = upper control limit, LCL = lower control limit, and d_2 is a constant from Table J, *IEE Volume III*.

3.6　Tool: 30,000-foot-level – Distribution Assessment

Roadmap steps: 3.2
Reference: *IEE Volume III*, Chapters 12 & 13
Minitab Syntax: Graph>Probability Plot

Percent characteristics of a population can be determined from the cumulative distribution function, CDF, which is the integration of the probability density function, PDF. Probability plots are useful in visually assessing how well data follow distributions. A basic concept behind probability plotting is that if data plotted on a probability distribution scale follow a straight line, then the population from which the samples are drawn can be represented by that distribution. There are many different types of probability coordinate systems to address data from differing distributions; e.g., normal, lognormal, or Weibull. Computer programs, such as Minitab, can generate probability plots conveniently and yield precise parameter estimations.

3.7 Tool: Process Capability/Performance Metric

Roadmap steps: 3.3
Reference: *IEE Volume III*, Chapters 12 & 13
Minitab syntaxes
- Graph:>Probability Plot (Scale – Percentile Lines – At Data Lines [specification limits])
- Graph:>Probability Plot (Scale – Percentile Lines – At Y Values [recommended values 10, 50, and 90])
- Stat>Quality Tools>Capability Analysis

Process capability/performance metrics applications are:
- Continuous data:
  - Long-term estimate considering subgrouping and a specification exists: When a 30,000-foot-level control chart indicates that the process is predictable and that there is more than one data point in a subgroup, a statistical computer analysis routine can be used that determines long-term capability by mathematically combining within and between subgroup variability to determine the long-term capability/performance metric relative to a specification(s). Non-normality needs to be addressed when making this assessment.
  - Probability plotting when there is a specification(s): A process at the 30,000-foot-level should be in control/predictable before a process capability/performance metric statement can be made. When the subgrouping variability is minimal relative to within variability, we can combine all the data in the appropriate probability distribution plot to make a statement relative to specifications.
  - Probability plotting when there is no specification(s): A process at the 30,000-foot-level should be in control/predictable before a process capability/performance metric statement can be made. When the subgrouping variability is minimal relative to within variability, we can combine all the data in the appropriate probability distribution plot to make a statement relative to 10, 50, and 90 percentile limits; i.e., an 80% frequency of occurrence region with median.
- Attribute data:
  - All data can be combined to describe the process capability/performance rate, noting that this would be the center-line of a 30,000-foot-level control chart when the data are untransformed and the subgroup sample size is consistent between sub-groupings.

3.8   *Reporting the Baseline Performance*

Roadmap steps: 3.2 and 3.3
Reference: *IEE Volume III*, Chapters 12 & 13

Reporting the results of the Measure-baseline phase output can be performed in many ways. In the IEE system, it is important to show graphics along with the conclusions in real business terms. The graphics and statistics or just the conclusion, alone, may not fully communicate to all audiences. A combination of both proper graphics and the business conclusion should be combined. Examples of this combined approach are included below for each typical case; Continuous data with a specification, Continuous data with no specification, Subgrouped continuous data with a specification, and attribute data. Each example is referenced to *IEE Volume III*, where the context of the data is provided.

IEE 30,000-foot-level report out – Continuous data with a specification (IEE V3, Figure 12.5)

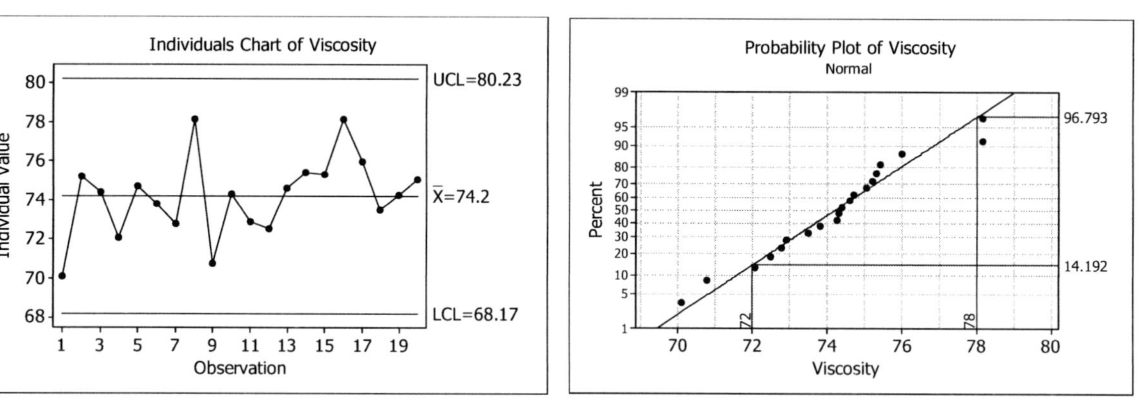

Predictable process with an approximate 17.4% non-conformance rate

IEE 30,000-foot-level report out – Continuous data without specification (IEE V3, Figure 12.14)

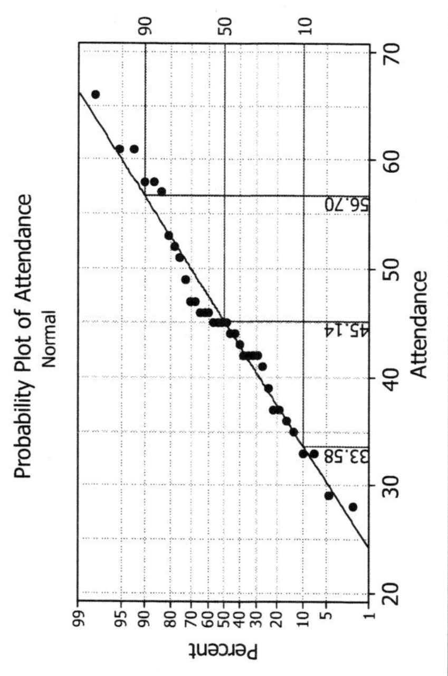
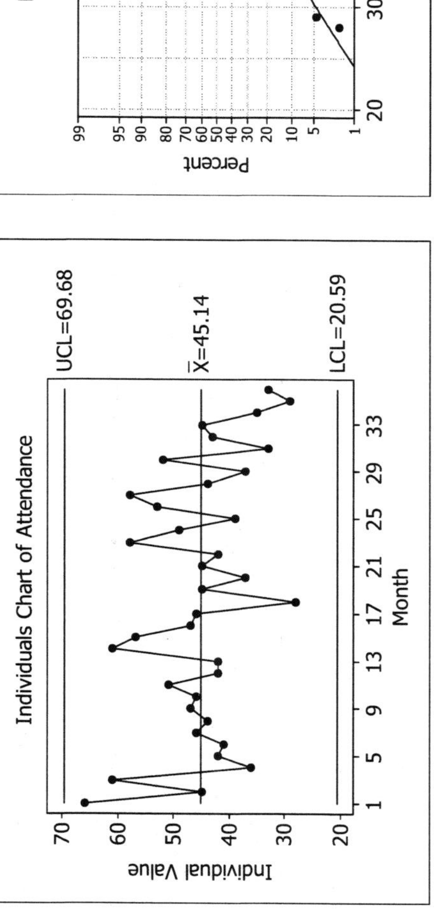

Predictable process with an approximate median attendance of 45 and 80% frequency of occurrence between 34 and 57

IEE 30,000-foot-level report out: Continuous data with a specification IEE V3 Figure 13.4 Individuals control chart of failure rate.

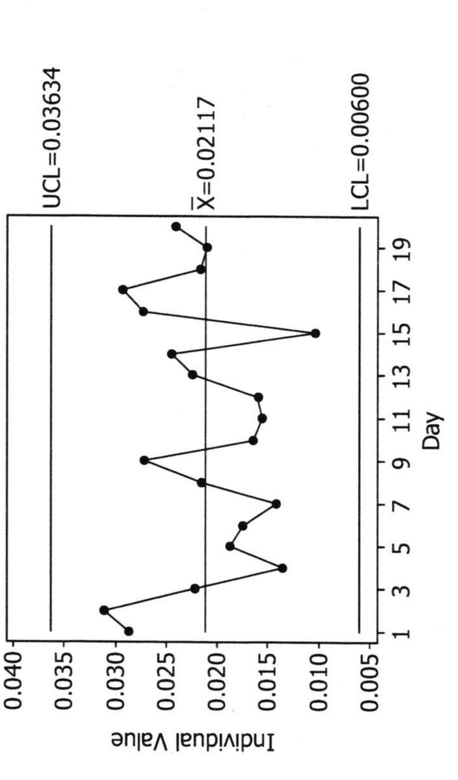

Predictable process with an approximate 2.1% non-conformance rate

IEE 30,000-foot-level report out: Subgrouped continuous data with a specification (IEE V3 Figure 12.10)

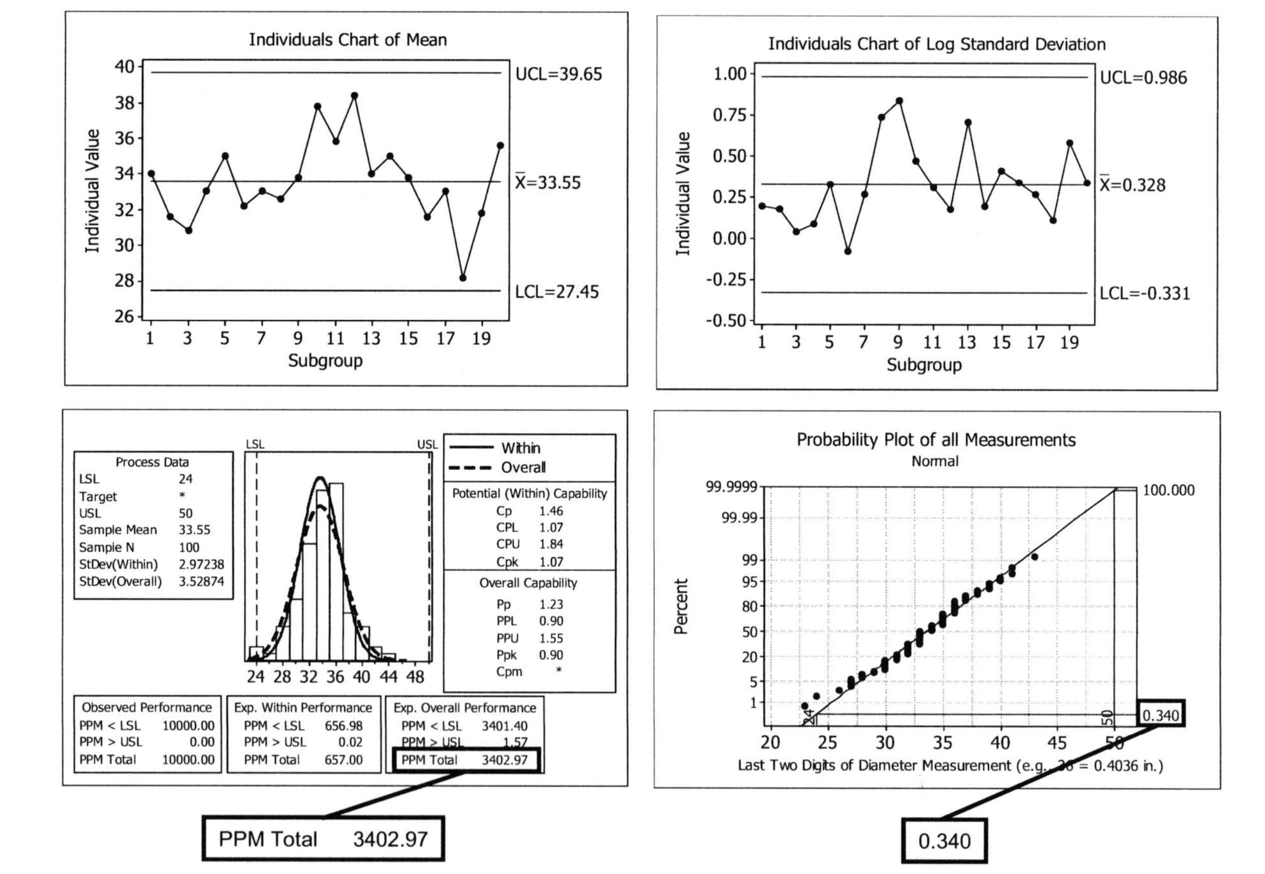

PPM Total 3402.97

0.340

Predictable process with an approximate 0.3% non-conformance rate

3.9   Confidence in Baselineing Conclusions

Roadmap steps 3.4
Reference: *IEE Volume III*, Chapters 20 and 21

- Purpose
  – Evaluate the confidence of your capability estimate to ensure that you do not convey an unreasonable belief in the mean or median performance.
- What it is
  – Small sample sizes are still able to provide a predictability and capability/performance estimate, but will also provide a wide confidence interval for each estimate. Evaluate the confidence in each estimate; if the uncertainty is quite high, then consider collecting more data before leaving this step.
  – If small sample sizes are all that are available, ensure that you fully disclose the uncertainty in your estimates.
  – Work to refine these estimates as more data are collected during the improvement project.

3.10 Narrowing the Project Scope

Roadmap steps 3.5 – 3.7

- Purpose
  – For attribute data, such as defect rate or yields, a Pareto chart may be used on all the data in the most recent predictable region to identify a segment of the problem to focus the improvement project efforts. This new project metric is generally called a 20,000-foot-level metric.
- What it is
  – If you narrow the project to a specific defect(s) or process step(s), roadmap steps 3.2 and 3.3 should be re-performed on the narrowed down data. The project should still include the baseline results of the 30,000-foot-level metric, since the improvement of this metric is the original goal of the project.
  – The project team may adjust the problem statement and SIPOC to reflect the new project scope, but should keep the original problem statement as a reference.

3.11 Application and Background

Application Examples of 30,000-foot-level metrics:
- Transactional 30,000-foot-level metric: One paid invoice was selected randomly each day from last year's invoices; i.e., Days Sales Outstanding (DSO), where the number of days beyond the due date was measured and reported. The DSO for each sample was reported in an individuals control chart, where no reason was identified for a few special cause data points. These data were plotted on a normal probability plot, where a null hypothesis for normality was rejected. A log-normal plot fit the data well. An individuals chart of the log-normal data did not indicate any special-cause conditions. The log-normal probability plot was used to estimate the proportion of invoices beyond 30, 60, and 90 days. An IEE project was initiated to improve the DSO metric.

- Transactional 30,000-foot-level metric: The mean and standard deviation of all DSOs were tracked using two individuals charts with a weekly subgrouping, where the standard deviation values had a log transformation. No special causes were identified. The long-term capability/performance of the process was reported as percentage non-conformance beyond 30, 60, and/or 90 days, using variance of components techniques or a statistical program that reports this metric under its $\bar{x}$ and s process capability/performance option.
- Manufacturing 30,000-foot-level metric (KPOV): One sample of a manufactured part was selected randomly each day over the last year. The diameter of the part was measured and plotted in a control chart. No special causes were identified. A null hypothesis for normality could not be rejected. The long-term process capability/performance was reported as the estimated ppm rate beyond the specification limits.
- Transactional and Manufacturing 30,000-foot-level cycle time metric (a Lean metric): One transaction was selected randomly each day over the last year, where the time from order entry to fulfillment was measured. The differences between these times relative to their due date were reported in an Individuals chart. No special causes were identified. A null hypothesis for normality could not be rejected. The long-term process capability/performance was reported as the estimated ppm rate beyond the due date for the transactions.
- Transactional and Manufacturing 30,000-foot-level inventory metric or satellite-level TOC metric (a Lean metric): Inventory was tracked monthly using a control chart. No special causes were identified. A null hypothesis for normality could not be rejected. The long-term process capability/performance was reported as the expected 80% month-to-month inventory levels and the associated monetary implications.
- Manufacturing 30,000-foot-level quality metric: Every week a high-volume manufacturer produces approximately the same number printed circuit boards. The weekly failure rate of the printed circuit boards is tracked on an individuals chart. No special causes were identified. The center line ppm rate of the individuals chart was reported as the capability/performance of the process.

3.12 Interpretation of Control Chart Patterns

Reference: *IEE Volume III*, Section 10.3

- Purpose
  - When a process is in control/predictable, the control chart pattern should exhibit natural characteristics as if it were from random data. Unnatural patterns involve the absence of one or more natural-pattern characteristics. Some examples of unnatural patterns are: mixture, stratification, instability, data transformation need, and/or a process shift. For identified unnatural 30,000-foot-level control chart patterns, a reason for the occurrence should be, when possible, determined and documented on the chart. Identified process shifts need staging so that data from each staged region determines the time-period's control limits. For each stability region, a process performance statement (e.g., percent non-conformance rate) can be made. Whenever there is a recent region of stability, the process can be said to be predictable, and the data from this region can be considered a random sample of the future, which presumes that the process inputs and implementation procedures remain unchanged from the most recent stability region.

- What it is
  - Facilitates the identification of process shifts in a 30,000-foot-level report-out that should be staged.
  - Helps identify when control chart subgrouping should be less frequent, since common-cause is occurring within subgroups.

- Helps identify when seasonal patterns should be tracked either on a monthly annual-rolling basis or independently; e.g., holiday season versus other times of year.
- Identifies when a process has changed to a new, improved level of performance because of a project execution.

It should be highlighted that whenever the process is stated to be out of control/unpredictable, the statement might have been made in error because there is a chance that either abnormally *good* or *bad* samples were drawn. This chance of error increases with the introduction of more criteria patterns when analyzing the charts.

Because the upper and lower control limits each are 3σ (sampling standard deviation), consider a control chart that is subdivided into three 3σ regions noted in the figure below. While statistical computer analysis programs may offer other tests, tests for out-of-control conditions relative to these zones are as follows:

- One point beyond zone A.
- Two out of three points in zone A or beyond.
- Four out of five points in zone B or beyond.
- Nine points in zone C or beyond.

From Figure 10.5 *Integrated Enterprise Excellence, Volume III – Improvement Project Execution: A Management and Black Belt Guide for Going Beyond Lean Six Sigma and the Balanced Scorecard,* Forrest W. Breyfogle III, Bridgeway Books, 2008.

4 P-DMAIC: Measure Phase – Consider Lean Tools

Purpose: To evaluate the process using lean tools and philosophy
Deliverables:
- A lean assessment of the process
- Applicable lean-tools applications

Reference: Chapter 14 of *Integrated Enterprise Excellence, Volume III* (Breyfogle 2008c)

4.1 Roadmap

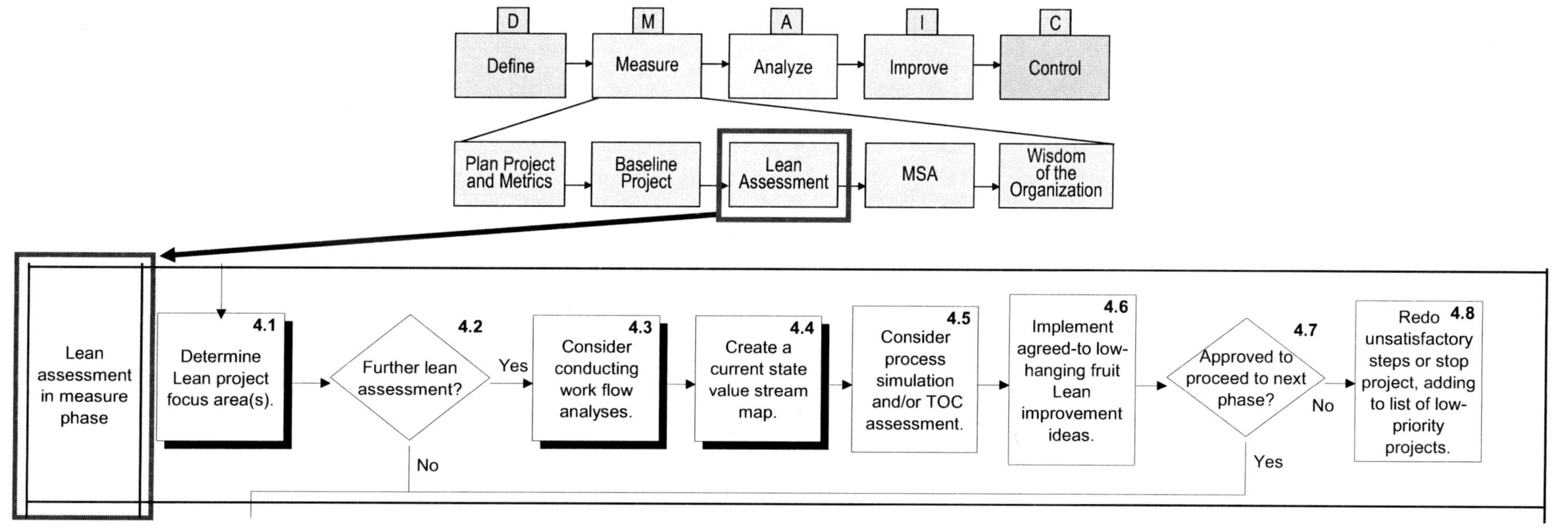

Step 4.1 drill down

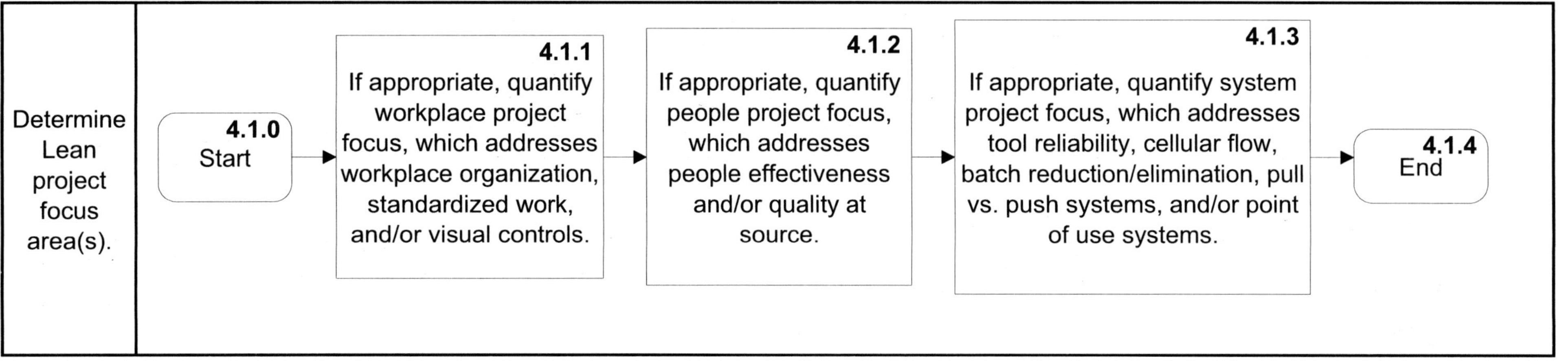

Step 4.3 drill down

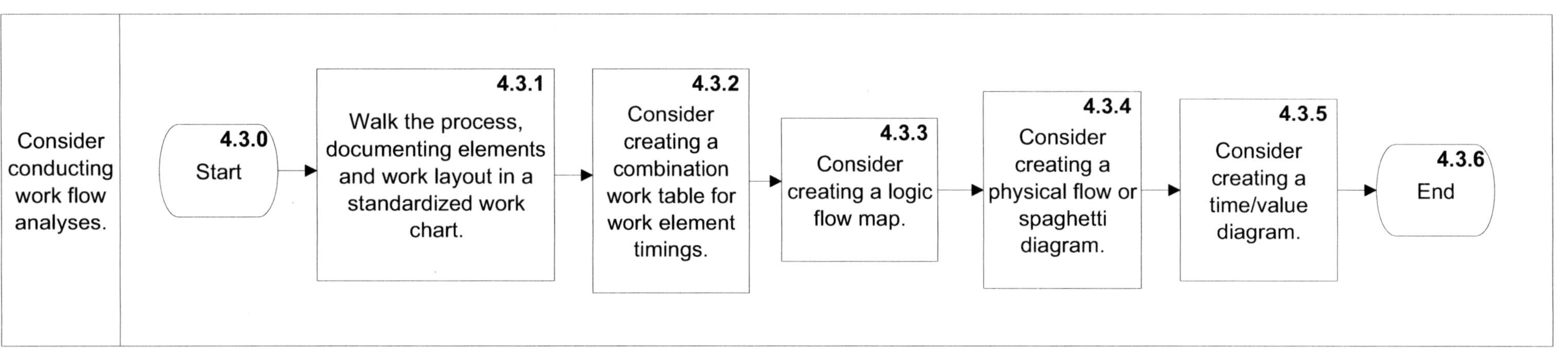

Create a current state value stream map.

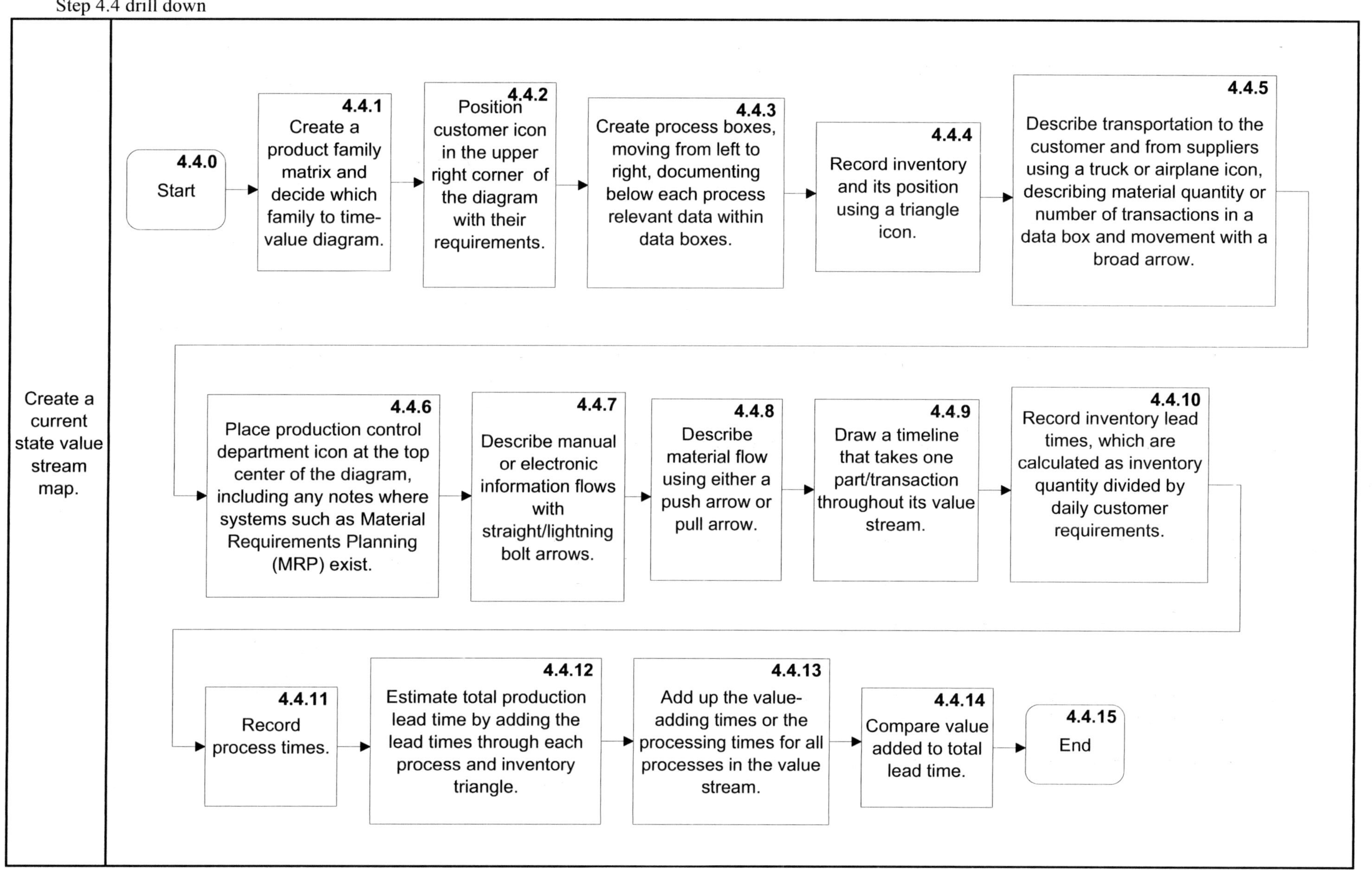

4.2 Check Sheet

Measure Phase: Lean Assessment Checklist		
Description	**Questions**	**Yes/No NA**
Tool/Methodology		
Lean tools	Is the KPOV a lean metric, like cycle time or inventory?	
	Are you addressing the *workplace* as a Lean project focus area, i.e., workplace organization, standardized work, and/or visual presentation?	
	Are you addressing *people* as a Lean project focus area, i.e., people utilization or quality at the source?	
	Are you addressing the *system* as a Lean project focus area, i.e., tool reliability, cellular flow, batch reduction/elimination, or pull vs. push systems?	
Standardized work chart, combination work table, logic flow diagram, and/or time value diagram	Have you conduced a work flow analysis; i.e., walked the process (documenting elements and work layout in a standardized work chart), created a combination work table for work element timings, created a logic flow diagram, and/or created a time value diagram?	
Value stream map	Have you created a current state value stream map?	
Assessment	Were any process improvements made?	
	If so, were they statistically verified with the appropriate hypothesis test?	
	Did you describe the change over time on a 30,000-foot-level control chart?	
	Did you calculate and display the change in the process capability/performance metric?	
	Have you documented and communicated the improvements?	
	Have you summarized the benefits and annualized financial benefits?	
Team		
Resources	Are all team members motivated and committed to the project?	
	Is process owner committed to the project?	
Next Phase		
Approval to proceed	Did the team adequately complete the above steps?	
	Has the project database been updated and communication plan followed?	
	Should an MSA be conducted for this project?	
	Is the team tracking with the project schedule?	
	Have schedule revisions been approved?	
	Are barriers to success identified and planned for?	

4.3 Application and Background

Application Example:
- An IEE project was created to improve the 30,000-foot-level metric, Days Sales Outstanding (DSO). A current state value stream map was created to describe how transactions flow through the process. A future state value stream map was created and implemented in the improvement phase to remove identified waste.

4.4 Tool: Determine Lean Project Focus Areas

Roadmap step: 4.1
Reference: *IEE Volume III*, Section 14.8

- Purpose
  - All improvement projects should include an evaluation of the process flow and efficiency.
  - This assessment is best performed by using Lean Assessment tools.
  - The outcome of this phase is to generate additional potential causes to be considered in the measure phase that are derived from the Lean view of a process.

- What it is
  - A Lean assessment is performed in order to identify the Lean concepts that may be applied to better understand the constraints and issues with the process being evaluated.

- Workplace Assessment (Roadmap step 4.1.1)
  - Workplace organization: Neat, clean, and safe environment with an arrangement that provides specific location for everything with an elimination of anything that is not required. Storage of materials is close to where used.
  - Standardized work: Operations are conducted by all using the best known sequence. Organizations have difficulty taking the time to standardize. If organizations standardize, they have difficulty sustaining it.
  - Visual controls: Signals that provide immediate understanding of situations and/or conditions. Controls need to be simple, efficient, self-regulated, and worker-managed. Examples are schedule/status boards, color coded files, good directional signals.
- People Assessment (Roadmap step 4.1.2)
  - People effectiveness: Strive for highly specific jobs with a rotation among team members. We want to have cross-trained and multi-skilled employees who can work many operations, not only in one area but in multiple areas. We want to create an environment where they have high responsibility and authority.
  - Quality at the source: People are to be certain that high-quality information and/or products are passed onto the next area. Adequate inspection tools are provided. Visual tools are provided to demonstrate acceptable standards.

- **System Assessment (Roadmap step 4.1.3)**
  - Workstation tool reliability: Operations tools and equipment are to be efficient and effective. Computer system response time is to be good and tool down time is minimal.
  - Cellular flow: Physical linkage of people with supporting hardware/software is in the most efficient and effective combination. It minimizes waste, maximizes value-add activities.
  - Batch reduction or elimination: Procedures that reduce WIP.
  - Pull versus push systems: Utilize pull systems which control the flow of resources over time, based on rules and system status. Avoid push systems that are based on schedules, forecasts, or when time is available to perform activities.
  - Point of use systems.

| Lean Area | | Project Importance | | |
Category	Principal	None	Some	Major
Workplace	Organization			
Workplace	Standardized work			
Workplace	Visual controls			
People	Effectiveness			
People	Quality at source			
System	Tool reliability			
System	Cellular flow			
System	Batch reduction or elimination			
System	Pull vs. push system			
System	Point of use systems			
Instructions:	Describe the level of project importance for each Lean principal			
	by entering an "X" in the appropriate box			

From Table 14.2 *Integrated Enterprise Excellence, Volume III – Improvement Project Execution: A Management and Black Belt Guide for Going Beyond Lean Six Sigma and the Balanced Scorecard,* Forrest W. Breyfogle III, Bridgeway Books, 2008.

4.5 Further Lean Assessment Needed?

- Purpose
  - To decide if there were any issues identified in the Lean Assessment that may need further evaluation as potential causes for the organizational problem.
- What it is
  - A Lean assessment is performed in order to identify the Lean concepts that may be applied to better understand the constraints and issues with the process being evaluated.
  - Any issue identified as "Major" on the Lean Assessment should be investigated further.

4.6 Tool: Workflow Analysis – Standardized Work

Roadmap step: 4.3.1
Reference: *IEE Volume III*, Section 14.10

- Purpose
  - Before suggesting or implementing changes, existing processes need to be understood.
  - This tool focuses on the movement of product or transactions within the work space.
- What it is
  - This is accomplished by walking and observing the current process in action. The Lean term is to "Walk the Line".
  - The standardized work chart example can be found in *IEE Volume III*, Table 14.4. This chart may also include a physical flow or spaghetti diagram.
  - Focus is on the typical or standard work process, not on the special-case processing.

4.7   Tool: Workflow Analysis – Combination Work Table

Roadmap step: 4.3.2
Reference: *IEE Volume III*, Section 14.11

- Purpose
  - This is a key tool to document sequencing issues among transaction processing, people, and equipment.
  - This tool focuses on the interaction between products/transactions with the people and the equipment over time.
- What it is
  - This tool will clearly demonstrate where products/transactions are waiting for the next step.
  - This tool will clearly demonstrate where the workforce is waiting for work to be executed.
  - This tool will clearly demonstrate where equipment is waiting for product/transactions or workers to use it.
  - This chart is more difficult to create than many lean charts, but it provides a clearer insight into the process than other lean tools are able to provide. The process steps are entered top to bottom, with the timing of each step. On the right, you diagram the movement of the workers over time as they interact with the process steps.
  - An example of the combination work chart can be found in *IEE Volume III*, Table 4.5.

4.8   Tool: Workflow Analysis – Logic Flow Map

Roadmap step: 4.3.3
Reference: *IEE Volume III*, Section 14.12

- Purpose
  - Use this tool when the identification of the value-added, non-value-added, and business value-added process steps needs to be highlighted.
  - This tool provides a process map that indicates the value of each step; steps may be identified by color or a notation.
- What it is
  - The Logic Flow Map is used as a tool to drill down or focus the project efforts into specific areas.
  - Follow the rules for assigning value, where value is only determined by the final customer.
  - General Flow Charting icons are used in these charts.

4.9 Tool: Workflow Analysis – Spaghetti Diagram or Physical Process Flow

Roadmap step: 4.3.4
Reference: *IEE Volume III*, Section 14.13

- Purpose
  - Use this tool when you have found major issues in the movement or transportation areas of the lean assessment.
  - It is used to show both movement of the workers and the movement of products/transactions.
- What it is
  - A diagram of the work area, generally drawn to scale or from a facilities drawing, is used as the template.
  - Observations are taken over multiple products/transactions, shifts, days… These observations are combined to identify the common paths that products/transactions and the workers take in the work area.
  - Every path is not diagramed, only the common paths. Avoid including special-case paths.
  - This is a very common diagram included in presentations that demonstrate work flow because the audience easily interprets the information.
  - Many low-hanging-fruit (LHF) improvements are identified and corrected after this analysis through a simple moving of equipment and supplies.
  - This tool can be used in both the E-DMAIC analyze phase and the P-DMAIC measure phase. When lead time is a 30,000-foot-level scorecard/dashboard enterprise value chain or project metric, the spaghetti diagram provides a picture of activities that can identify waste in transportation and motion. This picture can help identify where targeted improvement efforts should focus.

Example:

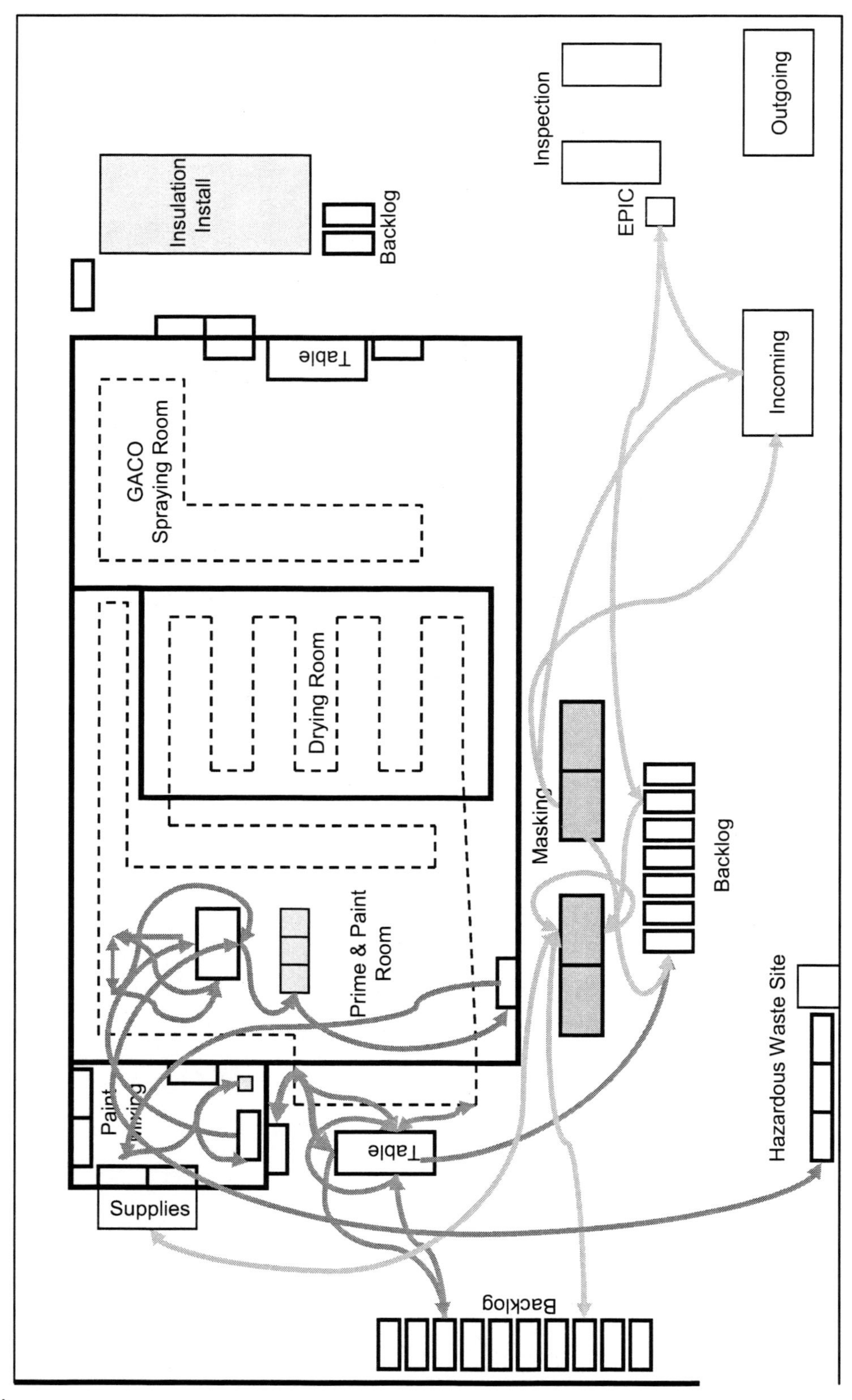

From Figure 14.2 *Integrated Enterprise Excellence, Volume III – Improvement Project Execution: A Management and Black Belt Guide for Going Beyond Lean Six Sigma and the Balanced Scorecard,* Forrest W. Breyfogle III, Bridgeway Books, 2008.

4.10 Tool: Workflow Analysis – Time Value Diagram

Roadmap step: 4.3.5
Reference: *IEE Volume III*, Section 14.15

- Purpose
  - Use this tool when the identification of time-based issues is key to the project.
  - This tool provides a simple diagram to show what happens over time for a product/transaction.
- What it is
  - The time value map should be considered for any project that has a primary or secondary goal to reduce lead time for a process.
  - It combines the value-added (VA) and non-value-added (NVA) concepts into a time based chart, which may provide clear guidance to where the improvement project should focus its efforts. The most common observation from this tool is that wait times are excessive in the processes and that only an effort to reduce the VA and NVA task times will not provide enough improvement for the project.
  - If the time value map indicates that there are a lot of issues to address, a follow-on value stream map may be needed.

Example:

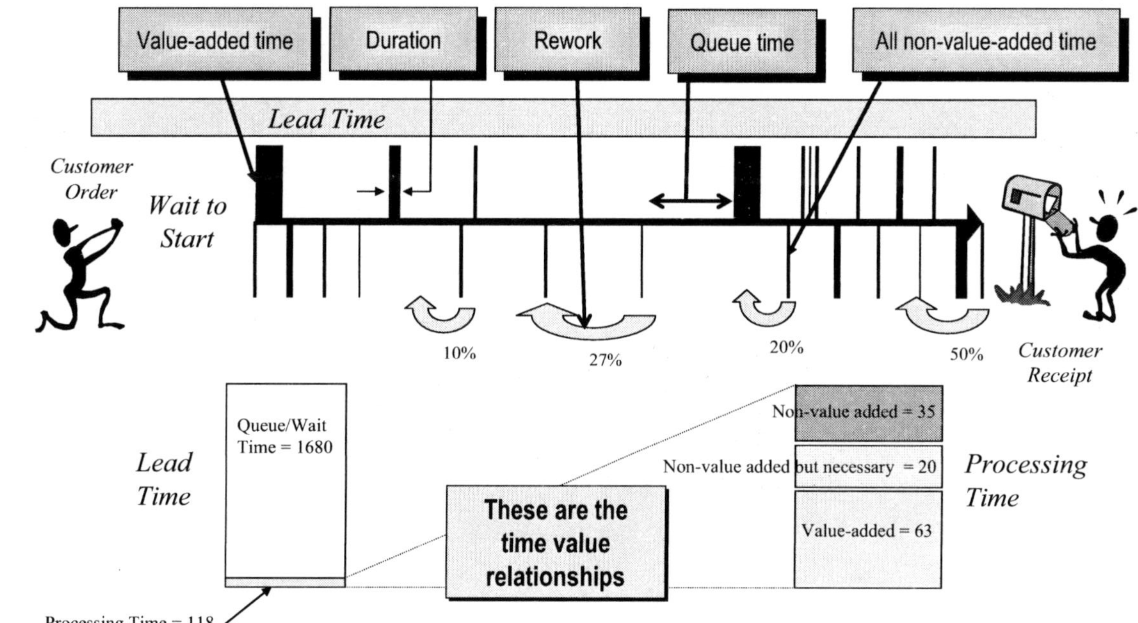

From Figure 14.4 *Integrated Enterprise Excellence, Volume III – Improvement Project Execution: A Management and Black Belt Guide for Going Beyond Lean Six Sigma and the Balanced Scorecard,* Forrest W. Breyfogle III, Bridgeway Books, 2008.

4.11 Tool: Create a Current State Value Stream Map

Roadmap step: 4.4
Reference: *IEE Volume III*, Section 14.17

- Purpose
  - Use this tool when you have identified significant issues with the product/transaction flow, information flow, and processing times.
  - This tool is considered to be the key point to document all information about the Lean issues in a process.
- What it is
  - A Value Stream Map (VSM) is considered as one of the most efficient methods to document significant process information.
  - A VSM is generally only created for high-level business processes, where there is a clear customer and supplier outside of the organization, or to say it another way, there is a clear value stream.
  - A value stream is a set of process steps that are executed in order to provide value to a customer. They exist for external customers along with internal customers of a support organization such as procurement, HR, and Facilities.
  - A standard set of icons is used in a VSM, which can be found with their definitions in *IEE Volume III*, figure 14.6. An example VSM along with a limited list of the most common icons is listed below.
  - A VSM can trace both product and information flow across organizational boundaries of a company. This mapping tool can describe how a high-level process is executed. VSMs show the sequential flow of transactions or items along with the information flow, such as ordering and customer feedback. A well-created VSM will show the process from the raw material supplier through the customer delivery along with the information flow from the customer to the business and to the raw material suppliers. In a transactional process, the customer and the supplier may be one in the same, but either way the map shows both the transaction flow and the information flow.
  - Although software exists that will create VSM diagrams and list the process data, most VSM efforts are created on large sheets of paper by the project team and used throughout the project in this form. Electronic diagrams are generally created in the end for presentation usage, although some will use the software in place of paper diagrams from the beginning of the project.

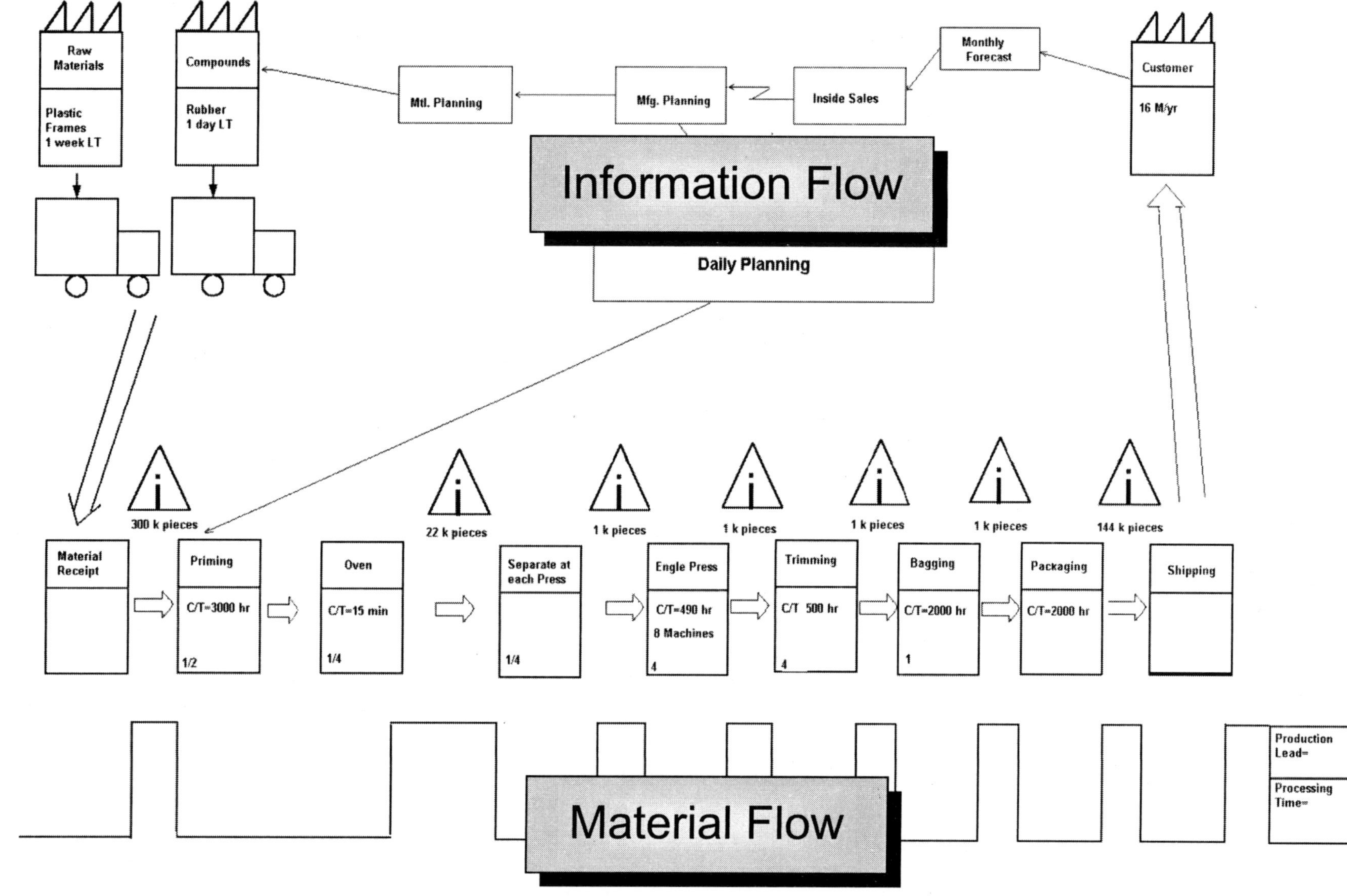

Raw Materials
Plastic Frames
1 week LT
Compounds
Rubber
1 day LT
Mtl. Planning
Mfg. Planning
Inside Sales
Monthly Forecast
Customer
16 M/yr
Information Flow
Daily Planning
300 k pieces
22 k pieces
1 k pieces
1 k pieces
1 k pieces
1 k pieces
144 k pieces
Material Receipt
Priming
C/T=3000 hr
1/2
Oven
C/T=15 min
1/4
Separate at each Press
1/4
Engle Press
C/T=490 hr
8 Machines
4
Trimming
C/T 500 hr
4
Bagging
C/T=2000 hr
1
Packaging
C/T=2000 hr
Shipping
Production Lead=
Processing Time=
Material Flow

A list of the most common VSM Icons

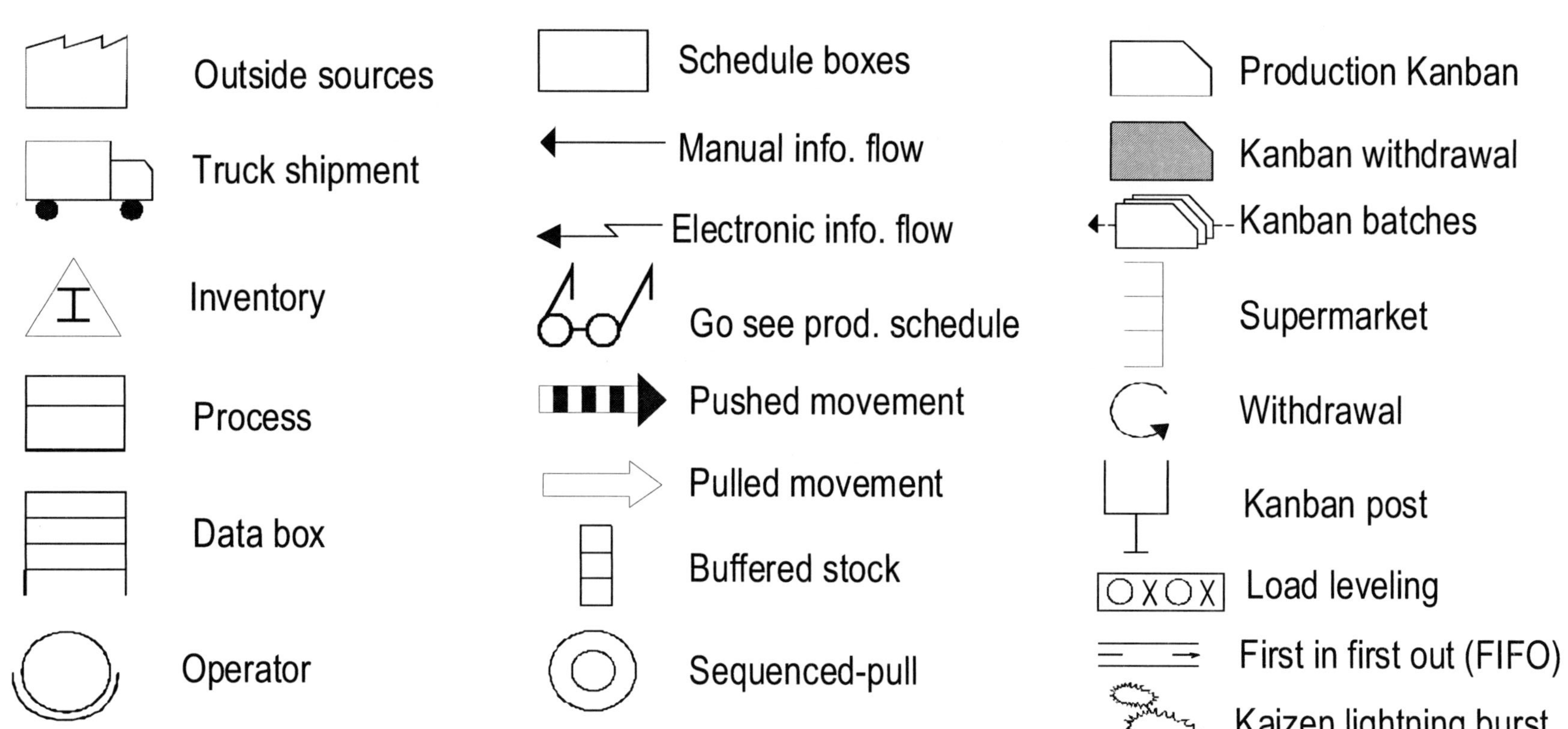

- Examples of VSM components:
  - Process Box Entries

Process Box Example

Assembly
C/T = 70 sec
C/O = 5 sec
Defects = 2.5%
2

- Inventory values
  - The times listed in the drop-down areas are the VA times in that process step.

    Note that you may document these quantities in counts or in time required to process the inventory.

Inventory Example

- Process Time Line
  - The top row of times documents the time in that process step and between process steps.
  - The times listed in the drop-down areas are the VA times in that process step.
  - The VA and Lead Time values are summed up and listed to the right of this time line. In some case an efficiency value is also reported; Process cycle efficiency = value-added time/total lead time.
  - This diagram provides a similar message as the time value map.

Lead Time
34.3 hrs
VA Time
18.25 min

4.12 Tool: Takt Time

Reference: *IEE Volume III*, Section 14.4

Takt time is customer demand rate; that is, the available work time per shift divided by customer demand rate per shift. This metric is expressed in units of time to produce one unit of product.

For example, determine the Takt time, given the following:

1000 parts or transactions per day; i.e., customer requirements, not capability
8 hour shifts
Two 15 minute breaks per shift
2 shifts per day

$$\text{Takt time} = \frac{(8.0 \text{ hr.} - .50 \text{ hr.}) \times 60 \text{ min./hr.} \times 60 \text{ sec./min.} \times 2 \text{ shifts/day}}{1000 \text{ transactions/day}} = 54 \text{ sec. per transaction}$$

The comparison of takt time to production capacity can highlight when either excess or insufficient process capacity exists. Takt time is important since it should be used to set the tempo of the organization.

4.13 Tool: Little's Law

Reference: *IEE Volume III*, Section 14.5

Little's law is:

$$\text{Lead time} = \frac{\text{WIP}}{\text{ACR}}$$

where WIP = Work in Process and ACR = Average Completion Rate

This equation quantifies the average length of time it takes to complete any work item or work items (lead time) from the amount of work that is waiting to be completed (WIP) and the average completion rate (transactions per day or week completed).

This relationship is more useful than one might initially think. Consider that we would like to get the lead time or average delivery time, but often it is very difficult to track individual transactions through all the process steps and then average these values. For example, the average duration to compete an insurance claim could be determined by dividing the number of claims in the overall system (WIP) by the average completion rate (i.e., average number of claims completed in a given period of time).

5 P-DMAIC: Measure Phase – Measurement Systems Analysis

Purpose: To determine current measurement system performance and validity

Deliverables:

- Measurement system analysis (MSA)
- Identification of measurement system issues
- A capable measurement system

Reference: Chapter 15 of *Integrated Enterprise Excellence, Volume III* (Breyfogle 2008c)

5.1 Roadmap

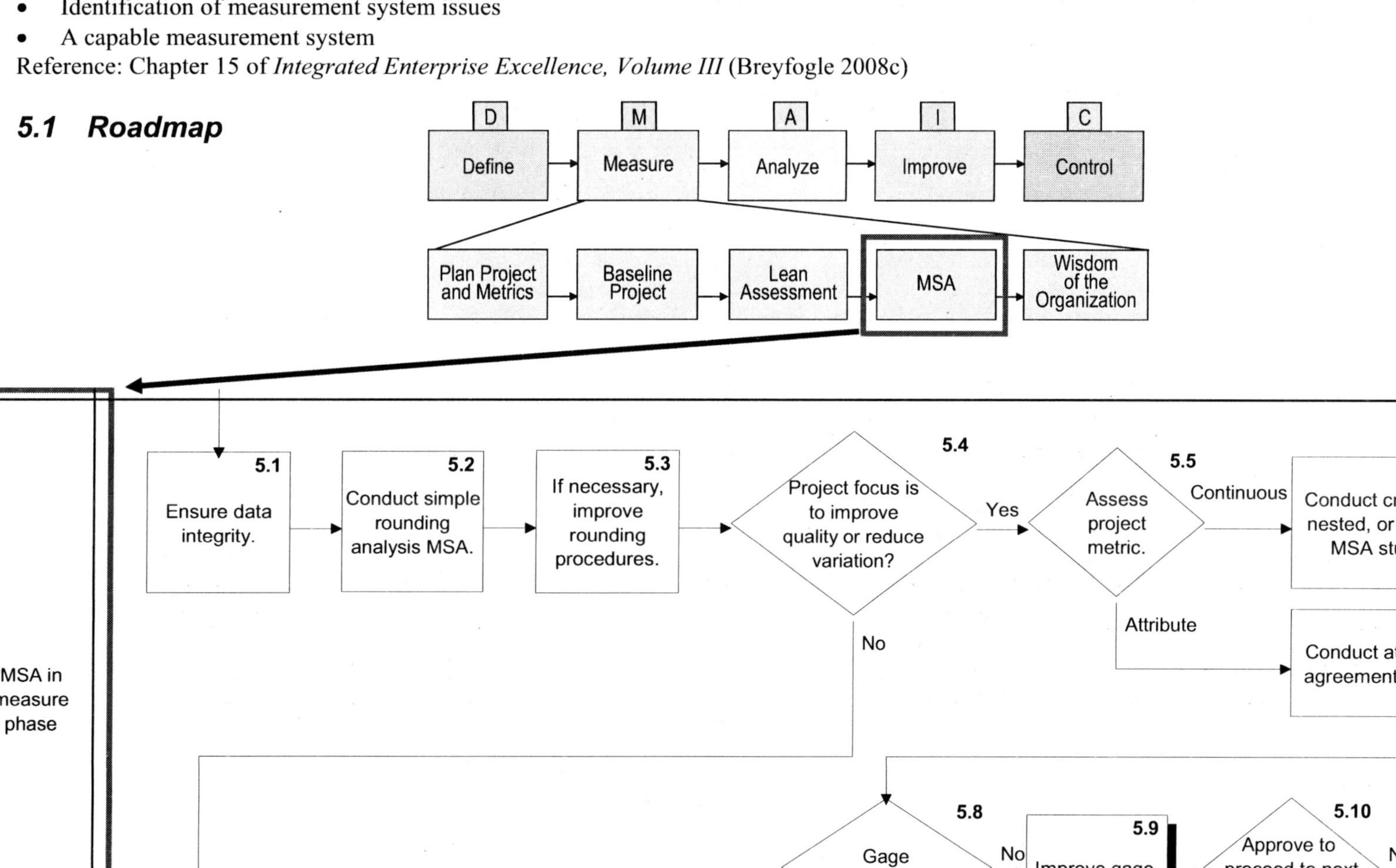

Step 5.8 drill down

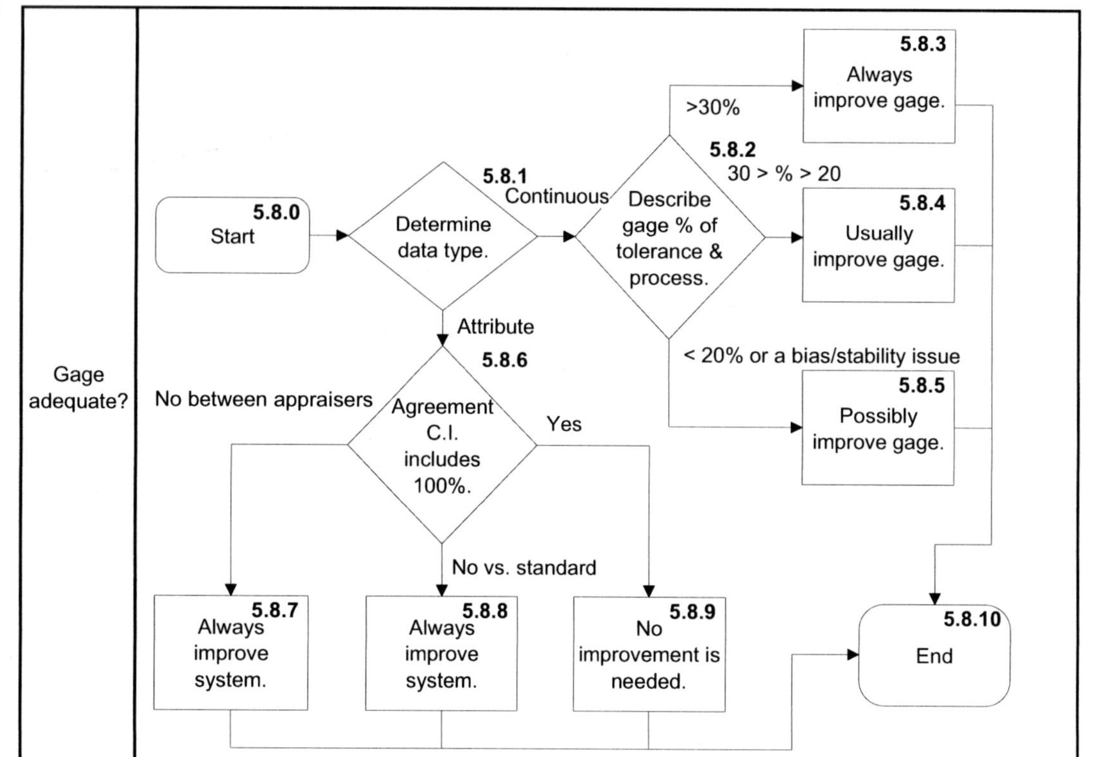

Step 5.9 drill down

5.2   Check Sheet

Measure Phase: Measurement Systems Analysis Check Sheet		
Description	**Questions**	**Yes/No NA**
Tool/Methodology		
Data integrity	Is there a common operational definition for the data being collected that reflects the needs of the customer?	
	Are the recorded data representative of the actual process?	
	Have you taken appropriate steps to error-proof the data collection process?	
Gage R&R	Was a Gage R&R needed?	
	If so, is the Measurement System satisfactory?	
	If the Measurement System was not satisfactory, have improvements been implemented to make it capable, or has the data collection plan been revised?	
Assessment	Were any process improvements made?	
	If so, were they statistically verified with the appropriate hypothesis test?	
	Did you describe the change over time on a 30,000-foot-level control chart?	
	Did you calculate and display the change in the process capability/performance metric?	
	Have you documented and communicated the improvements?	
	Have you summarized the benefits and annualized financial benefits?	
Team		
Resources	Are all team members motivated and committed to the project?	
	Is process owner supportive of MSA?	
Next Phase		
Approval to proceed	Did the team adequately complete the above steps?	
	Has the project database been updated and communication plan followed?	
	Is there a detailed plan for collecting Wisdom of the Organization?	
	Are barriers to success identified and planned for?	
	Is the team tracking with the project schedule?	
	Have schedule revisions been approved?	

5.3 Application and Background

Application Examples:

- Transactional 30,000-foot-level metric: DSO reduction was chosen as an IEE project. Focus was given to ensure that DSO entries accurately represented what happened within the process.
- Manufacturing 30,000-foot-level metric (KPOV): An IEE project was to improve the capability/performance of the diameter for a manufactured product; i.e., reduce the number of parts beyond the specification limits. A MSA was conducted of the measurement gage.
- Transactional and Manufacturing 30,000-foot-level cycle time metric (a Lean metric): An IEE project was to improve the time from order entry to fulfillment. Focus was given to ensure that the cycle time entries accurately represented what happened within the process.
- Transactional and Manufacturing 30,000-foot-level inventory metric or satellite-level TOC metric (a Lean metric): An IEE project was to reduce inventory. Focus was given to ensure that entries accurately represented what happened within the process.
- Manufacturing 30,000-foot-level quality metric: An IEE project was to reduce the number of defects in a printed circuit board manufacturing process. A MSA was conducted to determine if defects were both identified and recorded correctly into the company's database.

The reason for analyzing and improving a measurement system is to reduce accuracy and precision issues relative to process variation to get a truer picture of sources of process variation. These measurement issues are characterized by location and spread, which involve the MSA techniques of

- Location: stability, bias, linearity
- Spread: repeatability, reproducibility

5.4 Variability Sources in a 30,000-foot-level Metric

Consider that excess variability a 30,000-foot-level continuous-response metric result in an unsatisfactory process capability/performance metric. The black region in the following figure describes the measurement systems component to that variability, which is what a Measurement Systems Analysis (MSA) assesses.

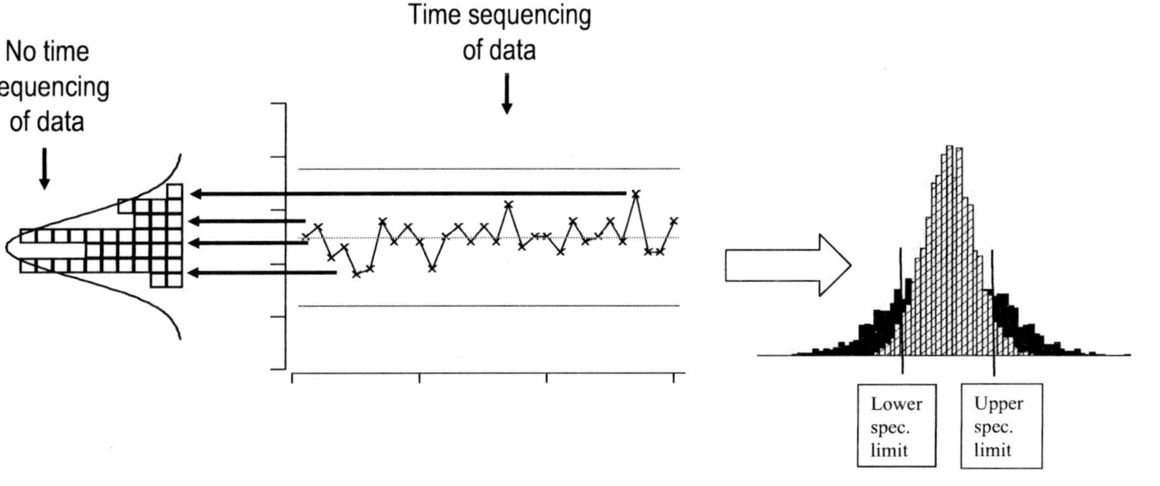

From Figure 15.1 *Integrated Enterprise Excellence, Volume III – Improvement Project Execution: A Management and Black Belt Guide for Going Beyond Lean Six Sigma and the Balanced Scorecard,* Forrest W. Breyfogle III, Bridgeway Books, 2008.

5.5 MSA: Data Integrity

Roadmap step: 5.1
Reference: *IEE Volume III*, Section 15.2

- Purpose
  - At this point in a project's execution, data need evaluation to verify that the values are complete and representative.
  - Many organizational problems are derived from making seemingly correct decisions from a data source that was not representing the performance it was expected to describe.
- What it is
  - A practitioner should validate the entire process that is producing data for the project. This should involve observing the process and recording the performance, then tracking the data through the system to ensure that the dataset contains proper values.

- Verify all automated data conversions that are programmed into Enterprise Resource Planning (ERP) or other electronic systems. They are routinely found to be different than expected, in areas of rounding or errors in conversion constants.
- Verify that all products/transactions that are processed end up in the data set. Specifically track transactions/products that experience rework or rejections to ensure that the entire time is included along with an indication of the additional processing. It is not unusual for organizations to report only the transaction/product data for items that experience the normal process.
- For defect type data, examine the classification system to ensure that the transactions/products are properly classified. You often find that multiple classifications are used for single defect types, which hides some of the issues. Many organizations only record one defect cause per product/transaction which may also be hiding the full impact of a problem.
- Determine what is recorded for a product/transaction that is found with an error or defect in the middle of processing that is corrected. Does it end up in the final quality reporting or do only the problems found in the final inspections get recorded?

Validating the integrity of a dataset can be challenging and time consuming, but this time investment can help practitioners avoid future project-execution issues. Often current business systems do not provide needed information; hence, when undertaking a project, one may need to set up a special collection system to ensure appropriate data are available for analyses; e.g., when areas of multiple-product/transaction defect tracking are to be available to assess their impact to process-rework/repair metric reports.

5.6 MSA: Simple Rounding MSA

Roadmap step: 5.2 & 5.3
Reference: *IEE Volume III*, Section 15.5

- Purpose
  - This is a quick look at the values being reported for your 30,000-foot-level metric to see if it is adequate for both the project and the future control plan.
- What it is
  - The amount of uncertainty of each data point is assumed to be the amount that it is rounded.
  - Reporting, for example, a lead time with integer days has an uncertainty of +/- ½ a day for the start and stop day, or a +/- 1 day uncertainty on the lead time.
  - Any continuous data point has an uncertainty of +/- half of the last unit reported.
  - Apply the same rules for uncertainty limits as you would for a continuous MSA, keeping the uncertainty less than 20% if possible.
  - For the example below, the uncertainty is 66.6% (2 days on a 3 day average). In this example, one would want to change the recording of lead time into hours and minutes rather than integer days.

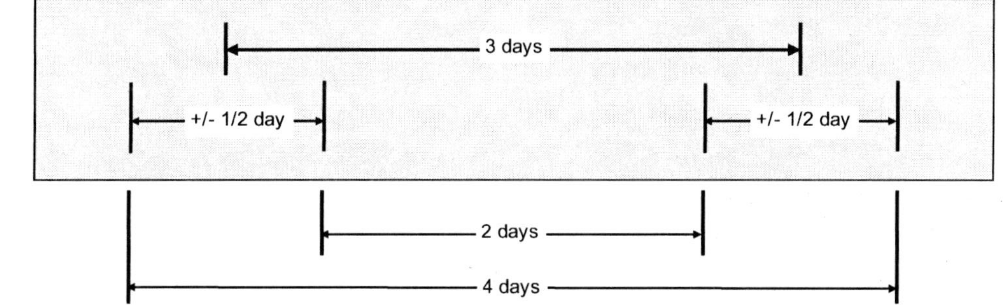

From Figure 15.15 *Integrated Enterprise Excellence, Volume III – Improvement Project Execution: A Management and Black Belt Guide for Going Beyond Lean Six Sigma and the Balanced Scorecard,* Forrest W. Breyfogle III, Bridgeway Books, 2008.

5.7 MSA: Focus on Quality or Variation Reduction?

Roadmap step: 5.4

- Purpose
  - Make a decision if there are possible issues in the data that will be used for the baseline and the analysis phase work. If so, perform a Measurement System Analysis.
- What it is
  - The value of an assessment of the measurement system is often underestimated.
  - In manufacturing environments, where there is a good calibration program, organizations often overly trust their measurement systems. Calibration systems only influence the average bias of a measurement system. They have no impact on the variation of the reported values.
  - In transactional systems and visual inspections, the quality of the decision is always over-estimated. If your project is dependent on a defect classification inspection or an approval step for a document, then you should seriously consider executing an attribute agreement analysis on every key decision step in the process. If an error at that step would change your improvement decisions, you are at risk in not providing a true improvement.

5.8 Tool: Gage R&R

Roadmap step: 5.6
Reference: *IEE Volume III*, Sections 15.9 – 15.13
Minitab Syntax: Stat>Quality Tools>Gage Study>Gage R&R (Crossed)

Consider that a 30,000-foot-level metric that has a continuous response does not have a satisfactory level of capability/performance because of excess variability. This variability (σ_T^2) can have many components, one of which is the measurement systems component. Mathematically, measurement systems analysis involves the understanding and quantification of measurement variance, as described in the following equation, in relation to process variability and tolerance spread:

$$\sigma_T^2 = \sigma_p^2 + \sigma_m^2$$

where

σ_T^2 = Total Variance

σ_p^2 = Process Variance

σ_m^2 = Measurement Variance

MSA assesses the statistical properties of repeatability, reproducibility, bias, stability, and linearity. Gage Repeatability and Reproducibility (R&R) studies address the variability of the measurement system, while bias, stability, and linearity studies address the accuracy of the measurement system.

An example of low measurement variability relative to part variability is described in the following Gage R&R analysis graph using the described equations,

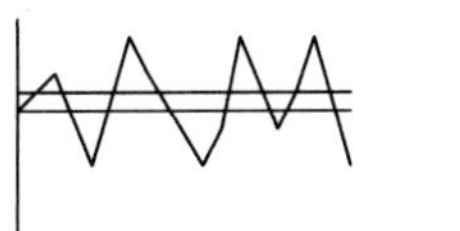

$$UCL_{\overline{x}} = \overline{\overline{x}} + A_2 \overline{R}$$

$$LCL_{\overline{x}} = \overline{\overline{x}} - A_2 \overline{R}$$

where $\overline{R}$ is within appraiser variability and A_2 is a constant determined from Table J (*Integrated Enterprise Excellence, V3*).

R&R analysis report-out options are:

Perspective	Approach	Advantages	Disadvantages
1	% contribution as ratio to total variance	Percentages add to 100%	Standard deviation is determined from distribution of test samples
2	% study	Easy to visualize	Standard deviation is determined from distribution of test samples Source percentages don't have a sum of 100%
3	Number of categories	Single number Easy to visualize	Standard deviation is determined from distribution of test samples Does not have much discrimination
4	% tolerance	Easy to visualize Response measured against customer needs	Source percentages don't have a sum of 100%
5	% process	Easy to visualize Compared to demonstrated process standard deviation that should originate from a large sample representative of the population	Source percentages don't have a sum of 100%

From Table 15.1 *Integrated Enterprise Excellence, Volume III – Improvement Project Execution: A Management and Black Belt Guide for Going Beyond Lean Six Sigma and the Balanced Scorecard,* Forrest W. Breyfogle III, Bridgeway Books, 2008.

68

Example:

- Process data was collected over a long period of time and compiled in a 30,000-foot-level control chart.
  - Process appeared predictable.
  - Specification was 100 +/- 15; i.e., process tolerance = 30.
  - Process capability/performance metric was unsatisfactory, where historical standard deviation was estimated to be 3.5.
- Gage R&R study was planned.
  - Five samples selected from a manufacturing process are to represent the normal spread of the process.
  - Two appraisers who normally do the measurements are chosen to participate in the study.
  - Each part is measured three times by each appraiser.
- Output

Gage R&R Study - ANOVA Method

Two-Way ANOVA Table with Interaction

Source	DF	SS	MS	F	P
Part	4	129.467	32.3667	13.6761	0.013
Appraiser	1	2.700	2.7000	1.1408	0.346
Part * Appraiser	4	9.467	2.3667	0.9221	0.471
Repeatability	20	51.333	2.5667		
Total	29	192.967			

Where ANOVA equals analysis of variance, SS equals sum of squares, MS equals mean squares, F equals F statistic, and P equals probability. Since P is less than 0.05 for "Part", we would reject the null hypothesis that the difference between parts is zero with a probability of being wrong less than 0.05.

Source	VarComp	%Contribution (of VarComp)
Total Gage R&R	2.5444	33.85
Repeatability	2.5333	33.70
Reproducibility	0.0111	0.15
Appraiser	0.0111	0.15
Part-To-Part	4.9722	66.15
Total Variation	7.5167	100.00

The best estimate for each of the variance components is shown above, along with its percent of contribution.

Source	StdDev (SD)	Study Var (6 * SD)	%Study Var (%SV)	%Tolerance (SV/Toler)	%Process (SV/Proc)
Total Gage R&R	1.59513	9.5708	58.18	31.90	45.58
Repeatability	1.59164	9.5499	58.05	31.83	45.48
Reproducibility	0.10541	0.6325	3.84	2.11	3.01
Appraiser	0.10541	0.6325	3.84	2.11	3.01
Part-To-Part	2.22985	13.3791	81.33	44.60	63.71
Total Variation	2.74165	16.4499	100.00	54.83	78.33

Number of Distinct Categories = 1

From the above, we can describe the overall gage R&R results from various perspectives.

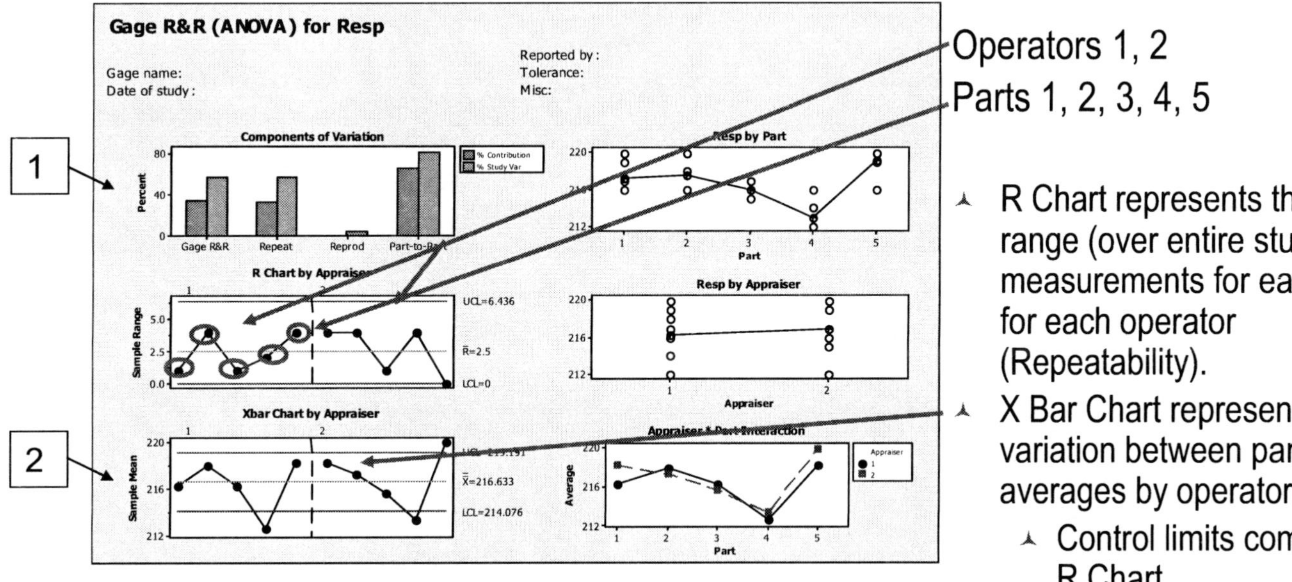

From Figure 15.1 *Integrated Enterprise Excellence, Volume III – Improvement Project Execution: A Management and Black Belt Guide for Going Beyond Lean Six Sigma and the Balanced Scorecard,* Forrest W. Breyfogle III, Bridgeway Books, 2008.

Notes:
1. On Chart 1, ideally you want Gage R&R variability to be small in comparison to part-to-art variability.
2. On Chart 2, unlike traditional control charts, you would like to see the parallel lines close together relative to the individual plotted points.

5.9   MSA: Attribute Agreement Study

Roadmap step: 5.7
Reference: *IEE Volume III*, Section 15.16
Minitab Syntax: Quality Tools>Attribute Agreement Analysis

- Purpose
  - Assess the consistency of an attribute decision process. It may be a defect classification, a process sequence decision, a rework decision, or an approval decision. If these steps are not performed in a consistent manner, then the reported data may not be representative of the true issues.
- What it is
  - The goal of this analysis is to verify that the measurement (decision) system will make a consistent decision across all appraisers, products/transactions, and conditions. No standard is needed for this analysis, but it is beneficial.
  - A greater number of samples are required for this test than is used in the continuous MSA testing. Most samples should have a condition that is very close to the decision point. This will allow for a better assessment of the decision criteria assessment.
  - The general form of the test is to have multiple appraisers assessing multiple samples, more than one time. That provides an equivalent to repeatability (appraisers providing the same decision on the same sample) and reproducibility (multiple appraisers providing the same decision across the same sample).The goal is to have the highest % agreement that is possible in every comparison.
  - Fleiss Kappa statistics are provided for using a pass/fail decision assessment. The Kendal's correlation coefficient is used with the decision and provides an ordinal output, such as a likert scale or a scoring that has order.
  - For the example output shown below, a key output is the assessment disagreement section. For this evaluation, one needs to include a standard into the analysis to generate this output. The legend at the bottom of the output describes the coding. In this section, one can determine if the appraisers are being either too restrictive or too loose with the requirements. In this example, the appraisers are too restrictive and are failing samples that should have passed, but they are always rejecting the non-conforming items. The last column shows that there are a significant number of samples on which the appraisers did not even repeat the same decision on the same sample.

Assessment Disagreement

Appraiser	# P / F	Percent	# F / P	Percent	# Mixed	Percent
A	0	0.00	1	14.29	4	20.00
B	0	0.00	2	28.57	10	50.00

P / F: Assessments across trials = P / standard = F.
F / P: Assessments across trials = F / standard = P.
Mixed: Assessments across trials are not identical.

6 P-DMAIC: Measure Phase – Organizational Wisdom

Purpose: To include a broad range of inputs from experienced members of the organization describing the current process

Deliverables:

- Detailed process description (process map)
- List of low-hanging-fruit problems for immediate improvement
- A prioritized list of potential problem causes to evaluate in analyze phase

Reference: Chapter 16 of *Integrated Enterprise Excellence, Volume III* (Breyfogle 2008c)

6.1 Roadmap

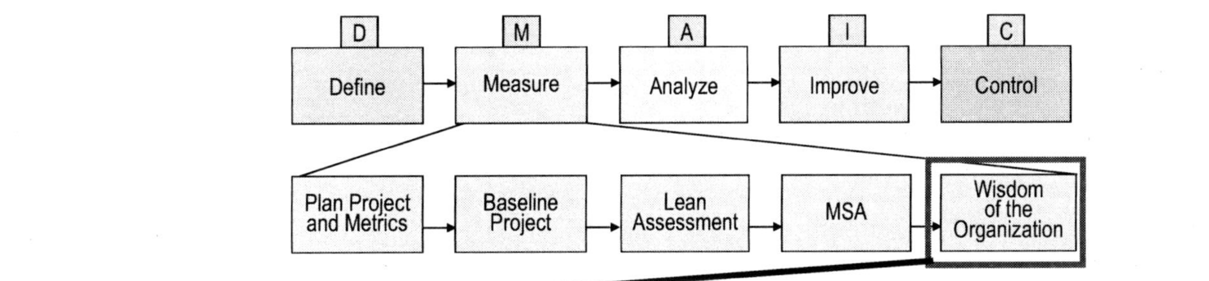

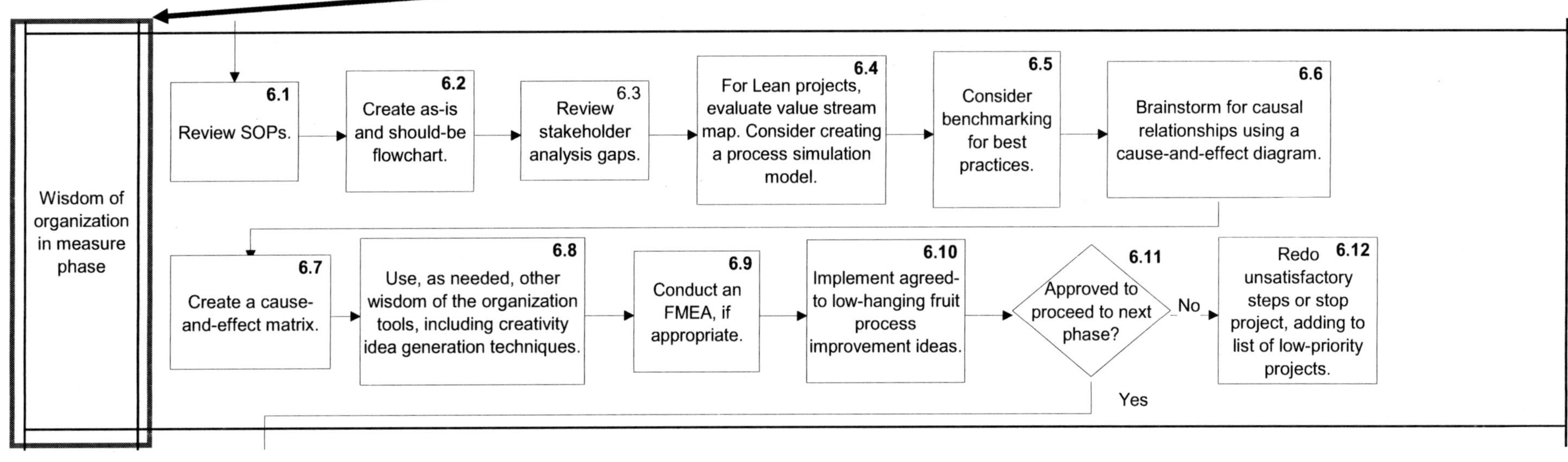

6.2 Check Sheet

Measure Phase: Wisdom of the Organization Check Sheet		
Tool/Methodology	**Questions**	**Yes/No NA**
Process flowchart	Was a process map created at the appropriate level of detail?	
	Does the flowchart include critical suppliers and end customers?	
Cause-and-Effect Diagram	Was a brainstorming session held with a cross-functional team to collect the Wisdom of the Organization inputs?	
Cause-and-Effect Matrix	Were the results of the Cause-and-Effect Diagram prioritized with the C&E Matrix?	
	Were there any "low-hanging-fruit" opportunities that can be fixed immediately?	
FMEA	Was an FMEA conducted with resulting action items?	
Assessment	Were any process improvements made?	
	If so, were they statistically verified with the appropriate hypothesis test?	
	Did you describe the change over time on a 30,000-foot-level control chart?	
	Did you calculate and display the change in the process capability/performance metric?	
	Have you documented and communicated the improvements?	
	Have you summarized the benefits and annualized financial benefits?	
Team		
Resources	Are all team members motivated and committed to the project?	
	Does the process owner agree with the major outcomes that came from wisdom of the organization assessment?	
Next Phase		
Approval to proceed	Did the team adequately complete the above steps?	
	Has the project database been updated and communication plan followed?	
	Should this project proceed to the Analyze Phase?	
	Is there a detailed plan for the Analyze Phase?	
	Are barriers to success identified and planned for?	
	Is the team tracking with the project schedule?	
	Have schedule revisions been approved?	

6.3 Application

Application Examples:

- Flow chart
  - An IEE project was created to improve the 30,000-foot-level metric, Days Sales Outstanding (DSO). A process flow chart was created to describe the existing process.
  - An IEE project was created to improve the 30,000-foot-level metric, the diameter of a manufactured part. A process flow chart was created to describe the existing process.
- Cause-and-effect Diagram
  - An IEE project was created to improve the 30,000-foot-level metric, Days Sales Outstanding (DSO). A process flow chart was created to describe the existing process. A team created a cause-and-effect diagram in a brainstorming session to trigger a list of potential causal inputs and improvement ideas.
  - An IEE project was created to improve the 30,000-foot-level metric, the diameter of a manufactured part. A process flow chart was created to describe the existing process. A team created a cause-and-effect diagram in a brainstorming session to trigger a list of potential causal inputs and improvement ideas.
- Cause-and-effect Matrix
  - Transactional 30,000-foot-level metric: DSO reduction was chosen as an IEE project. The team used a cause-and-effect matrix to prioritize items from a cause-and-effect diagram.
  - Manufacturing 30,000-foot-level metric (KPOV): An IEE project was to improve the capability/performance of the diameter of a manufactured product; i.e., reduce the number of parts beyond the specification limits. The team used a cause-and-effect matrix to prioritize items from a cause-and-effect diagram.
  - Transactional and Manufacturing 30,000-foot-level cycle time metric (a Lean metric): An IEE project to improve the time from order entry to fulfillment was measured. The team used a cause-and-effect matrix to prioritize items from a cause-and-effect diagram.
  - Transactional and Manufacturing 30,000-foot-level inventory metric or satellite-level TOC metric (a Lean metric): An IEE project was to reduce inventory. The team used a cause-and-effect matrix to prioritize items from a cause-and-effect diagram.
  - Manufacturing 30,000-foot-level quality metric: An IEE project was to reduce the number of defects in a printed circuit board manufacturing process. The team used a cause-and-effect matrix to prioritize items from a cause-and-effect diagram.
- Failure Mode and Effects Analysis (FMEA)
  - Transactional 30,000-foot-level metric: DSO reduction was chosen as an IEE project. The team used a cause-and-effect matrix to prioritize items from a cause-and-effect diagram. An FMEA was conducted of the process steps and/or highest categories from the cause-and-effect matrix.
  - Manufacturing 30,000-foot-level metric (KPOV): An IEE project was to improve the capability/performance of the diameter of a manufactured product; i.e., reduce the number of parts beyond the specification limits. The team used a cause-and-effect matrix to prioritize items from a cause-and-effect diagram. An FMEA was conducted of the process steps and/or highest categories from the cause-and-effect matrix.
  - Transactional and Manufacturing 30,000-foot-level cycle time metric (a Lean metric): An IEE project to improve the time from order entry to fulfillment was measured. The team used a cause-and-effect matrix to prioritize items from a cause-and-effect diagram. An FMEA was conducted of the process steps and/or highest categories from the cause-and-effect matrix.

- Transactional and Manufacturing 30,000-foot-level inventory metric or satellite-level TOC metric (a Lean metric): An IEE project was to reduce inventory. The team used a cause-and-effect matrix to prioritize items from a cause-and-effect diagram. An FMEA was conducted of the process steps and/or highest categories from the cause-and-effect matrix.
- Manufacturing 30,000-foot-level quality metric: An IEE project was to reduce the number of defects in a printed circuit board manufacturing process. The team used a cause-and-effect matrix to prioritize items from a cause-and-effect diagram. An FMEA was conducted of the process steps and/or highest categories from the cause-and-effect matrix.

6.4 Review Standard Operating Procedures

Roadmap step: 6.1
Reference: *IEE Volume III*, Section 16.2

- Purpose
  - Before initiating the collection of wisdom from the organization, a review of the Standard Operating Procedure (SOP) should be performed.
  - This allows an understanding of the key process operations and allows the practitioner to better lead the later steps of this phase.
- What it is
  - Many organizations do not exactly follow their process documentation. There may be operations that workers perform differently and/or short cuts may be taken. It is best to know the SOP before beginning observations or discussions with the process users.
  - One common characteristic often found is that the SOP does not provide much processing guidance. The SOP might describe the product/transaction end state and leave the actions up to the worker. This situation can work well for ISO (International Organization for Standardization) certification, but it can lead to a large amount of processing variability, which can be a project factor that warrants investigation.

6.5 Tool: Flowchart

Roadmap step: 6.2
Reference: *IEE Volume III*, Section 16.2

- Purpose
  - Provide a graphic that represents the sequencing of the process that can be used for communication to others.
  - Provides a discussion that uncovers the un-documented activities and differences in workers and equipment.
- What it is
  - A best practice is to generate three different process flowcharts.
    - Flowchart the SOP directed actions. It is common to find gaps in the instructions and guidance that will not really work.

- Flowchart the process as one observes it being executed. This helps the practitioner understand the process better before the improvement team flow charting exercise.
- Using the improvement team and possible additional process users, flow chart the process as they describe their actions. The process users will generally bring up differences in individual practices and other key observations. Chart the process just as they describe it.

- After all three flow charts are completed, bring out the first two and share them with the team. Lead a discussion on why they are different. Recognize that every difference is a possible improvement opportunity.

Frequently used symbols to describe the activities associated with a process map are:

Terminal: Symbol that defines start and end of a flowchart.

Activity symbol: Symbol that contains a description of a step of the process.

Decision symbol: Symbol that contains a question following an activity symbol; e.g., passes test? The process branches into two or more paths. Each path is labeled to correspond to the answer of the question.

On-page connector: Symbol identifies the connection points in a loop or the continuation in a flow. Tie-in symbols contain the same letter.

Off-page connector: Initiating symbol contains a letter or number in the form *to page x*, while the receiving symbol contains a letter or number in the form *from page y*.

Flowchart example:

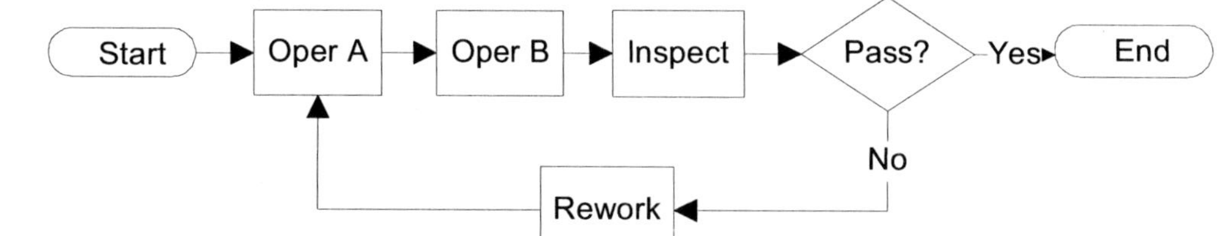

From Figure 16.1 *Integrated Enterprise Excellence, Volume III – Improvement Project Execution: A Management and Black Belt Guide for Going Beyond Lean Six Sigma and the Balanced Scorecard,* Forrest W. Breyfogle III, Bridgeway Books, 2008.

6.6　Assessment of Lean Value Stream Map and Simulation modeling

Roadmap step: 6.2
Reference: *IEE Volume III*, Sections 16.2 and 16.3

- Purpose
  - If a VSM was generated in the lean assessment phase, you should update it using the team inputs based on knowledge developed in the SOPs and standard flow charting.
  - After completing the flow charting, consider converting the flow chart into a working simulation that can be used to test assumptions and generate data that can be compared with actuals.
- What it is
  - Simulations can be used to evaluate improvements and hypothesis ideas that can not be evaluated in an operating process.
  - Simulations are generally most beneficial in transactional and non-manufacturing processes because they are so difficult to modify to test ideas.

6.7　Tool: Benchmarking

Roadmap step: 6.4
Reference: *IEE Volume III*, Section 16.4

With benchmarking, we learn from others. Benchmarking involves the search of an organization for the best practices, adaptation of the practices to its processes, and improving with the focus of becoming the best in class. Benchmarking can involve comparisons of products, processes, methods, and strategies. Internal benchmarking makes comparisons between similar operations within an organization. Competitive benchmarking makes comparisons with the best direct competitor. Functional benchmarking makes comparisons of similar process methodologies. Generic benchmarking makes comparisons of processes with exemplary and innovative processes of other companies. Sources of information for benchmarking include the internet, in-house published material, professional associations, universities, advertising, and customer feedback.

6.8 Tool: Brainstorming

Roadmap step: 6.5
Reference: *IEE Volume III*, Chapter 16.5

- Purpose
  - This is the point where you collect the cause and improvement ideas from the project team and the workforce.
- What it is
  - A brainstorming session is a very valuable means of generating new ideas and involving a group.
  - Many methods to brainstorm are available. The choice of a method should factor in what the improvement team leader is comfortable with and the level of pre-existing process knowledge.
  - The most common Lean Six Sigma method is to brainstorm information and then document it on a Cause and Effect Diagram (Ishikawa or Fishbone Diagram)
  - Other successful tools are the Why-Why Diagram, a fault tree diagram, or affinity diagrams.
  - A best practice is not to leave this idea generation phase without performing a few additional actions.
    - Using a group discussion, combine similar causes into a single item.
    - If some causes are too general, such as "Training", use the 5-why technique to drill down into these causes until you have a list of actionable causes that can be evaluated.

Example: Training is listed on the brainstorming exercises.
- Ask why training is listed
- The answer may be that the workers are doing things wrong
  - Ask what are they doing wrong (this is probably the true causes you need to know)
- The answer might be that they are not following the process
  - Ask what steps are not being followed (this is probably the true causes you need to know)
- The answer might be that they do not know enough to do the process properly.
  - Ask what skills they lack. (this is probably the true causes you need to know)

There will invariably be improved project efficiency and an overall reduction project duration when adequate time is spent on the creation of a brainstorming list and its causal prioritization.

6.9   *Tool: Cause-and-effect Diagram*

Roadmap step: 6.5
Reference: *IEE Volume III*, Section 16.6
Minitab Syntax: Stat>Quality Tools>Cause-and-Effect

This technique is useful to trigger ideas when conducting brainstorming sessions in which individuals list the perceived sources (causes) of a problem (effect). A cause-and-effect diagram provides a means for teams to focus on the creation of a list of process input variables, by categories, which could affect key process output variables.   With this strategy, we can address strata issues based on key characteristics; e.g., who, what, where, and when. The analysis of this stratification later through both graphical and analytical techniques can provide needed insight for pattern detection, which provides an opportunity for focused improvement efforts. When constructing a cause-and-effect diagram, it is often appropriate to consider six areas or causes that can contribute to a characteristic response or effect: materials, machine, method, personnel, measurement, and environment. Each one of these characteristics is then investigated for subcauses. Subcauses are specific items or difficulties that are identified as a factual or potential cause to the problem (effect).

Example:

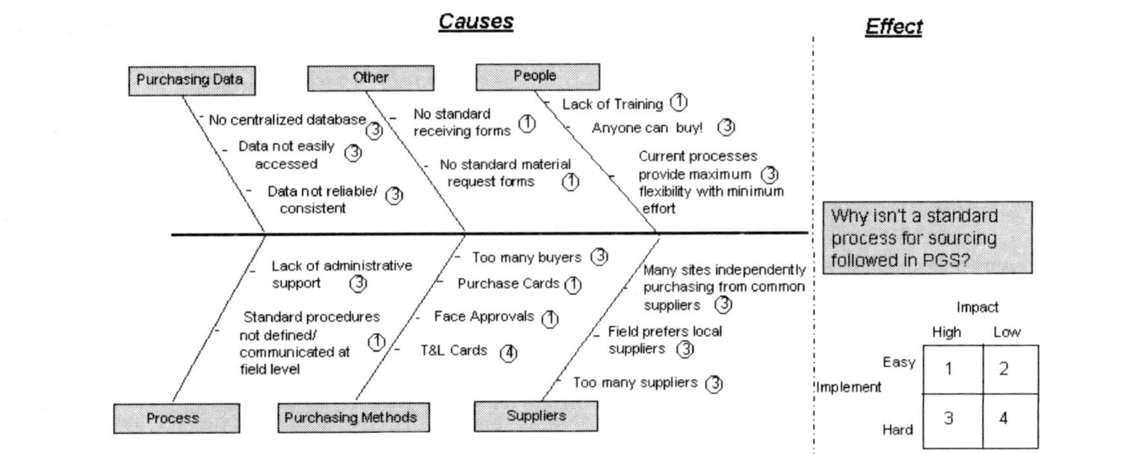

From Figure 16.6 *Integrated Enterprise Excellence, Volume III – Improvement Project Execution: A Management and Black Belt Guide for Going Beyond Lean Six Sigma and the Balanced Scorecard,* Forrest W. Breyfogle III, Bridgeway Books, 2008.

6.10 Tool: Other Brainstorming Tools

Roadmap step: 6.5
Reference: *IEE Volume III*, Section 14.14

- What it is
  - Why-Why or Fault Tree diagram may be beneficial when the system is quite well known. This may be especially beneficial when examining a defect generation problem. (Shown on the right)
  - Both methods start with the problem and build out in logical steps. The advantage of this methodology over a cause-and-effect diagram is in the inherent hierarchy that is developed with each cause in the tree being recognized as a possible effect from an earlier cause.
  - All causes on the bottom or far right are the causes to be carried into the later wisdom of the organization steps.

6.11 Tool: Cause-and-effect Matrix

Roadmap step: 6.7
Reference: *IEE Volume III*, Section 16.7

- Purpose
  - This tool is used to take the list of causes and prioritize them so that they can be addressed in order.
- What it is
  - The cause-and-effect matrix is a tool that can aid with the prioritization of importance of process input variables. This relational matrix prioritization by a team can help with the selection of what will be monitored to determine if there is a cause-and-effect relationship and whether key process input controls are necessary. The results of a cause-and-effect matrix can lead to other activities such as failure mode and effects analysis (FMEA), multi-vari charts, correlation analysis, and design of experiments (DOE).

Example format:

		Key process output variables (with prioritization)						Results	Percentage
		A	B	C	D	E	F		
		5	3	10	8	7	6		
	1	4	3		3			53	5.56%
	2	10		4	6		6	174	18.24%
Key	3		4					0	0.00%
process	4			9	5	9	8	241	25.26%
input	5	4				6		62	6.50%
variables	6		6		5		2	52	5.45%
	7	5		4		5		100	10.48%
	8		3		4		5	62	6.50%
	9	6		3		2		74	7.76%
	10		2	4				40	4.19%
	11	4			4	2	5	96	10.06%

From Table 16.1 *Integrated Enterprise Excellence, Volume III – Improvement Project Execution: A Management and Black Belt Guide for Going Beyond Lean Six Sigma and the Balanced Scorecard,* Forrest W. Breyfogle III, Bridgeway Books, 2008.

6.12 Tool: Affinity Diagram

Roadmap step: 6.7
Reference: *IEE Volume III*, Section 16.8

- Purpose
  - This tool is used to focus an effort that has too many options or directions it could take.
- What it is
  - Using an affinity diagram, a team can organize and summarize the natural grouping from a large number of ideas and issues that could have been created during a brainstorming session.
  - From this summary, teams can better understand the essence of problems and breakthrough solution alternatives.
  - This tool also allows a group with significantly different status or influence levels to work without inhibiting the inputs, far better than traditional brainstorming will perform.

To create an affinity diagram, record each brainstorming idea individually on a self-stick removable note, using at a minimum a noun and verb to describe each item. An affinity diagram often addresses 40-60 items but can assess 100-200 ideas. Next, place the self-stick removable note on a wall and ask everyone, without talking, to move the notes to the place where they think the issue best fits. Upon completion of this sorting, create a summary or header sentence for each grouping. Create subgroups for large groupings as needed with a subhead description.

6.13 Tool: Nominal Group Technique (NGT)

Roadmap step: 6.7
Reference: *IEE Volume III*, Section 16.9

Nominal group technique expedites team consensus on relative importance of problems, issues, or solutions. A basic procedure for conducting an NGT session is described below; however, voting procedures can differ depending upon team preferences and the situation.

An NGT is conducted by displaying a generated list of items, perhaps from a brainstorming session, on a flipchart or board. A final list is then created by eliminating duplications and making clarifications. The new final list of statements is then prominently displayed, and each item is assigned a letter, A, B, ..., Z. On a sheet of paper, each person ranks the statements, assigning the most important a number equal to the number of statements with the least important assigned the value of one. Results from the individual sheets are combined to create a total overall prioritization number for each statement.

6.14 Tool: Failure Mode and Effects Analysis (FMEA)

Roadmap step: 6.8
Reference: *IEE Volume III*, Sections 16.12 through 16.16

- Purpose
  - This tool is used to further develop the top causes found in the cause-and-effect matrix.
  - This tool can also be used as a parallel tool to understand and prioritize risk factors in a process.
- What it is
  - Potential failure mode and effects analysis (FMEA) is a method that facilitates process improvement.
  - Using FMEAs, organizations can identify and eliminate concerns early in the development of a process or design and provide a form of risk analysis.
  - A review of the difference between Failure modes (how the process fails) and process effects (how the failure is recognized) is generally key to keeping the FMEA effort from failing.

The quality of procured parts or services can improve when organizations work with their suppliers to implement FMEAs within their organization. Properly executed FMEAs can improve internal and external customer satisfaction in addition to the bottom line of organizations. Design FMEA (DFMEA) applications include component, subsystem, and main system. Process FMEA (PFMEA) applications include assembly, machines, work stations, gages, procurement, training of operators, and tests.

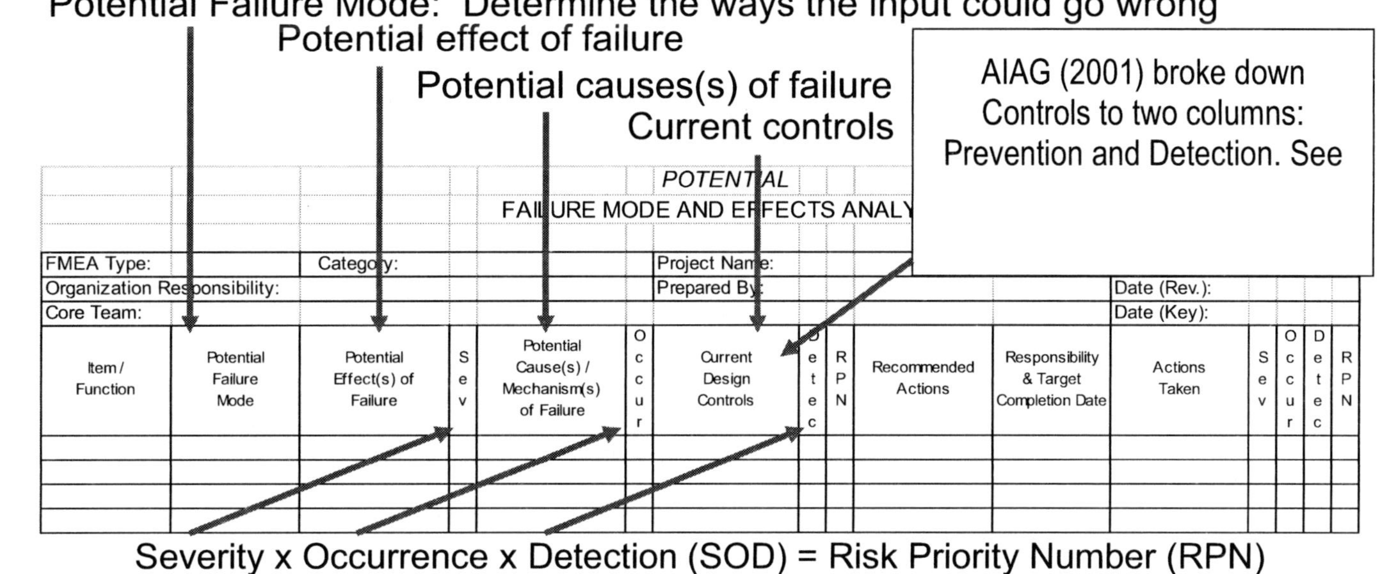

- The FMEA generation process can be performed more efficiently with little lost performance by following this guidance.
  - Fill out columns 1 – 3 (failure mode and effect columns) using only a Subject Matter Expert (SME)
    - o They will list the known process failure modes and how they were detected in the past.
  - Use the team to fill out columns 6 & 8 (Causes and detectability)
    - o This is where the benefit of objectivity is most beneficial.
  - End the meeting – Reconvene in a few days to finish.
  - Now Score each of the columns (4, 7, & 9) and calculate the RPN.
    - o Use the entire team for this effort.
  - Score entire columns before moving to the next column.
  - All scores in the same column should be reviewed for their relative order.

7   P-DMAIC: Analyze Phase

Purpose: To identify and analyze data for improvement opportunities
Deliverables:

- Data relationships between problem and causes based on evidence
- Validate input and output process variables
- Prioritized list of improvement opportunities to be evaluated in improve phase

Reference: Chapters 17 – 28 of *Integrated Enterprise Excellence, Volume III* (Breyfogle 2008c)

7.1   Roadmap

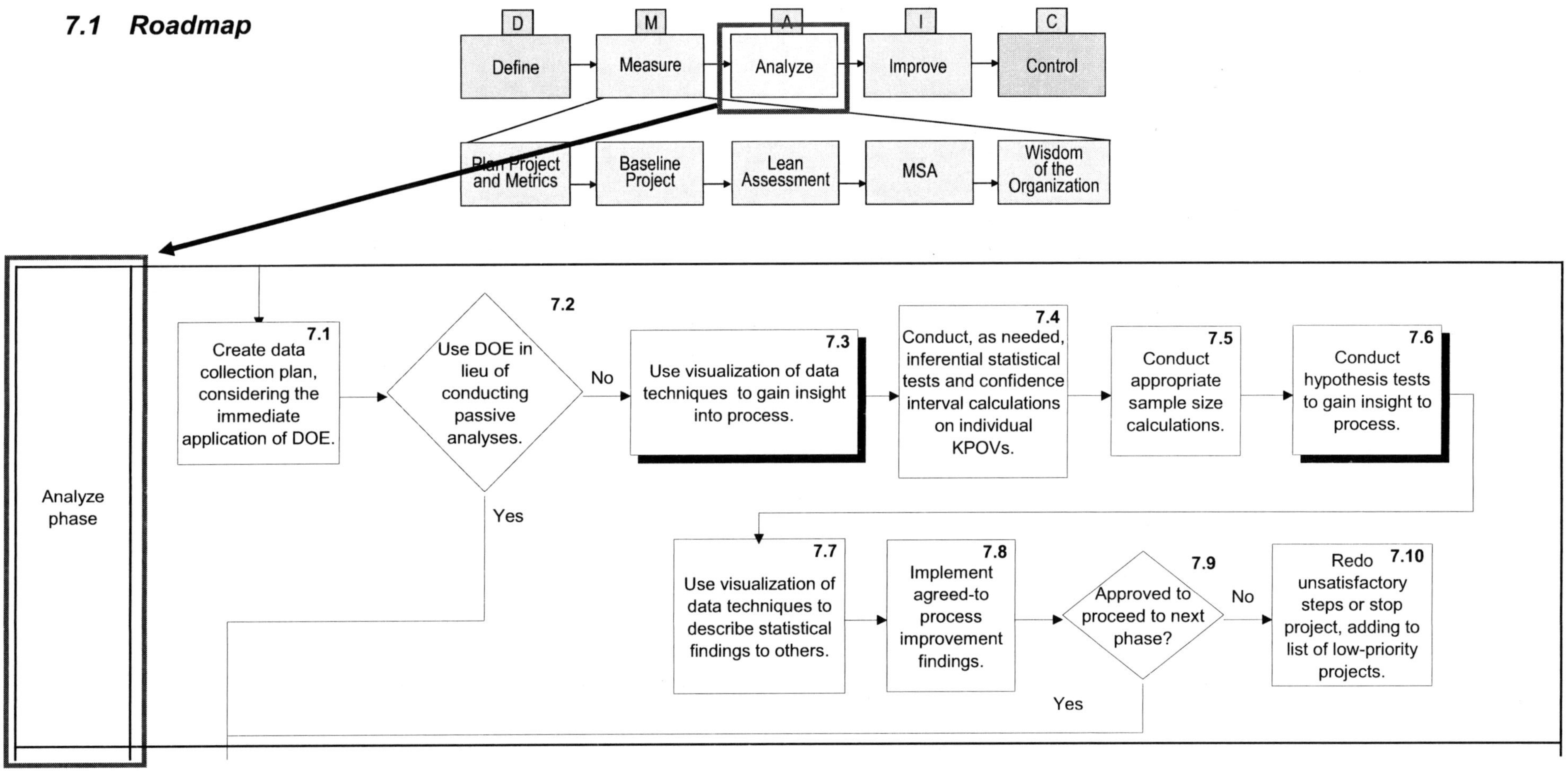

Step 7.6 Drill down (Part 1)

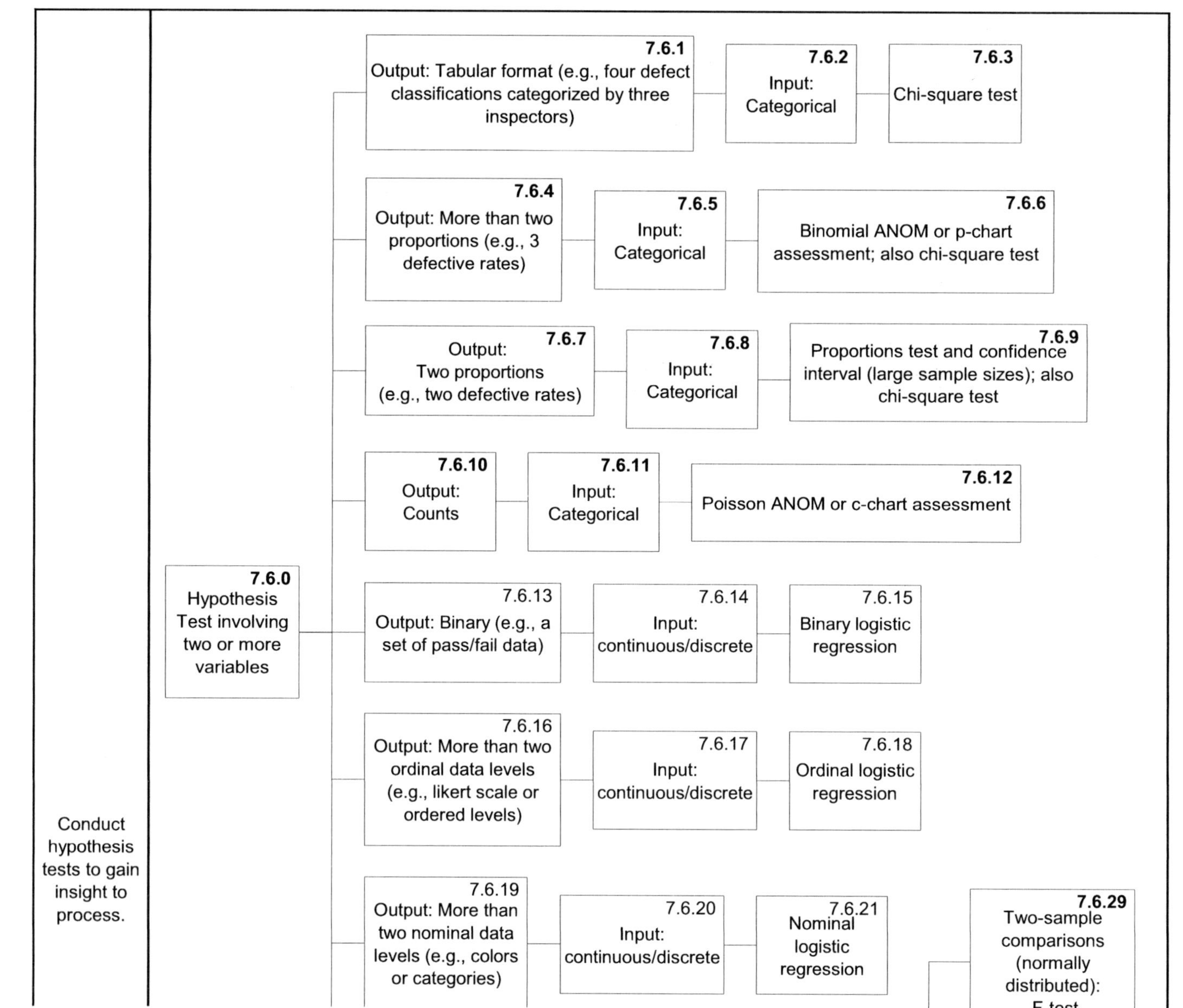

Step 7.6 Drill down (Part 2)

Conduct hypothesis tests to gain insight to process.

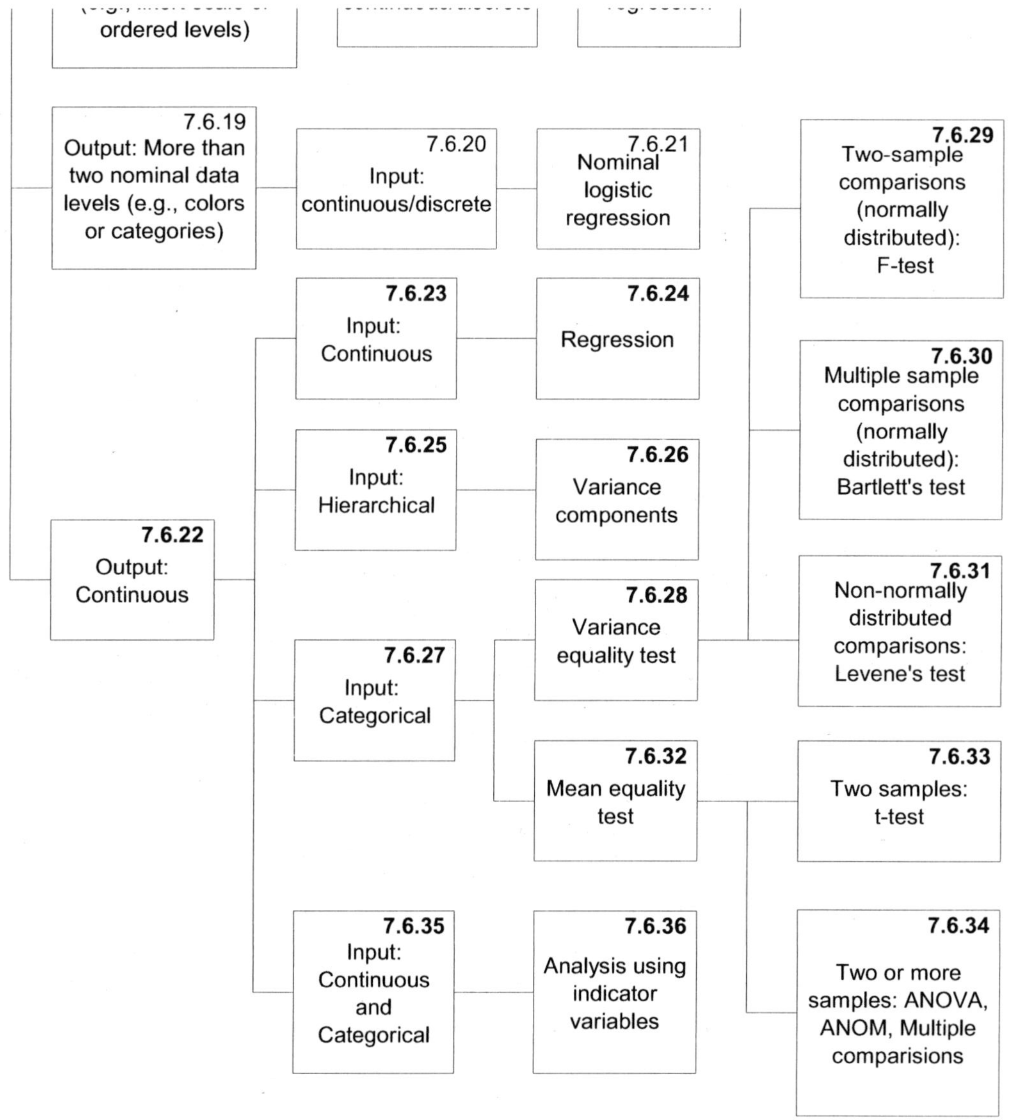

Step 7.3 Drill down

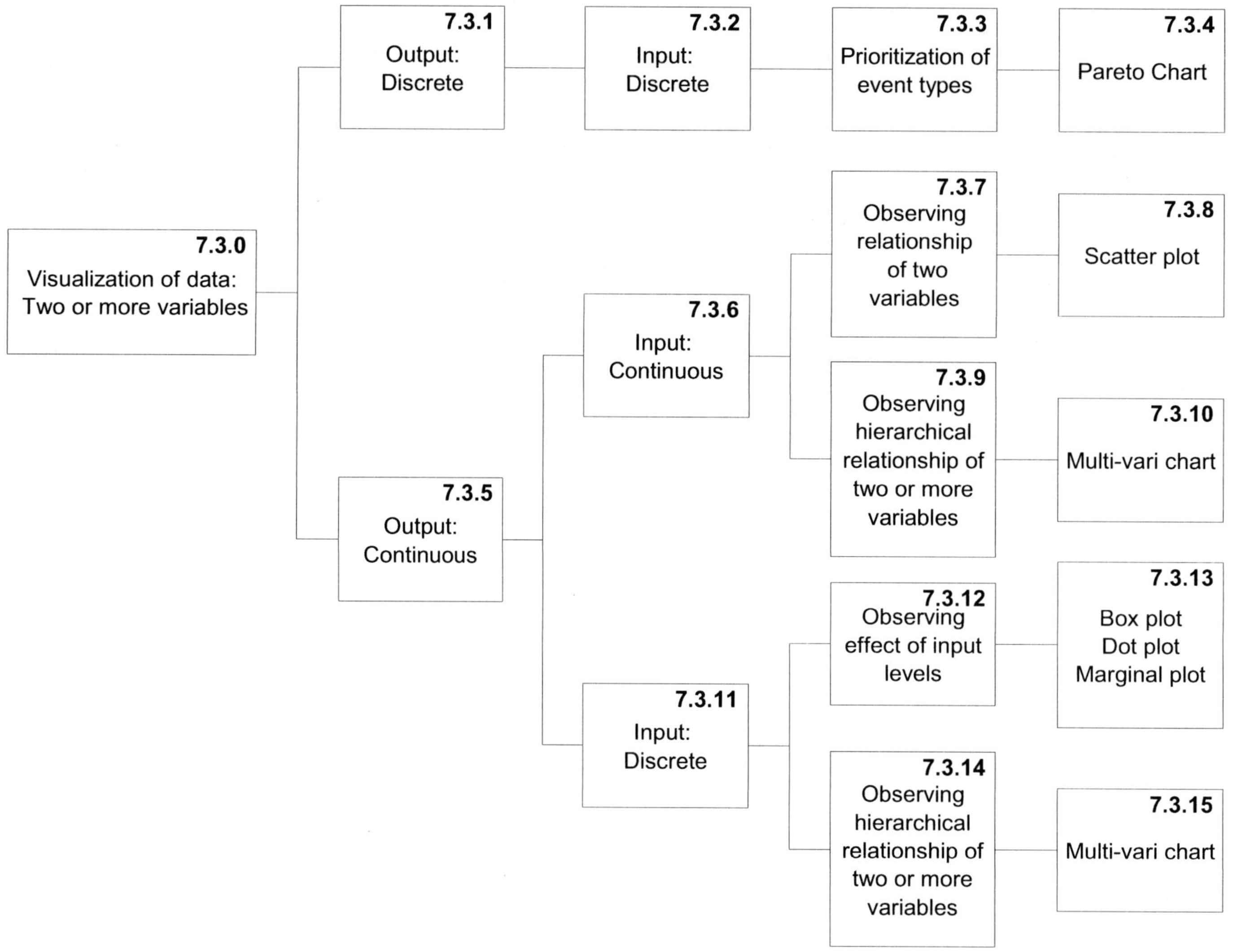

7.2 Check Sheet

Analyze Phase Check Sheet		
Description	**Questions**	**Yes/No NA**
Tool/Methodology		
Box plots, marginal plots, and multi-vari charts	Was the appropriate visualization of data technique used in order to gain process insight to the process?	
Pareto charts	If data are discrete, were Pareto Charts used to drill down to the KPIVs?	
Chi Square p-chart/u-chart (and/or ANOM)	If input data and output data are both discrete, was a chi-square test used to test for statistical significance and a p-chart or ANOM analysis (u-chart or ANOM analysis for count data) used to assess individual difference from the overall mean?	
Scatter Plots	If data are continuous, were scatter plots used to display the relationship between KPIVs and a KPOV?	
Comparison tests	Were statistical significance tests used to gain process insight?	
Variance components	If output data were continuous and inputs are hierarchical, was variance components considered to gain insight?	
Regression analysis	For continuous input and output data, was regression analysis used to compare the relationship between inputs and the output(s)?	
ANOVA / ANOM, Bartlett's /Levene's test	For discrete KPIVs and continuous KPOV data, was the appropriate tool used to compare populations for the different levels of KPIVs?	
Assessment	Were any process improvements made?	
	If so, were they statistically verified with the appropriate hypothesis test?	
	Did you describe the change over time on a 30,000-foot-level control chart?	
	Did you calculate and display the change in the process capability/performance metric?	
	Have you documented and communicated the improvements?	
	Have you summarized the benefits and annualized financial benefits?	
Team		
Resources	Are all team members motivated and committed to the project?	
	Does the process owner understand and support the major conclusins from the analyze phase?	
	Is the champion ready to remove potential obstacles to the upcoming changes?	
Next Phase		
Approval to proceed	Did the team adequately complete the above steps?	
	Has the project database been updated and communication plan followed?	
	Is DOE needed?	
	If so, should this project proceed to the Improve Phase?	
	Is there a detailed plan for the Improve Phase?	
	Has the team considered improvements to both the process mean and process variation?	
	Are barriers to success identified and planned for?	
	Is the team tracking with the project schedule?	
	Have schedule revisions been approved?	

7.3 Application and Background

Application Examples:

- An IEE project was created to improve the 30,000-foot-level metric, Days Sales Outstanding (DSO). One input that surfaced from a cause-and-effect diagram was the size of the invoice. A scatter plot and regression analysis of DSO versus size of invoice was created.
- DSO reduction was chosen as an IEE project. A cause-and-effect matrix ranked company as an important input that could affect the DSO response; i.e., the team thought that some companies were more delinquent in payments than other companies. From randomly sampled data, a statistical analysis was conducted to test the hypothesis of equality of means for the DSOs of these companies.
- Transactional 30,000-foot-level metric: DSO reduction was chosen as an IEE project. A cause-and-effect matrix ranked company as an important input that could affect the DSO response. The team wanted to estimate the variability in DSO between and within companies. A variance component analysis was conducted to test significance and estimate the components.

Background Reference: Chapters 18 through 28 of *Integrated Enterprise Excellence, Volume III* (Breyfogle 2008c)

7.4 Data Collection Plan (DCP) Needs, Source, and Types

Roadmap step: 7.1 and 7.2
Reference: *IEE Volume III*, Section 17.3

- Purpose
  - This step is to consider data collection as a process rather than a haphazard event.
  - A thorough planning effort prior to data collection can ensure that you only need to collect data one time for the entire analyze phase effort.
- What it is
  - Data collection is the execution of a systematic plan for taking measurements of key variables in an efficient and effective manner.
  - Data collection is the foundation of analyzing and understanding processes.
  - An operational definition for the collection of data is an easy-to-follow procedural translation for the measurements and their discussion.
  - If no historical data exists or a large set of historical data exists, it may be more efficient to create a Design of Experiments (DOE) matrix (methods found in the improve phase of this document) and then collect only the data that corresponds with the DOE observation combinations.
    - Only collect data from the process when the combination exists in the current process. This avoids the cost and effort to collect data that is not as useful.

- For existing historical data, extracting only the observations that match the conditions defined in the design of experiment will reduce the amount of data to possibly a manageable size, but it also can remove any correlation or biasing in the historical data set which improves the analysis confidence. This effort has been called a "Historical DOE".

A data collection plan (DCP) that accomplishes operational definition needs addresses:
- what to measure
- how to measure it
- when and where to measure it
- how many measurements to make
- how to record the data
- determine if customers and suppliers use the same measurement procedures, when appropriate
- a method to assess the variation of the data collection process

Populations are often too large to analyze in their entirety. A random sample of data from the population can be used to estimate characteristics of the population. Potential sources for information are:

Data Source	Pros	Cons
Historical	Cheap, Quick, Available, Familiar, Quantity	Accuracy, Relevance, Misleading, Outdated, May not be right variable
Current Process	Current Data, Relevant, Knowledge of Accuracy, No Additional Cost, Available	May be Long Collection Time, Data Collection tied to Process Cycle, Process May Change, May Not be Right Variable
New Process Measurement	Current Data, Right Variable, Knowledge of accuracy, New information, May be short term	Costs Money and Time, Process May Change, Impacts Process
Experimentation	Efficient, Effective, Economic, Provides New Process Knowledge (data)	Costs Money and Time, Requires Expertise, Could interfere with process or production

From Table 17.2 *Integrated Enterprise Excellence, Volume III – Improvement Project Execution: A Management and Black Belt Guide for Going Beyond Lean Six Sigma and the Balanced Scorecard,* Forrest W. Breyfogle III, Bridgeway Books, 2008.

7.5   Tools: Data Collection

Roadmap steps: 7.1 & 7.2
Reference: *IEE Volume III*, Section 17.4

Data collection tools, which are described in more detail below, include:
Check Sheets
- Used for manual collection of process data.
- May be collected at specific process steps or they may be attached to a product/transaction and filled out as it is processed.

Automated data collection
- Saves labor
- Sampling frequencies may be quick which can lead to auto-correlated data
- May need to use only a subset of this data, such as 1 point per hour or day to reduce auto-correlation.

Sampling
- Random
  - This effort is used to reduce the impact of time dependent changes on the process
  - It is not always the best method to sample. See the next two bullets.
- Stratified
  - This sampling involves segmenting your process data by categories or groupings and then randomly sampling within each category or group.
  - In this method, you adjust the sample size in each category or group to match the long term ratios of the process.
  - It allows a short term data set to be adjusted to represent the entire production period even though the data collection period was not representative of the entire period.
- Systematic
  - This is used for continuous processes where pure random sampling of the output is cumbersome.
  - If you know the process has random variation in its performance, you shift sampling to a fixed period of time or item counts. As long as the process variation sources are captured within the sample period, this method is superior to pure random sampling.

Surveys
- Questionnaires
  - These are very difficult to create. If possible, use your organization's market research department as a resource.
  - How the questions are written may bias the answers.
  - Very large sample sizes are needed to produce valid results.
  - Use this method as a last result.
- Interviews
  - These may be superior to questionnaires but they take significant resources and time to collect enough data to be representative.
  - If you hold interviews, be careful to ask open-ended questions and follow up to understand the responses. Avoid questions that may bias the answers.
- Infrequent sampling
  - If the goal is to understand the long term performance of a process, collecting data infrequently rather than at a 100% level is usually more efficient.
  - If you can afford to collect 100 data points, it is generally better to have 1/day over 100 days than it is to collect 10/day for 10 days.
- Design of experiments (DOE)
  - If a change is being evaluated, a DOE can provide independency insight with other process state conditions.
  - If there are no existing data in certain process conditions that need evaluation, it is better to collect this data using DOE methods than to use one-at-a-time testing.
  - These methods provide insight into interactions and interdependencies between process causes and settings which may be key to the analyze phase efforts.

Note: It can save time to format data collection sheets to match the format that would be entered into analysis software. For analyses, data typically need to be in columns, where each row is an observation.

7.6 *Visualization of data to gain insight*

Roadmap step: 7.3
Reference: *IEE Volume III*, Chapter 18

- Purpose
  - Before performing statistical hypothesis tests, you should chart, graph, or plot the data.
- What it is
  - Creating a visualization of the data provides insight about the data that may be missed if you start with the statistical testing.
  - You may find non-normality, bad data points, data groups with very small sample sizes and other issues that may impact your analysis.
  - Visualization plots may provide an obvious answer, which indicates that a hypothesis test is not needed.

7.7 Tools: Comparison Tests, Continuous Response

Roadmap step: 7.6.33
Reference: *IEE Volume III*, Chapter 22
Minitab Syntax: Stat>Basic Statistics>2-Sample t

Application examples:

- Transactional 30,000-foot-level metric: DSO reduction was chosen as an IEE project. A cause-and-effect matrix ranked company as an important input that could affect the DSO response; i.e., the team thought that Company A was more delinquent in payments than other companies. From randomly sampled data, a t-test was conducted to test the hypothesis of equality of mean DSO of Company A to the other companies.
- Manufacturing 30,000-foot-level metric (KPOV): An IEE project was to improve the process capability/performance of the diameter of a manufactured product; i.e., reduce the number of parts beyond the specification limits. A cause-and-effect matrix ranked cavity of the two-cavity mold as an important input that could be yielding different part diameters. From randomly sampled data, a t-test was conducted to test the hypothesis of mean diameter equality for cavity 1 and cavity 2. An F-test was conducted to test the hypothesis of variability equality for cavity 1 and cavity 2.
- Transactional and Manufacturing 30,000-foot-level lead time metric (a Lean metric): An IEE project to improve the time from order entry to fulfillment was measured. A low-hanging-fruit change was made to the process. Using the 30,000-foot-level control chart data, a confidence interval was created to describe the impact of the change in mean system's lead time.

The methods discussed in this chapter can be used, for example, to compare two production machines or suppliers. Both mean and standard deviation output can be compared between the samples to determine whether a difference is large enough to be statistically significant. The comparison test of means is robust to the shape of the underlying distribution not being normal; however, this is not true when comparing standard deviations.

The null hypothesis for the comparison test is that there is no difference, while the alternative hypothesis is that there is a difference. When comparing the means of two samples, the null hypothesis is that there is no difference between the population means, while the alternative hypothesis is that there is a difference between the population means. A difference between two means could be single-sided, i.e., $\mu_1 > \mu_2$ or $\mu_1 < \mu_2$, or double-sided, i.e., $\mu_1 \neq \mu_2$. The following table summarizes the equations and tables to use when making these comparisons to determine whether there is a statistically significant difference at the desired level of risk. The null hypothesis rejection criterion is noted for each of the tabulated scenarios.

$$\sigma_1^2 = \sigma_2^2 \qquad\qquad \sigma_1^2 \neq \sigma_2^2$$

σ is Known

$$Z_0 = \frac{\left| \overline{x}_1 - \overline{x}_2 \right|}{\sigma \sqrt{\dfrac{1}{n_1} + \dfrac{1}{n_2}}} \qquad\qquad Z_0 = \frac{\left| \overline{x}_1 - \overline{x}_2 \right|}{\sqrt{\dfrac{\sigma_1^2}{n_1} + \dfrac{\sigma_2^2}{n_2}}}$$

Reject H_0 if $Z_0 > Z_\alpha$ $\qquad\qquad$ Reject H_0 if $Z_0 > Z_\alpha$

σ is Unknown

$$t_0 = \frac{\left| \overline{x}_1 - \overline{x}_2 \right|}{s \sqrt{\dfrac{1}{n_1} + \dfrac{1}{n_2}}} \qquad\qquad t_0 = \frac{\left| \overline{x}_1 - \overline{x}_2 \right|}{\sqrt{\dfrac{s_1^2}{n_1} + \dfrac{s_2^2}{n_2}}}$$

Reject H_0 if $t_0 > t_\alpha$ $\qquad\qquad$ Reject H_0 if $t_0 > t_\alpha$

$$v = n_1 + n_2 - 2$$

$$s = \sqrt{\frac{(n_1 - 1)s_1^2 + (n_2 - 1)s_2^2}{n_1 + n_2 + 2}} \qquad\qquad v = \frac{\left[\left(s_1^2 / n_1 \right) + \left(s_2^2 / n_2 \right) \right]^2}{\dfrac{\left(s_1^2 / n_1 \right)^2}{n_1 + 1} + \dfrac{\left(s_2^2 / n_2 \right)^2}{n_2 + 1}} - 2$$

Z table and t table are in Appendix B

Example computer output (*IEE Volume III*, Example 22.1)

Two-Sample T-Test and CI: Current Design, New Design

```
Two-sample T for Current Design vs New Design

                N     Mean   StDev   SE Mean
Current Design  14   0.955   0.195    0.052
New Design      14   0.631   0.102    0.027


Difference = mu (Current Design) - mu (New Design)
Estimate for difference:  0.323786
95% CI for difference:  (0.200473, 0.447099)
T-Test of difference = 0 (vs not =): T-Value = 5.50   P-Value = 0.000   DF = 19
```

7.8   Tool: Comparing Proportions

Roadmap step: 7.6.3
Reference: *IEE Volume III*, Section 23.5
Minitab Syntax: Stat>Tables>Chi-Square Test

The chi-square distribution can be used to compare the frequency of occurrence for categorical variables. Within this test, often called a χ^2 goodness-of-fit test, we compare an observed frequency distribution with a theoretical distribution. An example application is that a company wants to determine if inspectors categorize failure similarly. Consider that inspectors are described as A_1, A_2, and so forth, while types of failures are B_1, B_2, and so forth. The chi-square test assesses the association or lack of independency in a two-way classification. This procedure is used when testing to see if the probabilities of items or subjects being classified for one variable depend on the classification of the other variable.

    Data compilation and analysis are in the form of the following *contingency table*, in which observations are designated as O_{ij} and expected values are calculated to be E_{ij}. Expected counts are printed below observed counts. The column totals are the sum of the observations in the columns; the row totals are the sum of the observations in the rows. An example computer analysis output is:

Chi-Square Test: Insp 1, Insp 2, Insp 3

```
Expected counts are printed below observed counts
Chi-Square contributions are printed below expected counts

            Insp 1  Insp 2  Insp 3   Total
      1         27      25      22      74
            24.67   24.67   24.67
            0.221   0.005   0.288

      2          3       5       8      16
             5.33    5.33    5.33
            1.021   0.021   1.333

Total         30      30      30      90

Chi-Sq = 2.889, DF = 2, P-Value = 0.236
```

7.9   Tool: Difference in Two Proportions

Roadmap step: 7.6.9
Reference: *IEE Volume III*, Section 23.10
Minitab Syntax: Stat>Basic Stat>2 Proportions

When there are only two proportions, there is an alternative approach to the chi-square test. The following example illustrates the two-proportion analysis methodology: Consider that a team believed that they had made improvements to a process. They needed to test this hypothesis statistically and wanted to determine the 95% confidence interval for the improvement in PPM rate, given the following data:

Before improvement: 6290 defects out of 620000
After improvement: 4661 defects out of 490000

A computer analysis yielded

Test and CI for Two Proportions

```
Sample     X        N   Sample p
1        6290   620000   0.010145
2        4661   490000   0.009512


Difference = p (1) - p (2)
Estimate for difference:  0.000632916
95% CI for difference:  (0.000264020, 0.00100181)
Test for difference = 0 (vs not = 0):   Z = 3.36   P-Value = 0.001

Fisher's exact test: P-Value = 0.001
```

7.10 Tools: Scatter Plot, Correlation, and Regression Analysis

Roadmap steps: 7.3, 7.4, 7.6
Reference: *IEE Volume III*, Sections 25.3, 25.4 and 25.6
Minitab syntaxes:
- Graph>Scatterplot
- Stat>Basic Statistics>Correlation
- Stat>Regression>Regression
- Stat>Regression>Fitted Line Plot

Tools:
- Scatter Plot: A scatter plot or dispersion graph shows the relationship between two variables pictorially. It gives a simple illustration of how one variable can influence the other. Care must be exercised when interpreting dispersion graphs. A plot that shows a relationship does not prove a true cause-and-effect relationship; i.e., it does not prove causation. Happenstance data can cause the appearance of a relationship. For example, the phase of the moon could appear to affect a process that has a monthly cycle. When constructing a dispersion graph, first define clearly the variables that are to be evaluated. Next, collect at least 30 data pairs (50 or 100 pairs is better). Data pairs are plotted using the horizontal axis for probable cause and the vertical axis for probable effect.
- Correlation coefficient: A statistic that represents the strength of a linear relationship between two variables is the sample correlation coefficient (r). A correlation coefficient can take values between -1 and +1. A negative one indicates perfect negative correlation, while a positive one indicates perfect positive correlation. Zero indicates no correlation.

- Coefficient of determination (R2): The coefficient of determination can be determined from the square of the correlation coefficient. The coefficient of determination can be presented as an R-Sq and R-Sq(adj) percentage in an analysis output. This value represents the proportion of the variability accounted for by the model, where the R2 (adj) adjusts for the degrees of freedom.
- Simple Linear Regression: Correlation only measures association, while regression model methods serve to develop quantitative variable relationships that are useful for estimation and prediction. In regression equations, the independent variable is variable x, while the dependent variable is y. This section focuses on regression models that contain linear variables; however, regression models can also include quadratic and cubic terms; i.e., model tool contains non-linear parameters.
- Prediction Interval (PI) and Confidence Interval (CI) Bands: Confidence bands reflect the confidence intervals on the equation coefficients. The prediction bands reflect the confidence interval for the PI percentage of population responses at any given level of the independent variable.
- Residual analysis: For our analysis, modeling errors are assumed to be normally and independently distributed with mean zero and a constant but unknown variance. An abbreviation for this assumption is NID(0, σ^2). An important method for testing this assumption is residual analysis, where a residual is the difference between the observed value and the corresponding fitted value. Residual analyses play an important role in investigating the adequacy of the fitted model and in detecting departures from the model. Residual analysis techniques include the following:
- Checking the normality assumption through a normal probability plot and/or histogram of the residuals.
- Checking for correlation between residuals by plotting residuals in time sequence.
- Checking for correctness of the model by plotting residuals versus fitted values.

Simple Linear Regression Example Output:

The regression equation is

```
Delivery Time (y) = 3.32 + 2.18 Cases

Predictor        Coef        StDev          T          P
Constant        3.321        1.371       2.42      0.024
Cases          2.1762       0.1240      17.55      0.000

S = 4.181      R-Sq = 93.0%      R-Sq(adj) = 92.7%
```

Analysis of Variance

```
Source           DF          SS          MS          F          P
Regression        1       5382.4      5382.4     307.85      0.000
Residual Error    23       402.1        17.5
Total             24      5784.5
```

Residual Plots

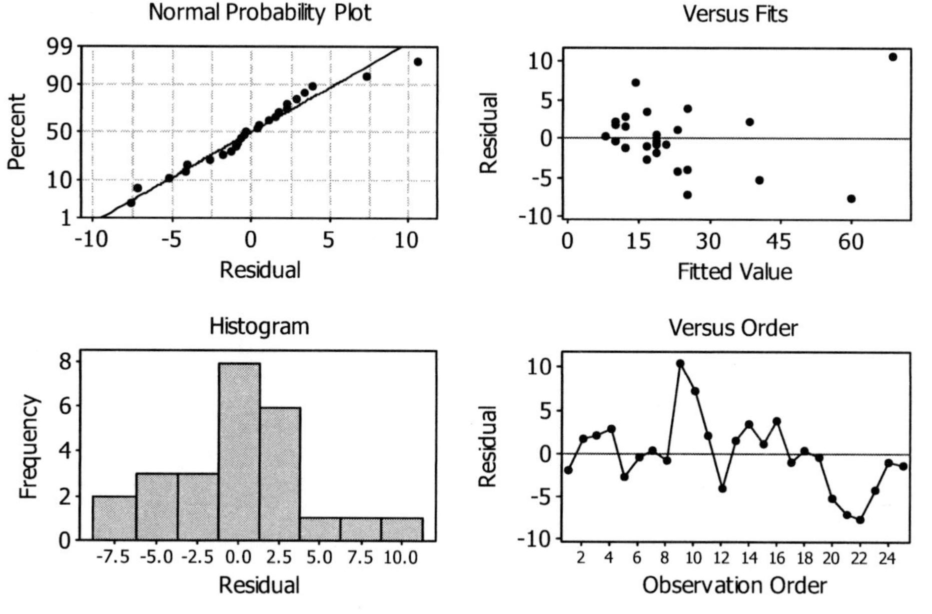

From Figure 25.4 *Integrated Enterprise Excellence, Volume III – Improvement Project Execution: A Management and Black Belt Guide for Going Beyond Lean Six Sigma and the Balanced Scorecard,* Forrest W. Breyfogle III, Bridgeway Books, 2008.

Prediction interval and confidence interval bands plot

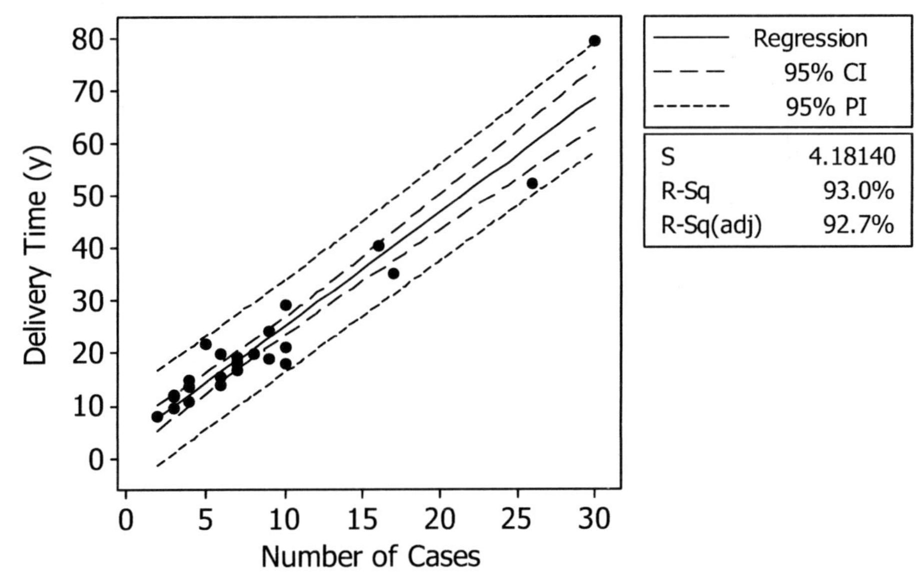

From Figure 25.3 *Integrated Enterprise Excellence, Volume III – Improvement Project Execution: A Management and Black Belt Guide for Going Beyond Lean Six Sigma and the Balanced Scorecard,* Forrest W. Breyfogle III, Bridgeway Books, 2008.

7.11 Tools: Marginal Plot Analysis of Variance (ANOVA), Analysis of Means (ANOM), Multiple Comparisons, and Equality of Variances

Roadmap steps: 7.3, 7.4, 7.6
Reference: *IEE Volume III*, Sections 18.4, 26.2 – 26.14
Minitab syntaxes:
- Graph>Marginal Plot
- Graph>Individual Value Plot
- Stat>ANOVA>One Way
- Stat>ANOVA>Analysis of Means
- Stat>ANOVA>One Way>Multiple Comparisons
- Stat>ANOVA>Test for Equal Variances

Tools:

- Marginal Plot: A marginal plot permits the visualization of the distribution of data by stratification relative to the overall sampled distribution.
- Individual Value Plot: An individual value plot permits the visualization of data by stratification.
- Analysis of Variance (ANOVA): Analysis of variance assesses the mean differences between samples taken at different factor levels to determine if these differences are large enough relative to error to conclude that the factor level causes a statistical significant difference in response. An expression for the null hypothesis (H_O) and alternative hypothesis (H_A) is:

$$H_0: \mu_1 = \mu_2 = ... = \mu_a$$
$$H_A: \mu_i \neq \mu_j \text{ , for at least one pair } (i, j)$$

- Analysis of Means (ANOM): ANOM graphically assesses the individual hypotheses that each factor level mean is equal to the overall mean of all factor levels.
- Multiple Comparisons: Statistically compares the mean of each factor level to all other factor levels. One approach to accomplish this is through Tukey's multiple comparisons test.
- Equality of variance: Bartlett's test is frequently used to test this hypothesis when the normality assumption is valid and more than two categories are compared. Levene's test can be used when the normality assumption is questionable. An expression for this hypothesis is:

$$H_0 : \sigma_1^2 = \sigma_2^2 = ... = \sigma_a^2$$
$$H_A : \text{above not true for at least one } \sigma_i^2$$

Example: Marginal Plot, Individual Value Plot, ANOVA, ANOM, Multiple Comparisons, Equality of Variance Output (Examples 24.1 and 24.2)

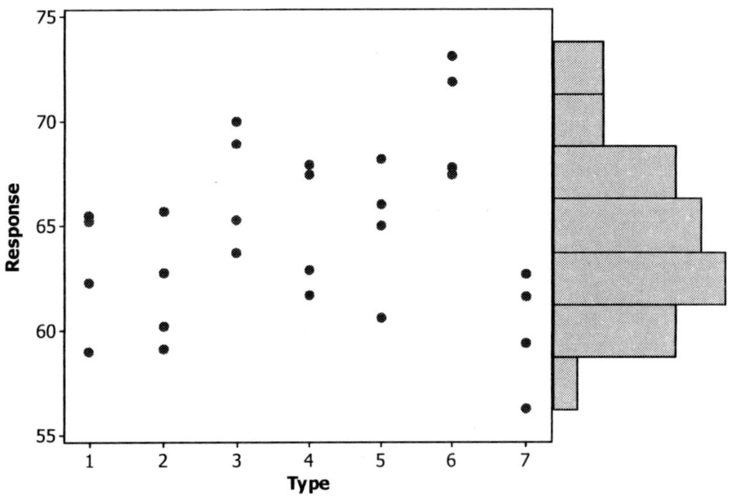

Individual Value Plot

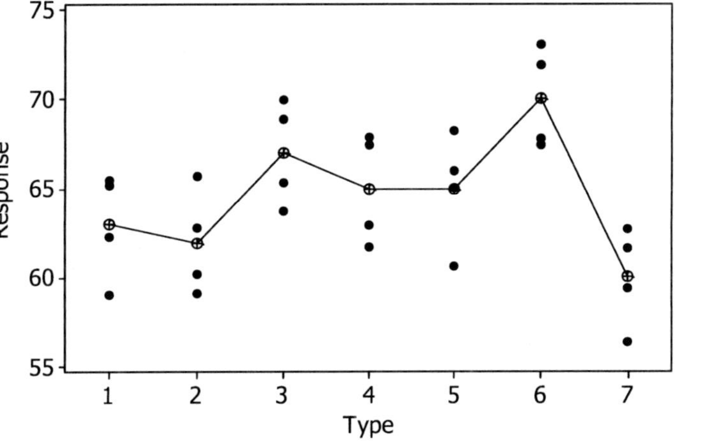

From Figure 26.2 *Integrated Enterprise Excellence, Volume III – Improvement Project Execution: A Management and Black Belt Guide for Going Beyond Lean Six Sigma and the Balanced Scorecard,* Forrest W. Breyfogle III, Bridgeway Books, 2008.

One-Way Analysis of Variance

Analysis of Variance for Response

```
Source     DF        SS        MS        F        P
Type        6    265.34     44.22     4.92    0.003
Error      21    188.71      8.99
Total      27    454.05

                                       Individual 95% CIs For Mean
                                       Based on Pooled StDev
Level       N      Mean     StDev  -------+---------+---------+---------
1           4    63.000     3.032            (-----*-----)
2           4    61.950     2.942         (-----*-----)
3           4    66.975     2.966                     (-----*-----)
4           4    64.975     3.134              (-----*-----)
5           4    64.950     3.193              (-----*-----)
6           4    70.050     2.876                          (-----*-----)
7           4    60.000     2.823      (-----*-----)
                                   -------+---------+---------+---------
Pooled StDev =     2.998            60.0      65.0      70.0
```

```
Tukey 95% Simultaneous Confidence Intervals
All Pairwise Comparisons among Levels of Type

Individual confidence level = 99.62%

Type = 1 subtracted from:

Type    Lower  Center   Upper  -------+---------+---------+---------+--
2      -7.945  -1.050   5.845            (------*------)
3      -2.920   3.975  10.870                 (------*------)
4      -4.920   1.975   8.870               (------*------)
5      -4.945   1.950   8.845               (------*------)
6       0.155   7.050  13.945                    (------*------)
7      -9.895  -3.000   3.895          (------*------)
                               -------+---------+---------+---------+--
                                    -10         0        10        20


Type = 2 subtracted from:

Type    Lower  Center   Upper  -------+---------+---------+---------+--
3      -1.870   5.025  11.920                  (------*------)
4      -3.870   3.025   9.920                (------*------)
5      -3.895   3.000   9.895                (------*------)
6       1.205   8.100  14.995                     (------*------)
7      -8.845  -1.950   4.945           (------*------)
                               -------+---------+---------+---------+--
                                    -10         0        10        20


Type = 3 subtracted from:

Type     Lower  Center   Upper  -------+---------+---------+---------+--
4       -8.895  -2.000   4.895           (------*------)
5       -8.920  -2.025   4.870           (------*------)
6       -3.820   3.075   9.970                (------*------)
7      -13.870  -6.975  -0.080      (------*------)
                                -------+---------+---------+---------+--
                                     -10         0        10        20
```

Significant differences between factor levels are identified by the individual conference interval not including the value of zero.

In this example the differences
Type 1 and 6
Type 2 and 6
Type 3 and 7
Type 6 and 7

```
Tukey 95% Simultaneous Confidence Intervals
All Pairwise Comparisons among Levels of Type

Individual confidence level = 99.62%

Type = 4 subtracted from:

Type      Lower   Center   Upper   -------+---------+---------+---------+--
5        -6.920   -0.025   6.870                (------*------)
6        -1.820    5.075  11.970                   (------*------)
7       -11.870   -4.975   1.920          (------*------)
                                  -------+---------+---------+---------+--
                                       -10         0        10        20


Type = 5 subtracted from:

Type      Lower   Center   Upper   -------+---------+---------+---------+--
6        -1.795    5.100  11.995                  (------*------)
7       -11.845   -4.950   1.945          (------*------)
                                  -------+---------+---------+---------+--
                                       -10         0        10        20

Type = 6 subtracted from:

Type      Lower   Center   Upper   -------+---------+---------+---------+--
7       -16.945  -10.050  -3.155   (------*------)
                                  -------+---------+---------+---------+--
                                       -10         0        10        20
```

Residual Analysis

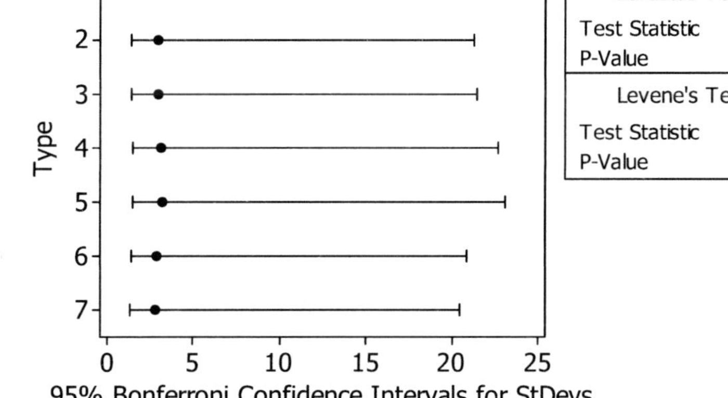

From Figure 26.3 Integrated Enterprise Excellence, Volume III – Improvement Project Execution: A Management and Black Belt Guide for Going Beyond Lean Six Sigma and the Balanced Scorecard, Forrest W. Breyfogle III, Bridgeway Books, 2008.

ANOM and Equality of Variance

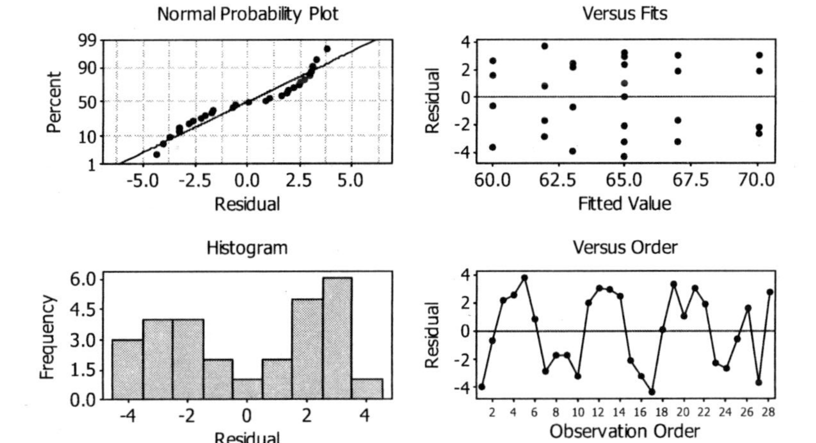

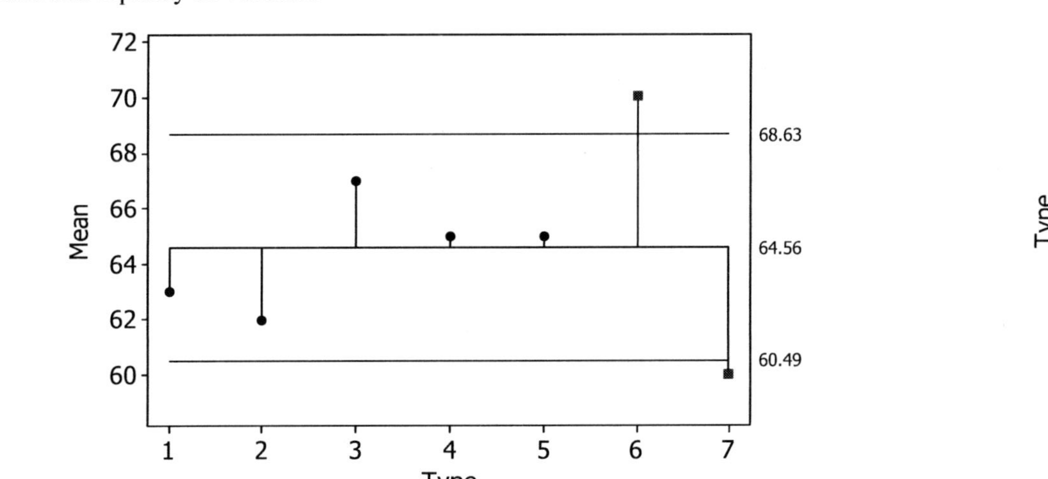

From Figure 26.4 Integrated Enterprise Excellence, Volume III – Improvement Project Execution: A Management and Black Belt Guide for Going Beyond Lean Six Sigma and the Balanced Scorecard, Forrest W. Breyfogle III, Bridgeway Books, 2008.

From Figure 26.3 Integrated Enterprise Excellence, Volume III – Improvement Project Execution: A Management and Black Belt Guide for Going Beyond Lean Six Sigma and the Balanced Scorecard, Forrest W. Breyfogle III, Bridgeway Books, 2008.

7.12 Tools: *Multi-vari chart and Variance Components*

Roadmap steps: 7.3, 7.4, 7.6
Reference: *IEE Volume III*, Section 18.5 and Chapter 24
Minitab syntaxes:
- Stat>Quality Tools>Multi-vari Chart
- Stat>ANOVA>Fully Nested ANOVA

Tools:
- Multi-vari chart: Within a discrete manufacturing environment, contributing factors to overall variability of a response include differences between time periods, production tool differences, part-to-part variations, and within-part variability. Within a continuous flow manufacturing process, contributing factors to overall variability include within shifts, across shifts, and across days/weeks/months. Multi-vari charts allow visual decomposition into components and the identification of the component that affects variability the most.
- Variance components analysis: The methodology is a random effects model or components of variance model, as opposed to a fixed-effects model. The statistical model for the random effects or components of variance model is similar to that of the fixed effects model. The difference is that in the random effects model, the levels (or treatments) could be a random sample from a larger population of levels. For this situation, we would like to extend conclusions, based on samples of levels, to all population levels whether explicitly considered or not. In this situation, the test attempts to quantify the variability from factor levels.

Examples

Multi-vari chart

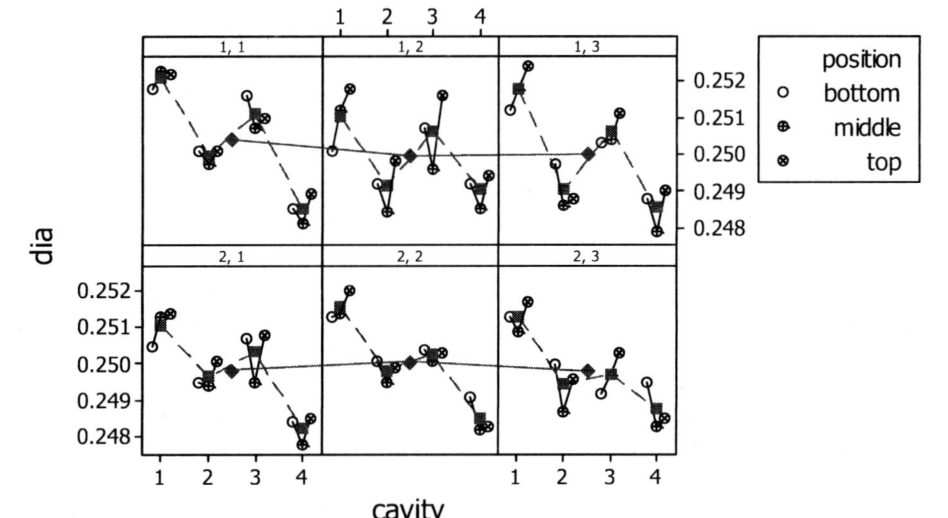

From Figure 18.6 *Integrated Enterprise Excellence, Volume III – Improvement Project Execution: A Management and Black Belt Guide for Going Beyond Lean Six Sigma and the Balanced Scorecard,* Forrest W. Breyfogle III, Bridgeway Books, 2008.

Fully Nested Analysis of Variance

Analysis of Variance for Diameter

Source	DF	SS	MS	F	P
Time	2	56.4444	28.2222	0.030	0.970
Cavity	9	8437.3750	937.4861	17.957	0.000
Part	12	626.5000	52.2083	1.772	0.081
Position	48	1414.0000	29.4583		
Total	71	10534.3194			

Variance Components

Source	Var Comp.	% of Total	StDev
Time	-37.886*	0.00	0.000
Cavity	147.546	79.93	12.147
Part	7.583	4.11	2.754
Position	29.458	15.96	5.428
Total	184.588		13.586

7.13 Tools: Logistic Regression

Roadmap steps: 7.6.13 – 7.6.21.
Reference: *IEE Volume III*, Section 28.10
Minitab syntaxes:

- Stat>Basic Statistics Stat>Regression>Binary Logistic Regression
- Stat>Basic Statistics Stat>Regression>Ordinal Logistic Regression
- Stat>Basic Statistics Stat>Regression>Nominal Logistic Regression
- Graph>Contour Plot

Background:
- Logistic regression fills a gap in most Lean Six Sigma analysis tool sets. The ability to create a Y=F(x) where the Y is an attribute and the x is one or more continuous variables.
- This tool could be widely used in transactional environments where the overall performance can be described with good/bad (binary) or a likert scale (ordinal) measurement of success.
- In some cases where the defect rate for all observations (batches or lots) is far from non-zero and nearly equals sample sizes, the calculated percentages with a standard linear regression can be used, but this does not always work well.
- Binary logistic regression is applicable when the response is binary, such as pass or fail, and inputs are continuous or attribute variables.
- The data format for this tool is similar to what you would use for linear regression. Each observation is in a row. A column is used for each predictor. There should be two or more columns describing the results; for a binary case it is typically a column for the number failed and a column for the total count for that observation. You do not enter the percentage values.
- The logistic regression tools can be used to perform a logistic ANOVA using indicator variables and to analyze a design of experiments that has a pass/fail or other attribute output.

Logistic regression is an extension to standard multiple linear regression. The attribute Y, such as a yield or categorization count is converted to a continuous variable through a link function, such as the logit function. This new value is analyzed to produce a predictive equation with coefficients, just as a standard regression. The difference is that the equation predicts the logit(p) value, which would need a reverse transformation back to a percentage that can be used in the decision-making process.

Variables are determined to be significant if they have a p-value >0.05, just as in standard regression. The real difference between linear regression and logistic regression is the equivalent of the residual analysis. Since the residual is not normally distributed, alternatives must be used in place of the standards used in linear regression.

- The logit function is used to link the probability for the following example

$$\text{Logit}(p) = \ln\left(\frac{p}{1-p}\right)$$

- This relationship is the logarithm of the ratio of the pass and fails probabilities.
  - The ratio of probabilities ranges from 0 to infinity.
  - Where the logarithm transforms the data so that it ranges from negative to positive infinity.
  - It is these infinite tails that allow the data to meet the requirements for the regression algorithm.

The equivalent of a residual analysis is performed with an analysis of the goodness-of-fit tests and a review of output charts.

- Smarter Solutions recommends that you do not accept the result if all three goodness-of-fit tests have p-values < 0.05.
- A check for outliers can be made with the "delta chi-square vs. percentage" chart. Any point that appears to have a higher delta chi-square value than the other points should be investigated just as an unusual observation would be in a standard regression.

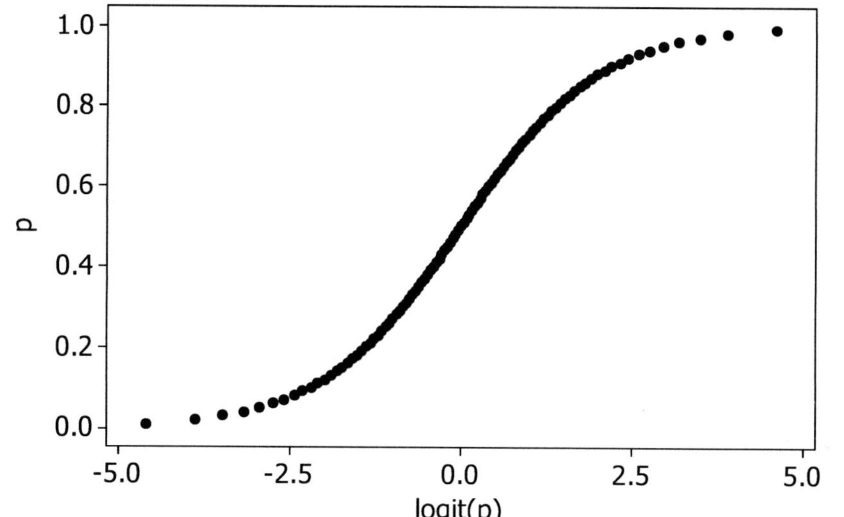

From Figure 28.1 *Integrated Enterprise Excellence, Volume III – Improvement Project Execution: A Management and Black Belt Guide for Going Beyond Lean Six Sigma and the Balanced Scorecard*, Forrest W. Breyfogle III, Bridgeway Books, 2008.

Conversion of the predicted value back to a percentage can be performed as shown below, where EPRO is the estimated probability;

$$\hat{p} = \frac{1}{1 + e^{-\text{logit}(\hat{p})}} = EPRO$$

$$\text{where } \text{logit}(p) = \ln\left(\frac{p}{1-p}\right) = constant + coef_1 * x_1 + coef_2 * x_2 + ...$$

Sample Binary Logistic Regression Output;

```
Link Function: Logit

Response Information

Variable   Value       Count
not ready  Event          12
           Non-event     375
Total      Total         387


Logistic Regression Table

                                         Odds      95% CI
Predictor        Coef     SE Coef    Z       P    Ratio  Lower  Upper
Constant      5.55917     1.11969  4.96  0.000
Heat        0.0820308   0.0237344  3.46  0.001   1.09   1.04   1.14
Soak        0.0567713    0.331212  0.17  0.864   1.06   0.55   2.03

Log-Likelihood = -47.673

Goodness-of-Fit Tests

Method         Chi-Square  DF       P
Pearson           13.5431  16   0.633
Deviance          13.7526  16   0.617
Hosmer-Lemeshow    7.3812   6   0.287
```


If you store the estimated probabilities for each observation, this column of data can be used to generate contour plots for pairs of predictors. This is generally an easier method to identify the optimal conditions than back-transforming the logit link function.

8 P-DMAIC: Improve Phase

Purpose: To improve process performance based on data analysis and other assessments

Deliverables:

- Quantified relationships between process inputs and outputs;
- Quantification of improved process predictability and capability;
- Implemented changes;
- Demonstrated improvement

Reference: Chapters 29 – 37 of *Volume III* (Breyfogle 2008c)

8.1 Roadmap

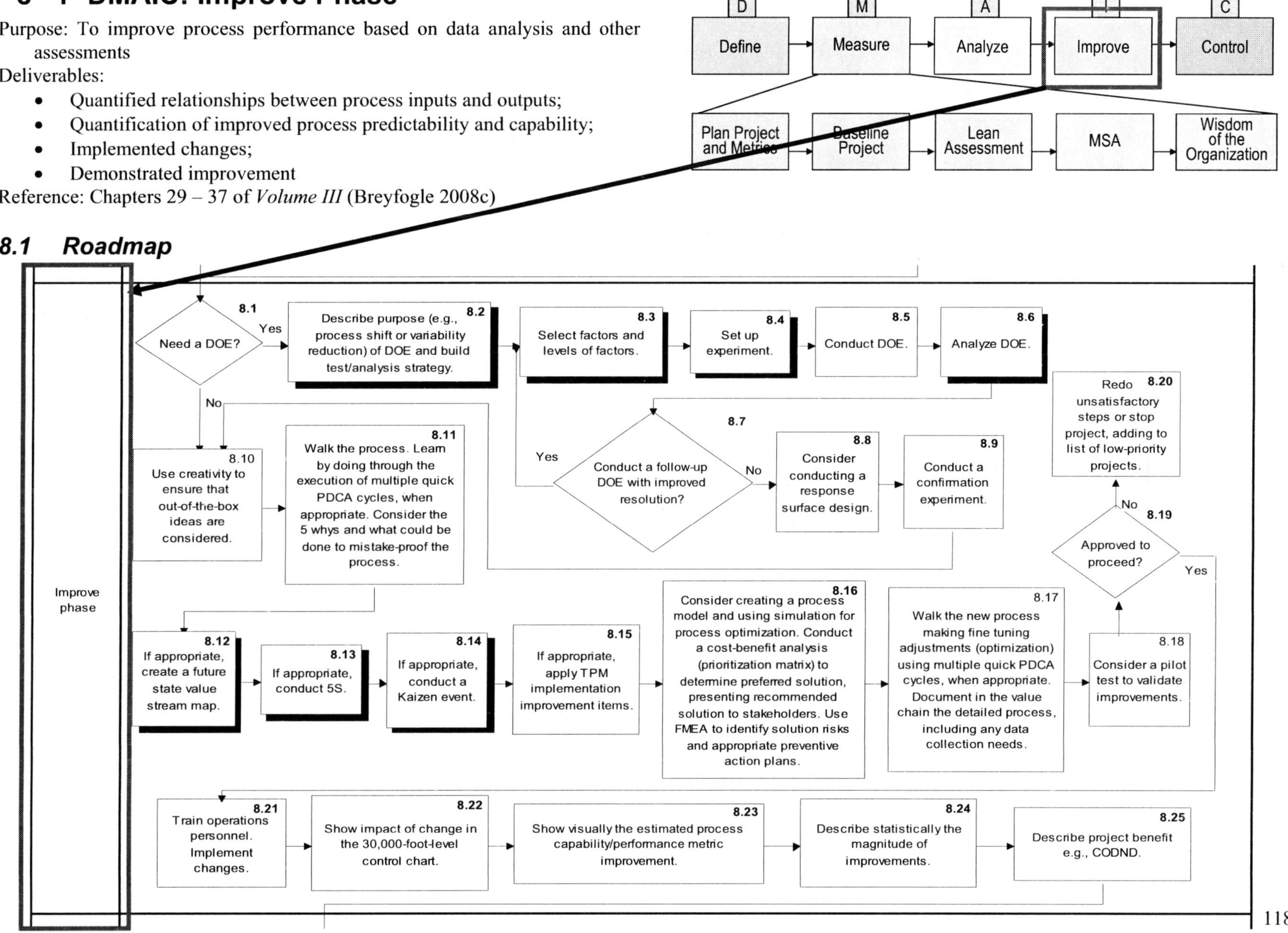

Step 8.2 drill down

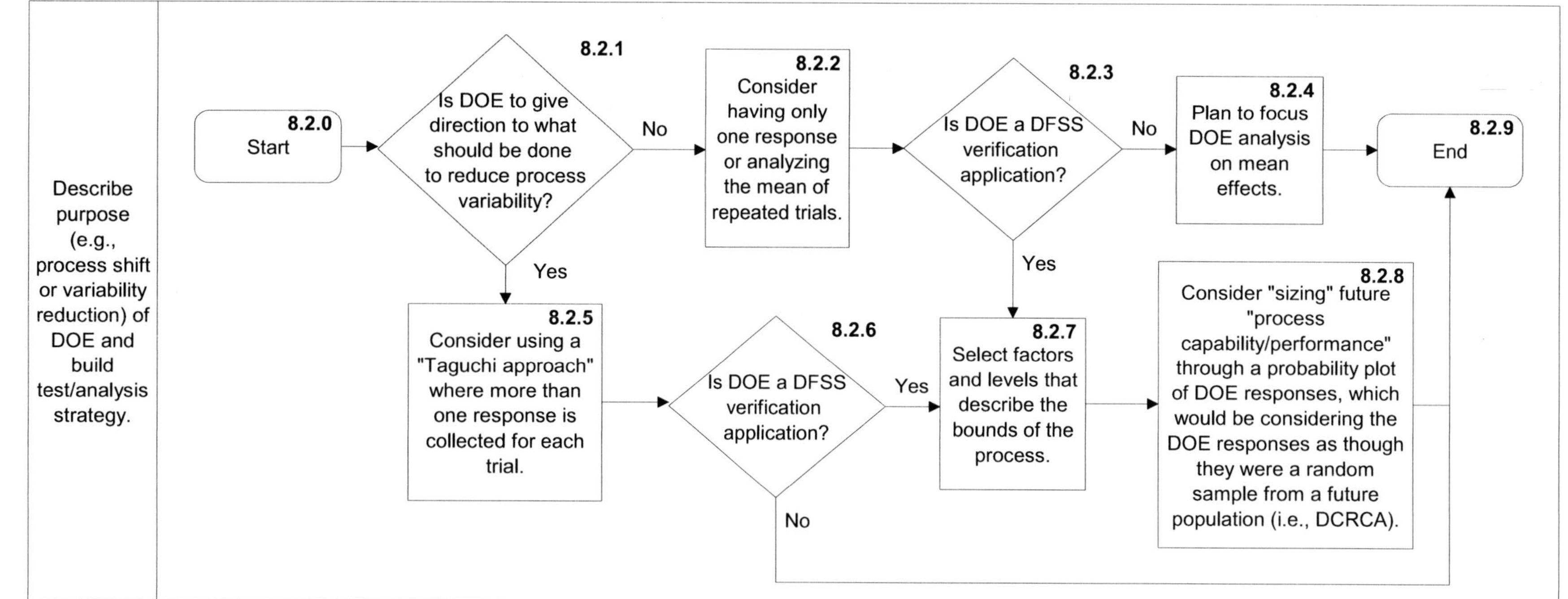

Step 8.3 drill down

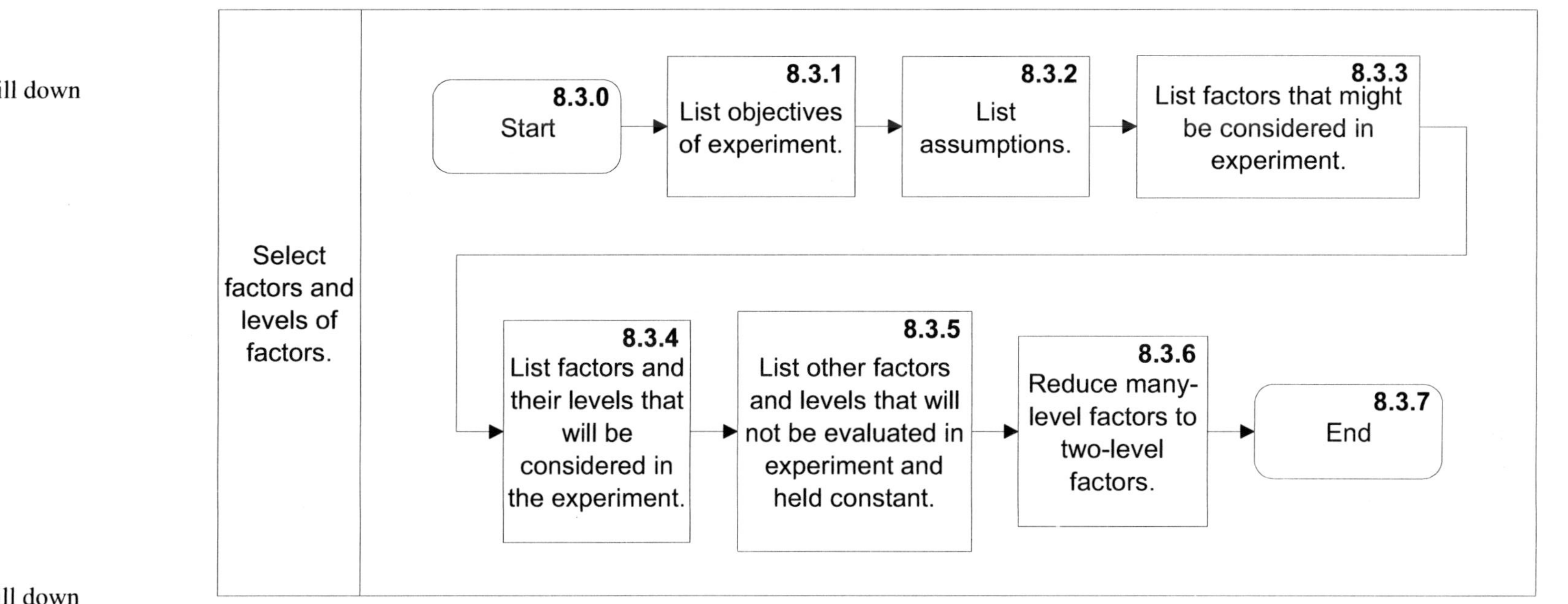

Step 8.4 drill down

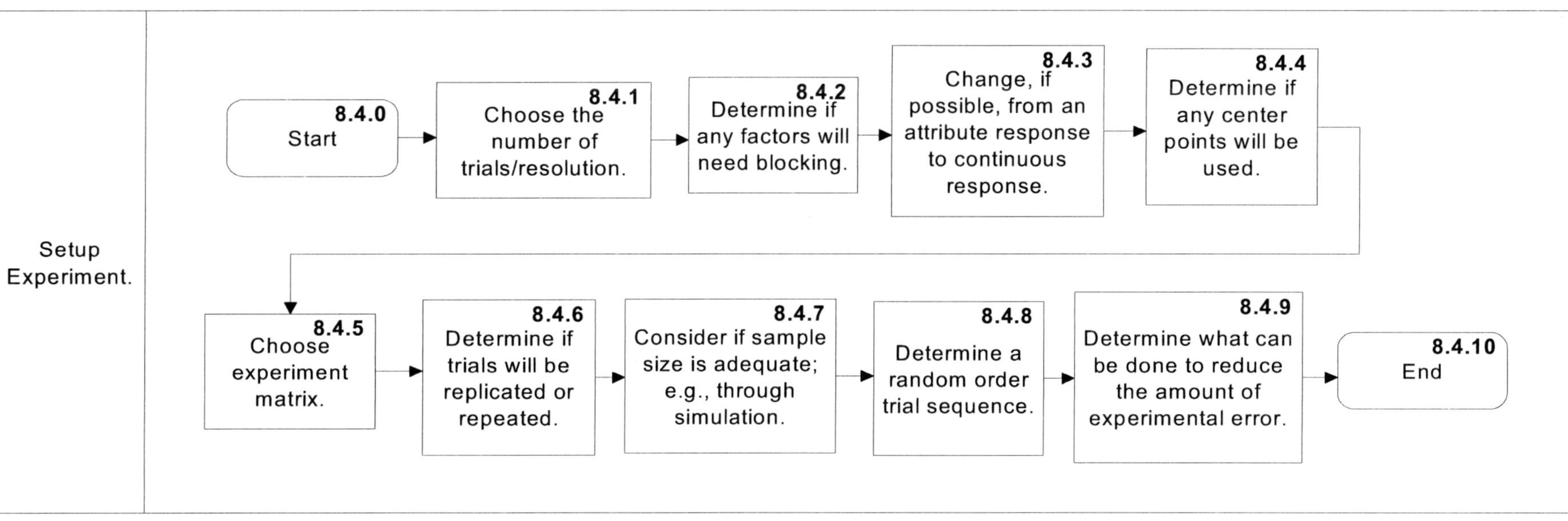

Step 8.6 drill down

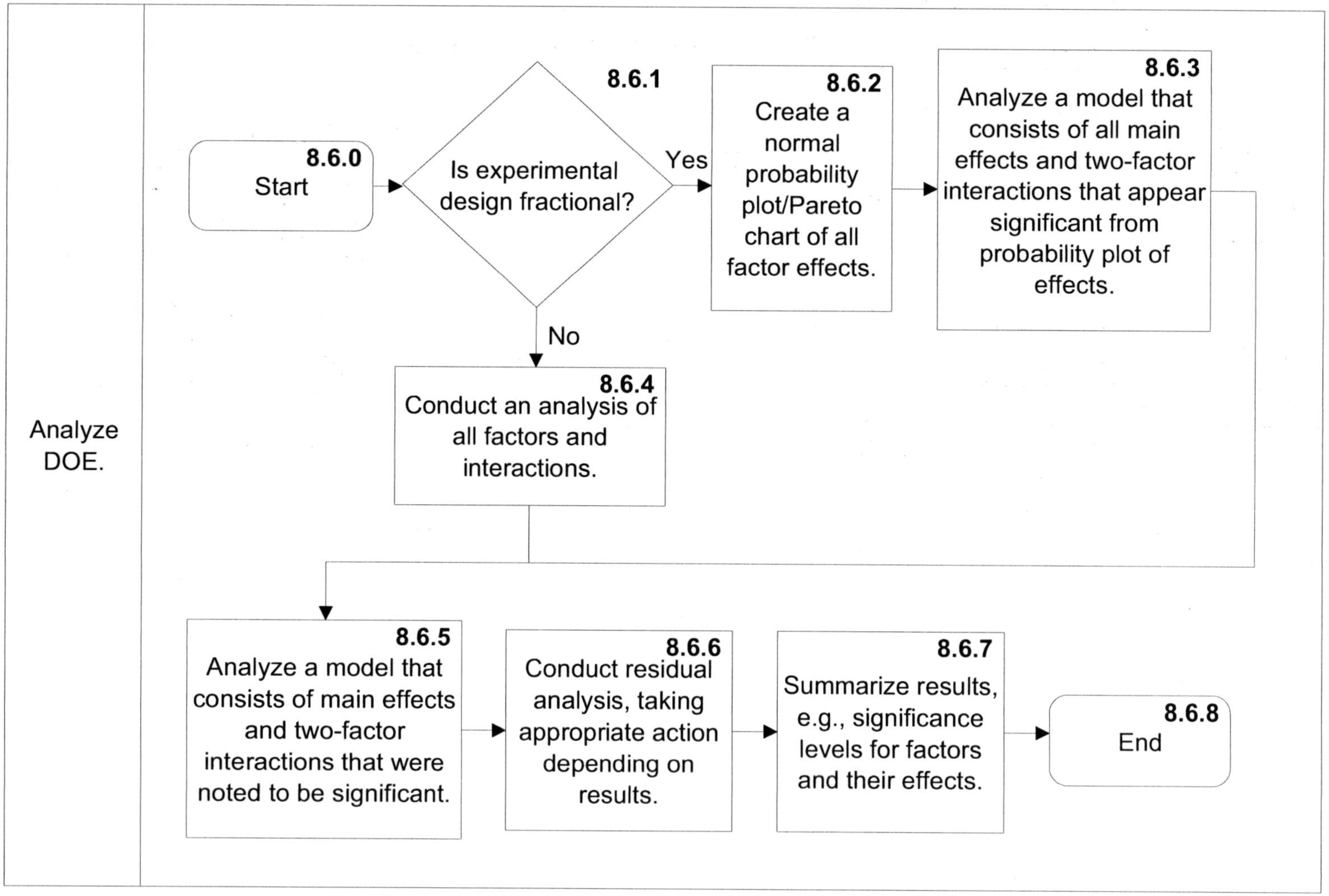

Analyze
DOE.

Step 8.12 drill down

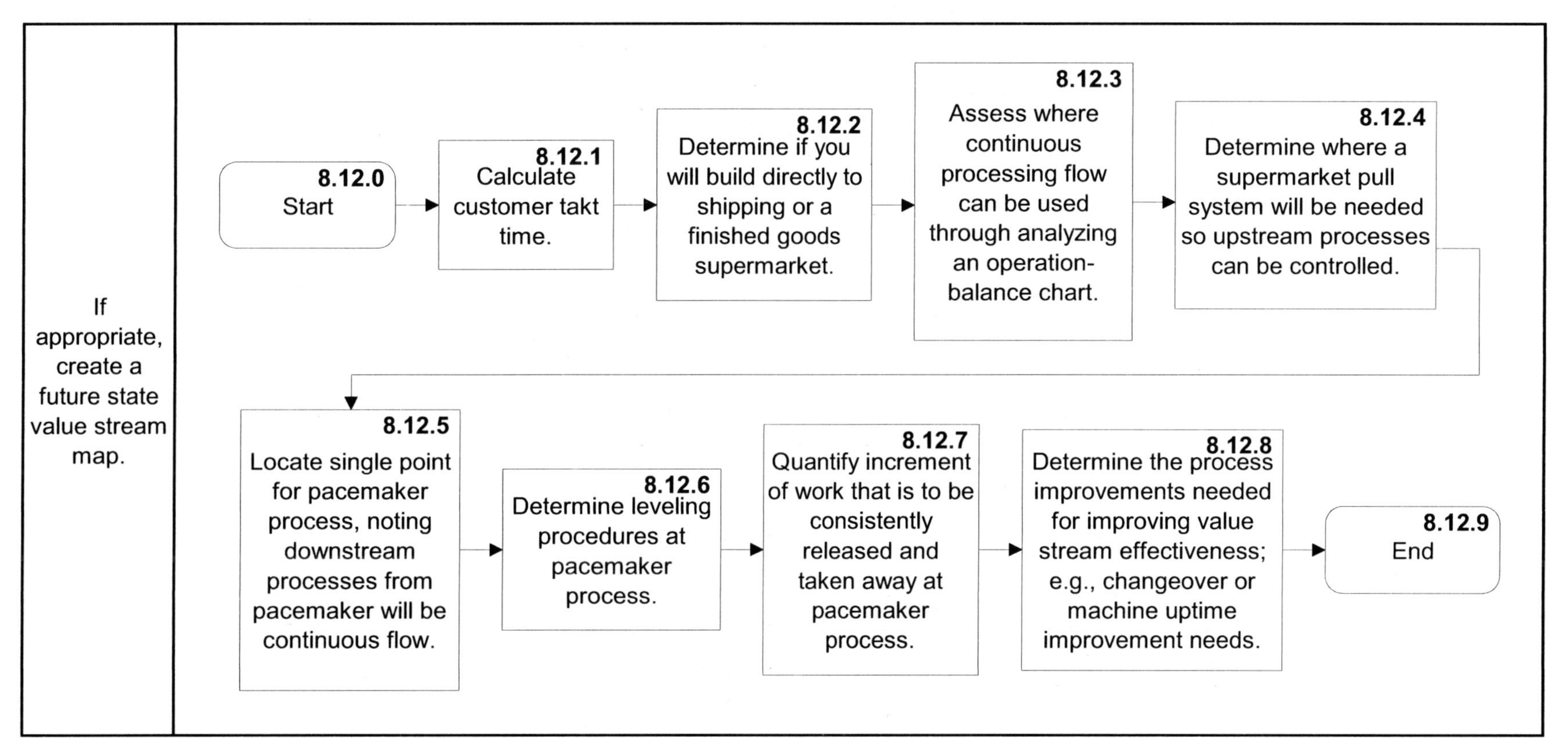

Step 8.13 drill down

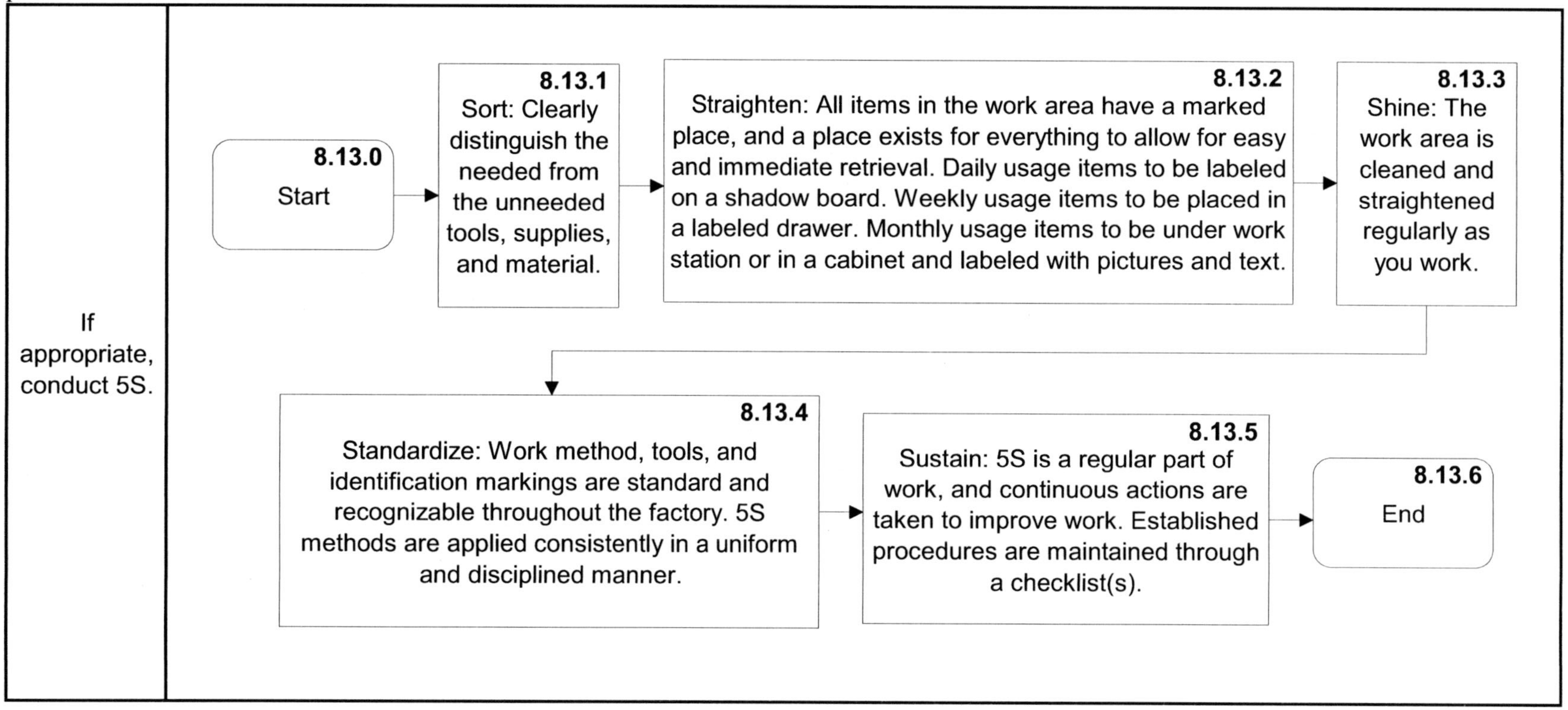

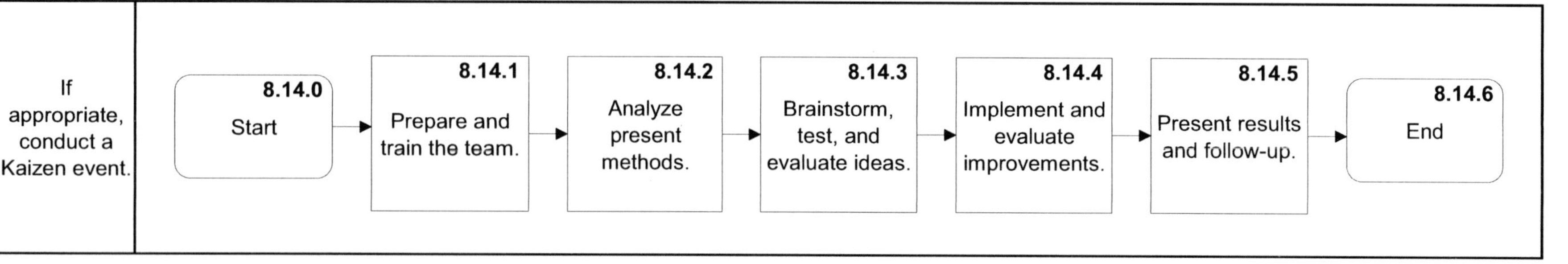

Step 8.14 drill down

8.2 Check Sheet

Improve Phase Check Sheet		
Descriptions	**Questions**	**Yes/No NA**
Tool/Methodology		
DOE	Was the DOE carefully planned, selecting the appropriate factors, levels, and response (mean and variance)?	
	Was appropriate randomization used?	
	Were results analyzed appropriately to determine KPIVs?	
	Is a follow-up DOE necessary?	
	Is Response Surface Methodology needed?	
	Was a confirmation experiment conducted?	
Improvement strategies	Did you create a future state value stream map?	
	Did you use 5S, Kaizen event, or TPM implementation strategy to facilitate improvements?	
Mistake-proofing	Were mistake-proofing options considered?	
Improvement recommendations	Are improvement recommendations well thought out?	
	Do improvement recommendations address the KPIVs determined in the Analyze Phase?	
	Is there an action plan for implementation of improvements with accountabilities and deadlines specified?	
Assessment	Were any process improvements made?	
	If so, were they statistically verified with the appropriate hypothesis test?	
	Did you describe the change over time on a 30,000-foot-level control chart?	
	Did you calculate and display the change in the process capability/performance metric?	
	Have you documented and communicated the improvements?	
	Have you summarized the benefits and annualized financial benefits?	
Team		
Team members	Are all team members motivated and committed to the project?	
Process owner	Does the process owner support the recommended improvements?	
Champion	Is champion ready to step in to promote the proposed changes, if needed and appropriate?	
Next Phase		
Approval to proceed	Did the team adequately complete the above steps?	
	Has the project database been updated and communication plan followed?	
	Should this project proceed to the Control Phase?	
	Is there a detailed plan for the Control Phase?	
	Are barriers to success identified and planned for?	
	Is the team tracking with the project schedule?	
	Have schedule revisions been approved?	

8.3   Applications

Application example
- An IEE project was to reduce DSO for an invoice. Wisdom of the organization and passive analysis led the creation of a DOE experiment that considered factors: size of order (large vs. small), calling back within a week after mailing invoice (yes vs. no), prompt to paying customer (yes vs. no), origination department (from passive analysis: least DSO vs. highest DSO average), stamping "past due" on envelope (yes vs. no)

8.4   Tool: Design of Experiments (DOE)

Roadmap steps: 8.3 – 8.6
Reference: *IEE Volume III*, Chapters 29-37
Minitab syntaxes:
- Stat>DOE>Factorial>Create Factorial Design
- Stat>DOE>Factorial>Analyze Factorial Design
- DOE>DOE>Factorial>Define Custom Factorial Design
- DOE>DOE>Factorial>Factorial Plots

DOE techniques offer a structured approach for changing many factor settings (input variables) within a process at once and observing the data collectively for improvements/degradations. DOE analyses not only yield a significance test of the factor levels but also give a response prediction model. These experiments can address all possible combinations of a set of input factors (a full factorial) or a subset of all combinations (a fractional factorial).

Tools:
- Interaction: Interaction is a description for the measure of the differential comparison of response for each level of a factor at each of the several levels of one or more other factors. In many situations, three-factor and higher interaction effects can be considered small relative to the main effects and two-factor interaction effects. Therefore, interactions higher than two can often be ignored. In such cases, a smaller number of trials are needed to assess the same number of factors.
- Two-level Factorial Designs: When many factors are considered, full factorials can yield a very large number of test experimental runs, whereas a fractional factorial, which has interaction confounding, can require a much reduced sample size. For example, a sixteen-trial, saturated fractional factorial experiment can assess fifteen two-level factors, while it would take 32,768 trials as a full factorial.
- Resolution: A fractional factorial design can assess the factors with various resolutions. A resolution V design evaluates the main effects and two-factor interactions independently. A resolution IV design evaluates main effects and confounded or mixed-up, two-factor interactions (i.e., there is aliasing of the two-factor interactions). A resolution III design evaluates the main effects, which are confounded with the two-factor interactions.
- DOE collective response capability assessment (DCRCA): DCRCA is the evaluation of the overall response of the DOE to specification limits. This type of plot can be very useful when attempting to project how a new process would perform relative to specification limits. If the levels of the DOE factors were

chosen to be the tolerance extremes for the new process and the response was the output of the process, this probability plot gives an overall picture of how we expect the process to perform later relative to specification limits.

Example:

The following factors and factor levels were chosen for a DOE

		Levels	
Factors and Their Designations		(−)	(+)
A: Motor temperature	(mot_temp)	Cold	Hot
B: Algorithm	(algor)	Current design	Proposed redesign
C: Motor adjustment	(mot_adj)	Low tolerance	High tolerance
D: External adjustment	(ext_adj)	Low tolerance	High tolerance
E: Supply voltage	(sup_volt)	Low tolerance	High tolerance

A 16-trial, resolution V DOE yielded the noted responses:

Trial #	--------------- Inputs -------------					Resp.
	mot_temp	algor	mot_adj	ext_adj	sup_volt	
1	+	-	-	-	+	5.6
2	+	+	-	-	-	2.1
3	+	+	+	-	+	4.9
4	+	+	+	+	-	4.9
5	-	+	+	+	+	4.1
6	+	-	+	+	+	5.6
7	-	+	-	+	-	1.9
8	+	-	+	-	-	7.2
9	+	+	-	+	+	2.4
10	-	+	+	-	-	5.1
11	-	-	+	+	-	7.9
12	+	-	-	+	-	5.3
13	-	+	-	-	+	2.1
14	-	-	+	-	+	7.6
15	-	-	-	+	+	5.5
16	-	-	-	-	-	5.3

The resolution V DOE alias structure was the following, where no two-factor interactions are confounded with either main effects or other two-factor interactions:

```
1   2   3   4   5   6   7   8    9   10  11    12     13      14    15
*A  *B  *C  *D  AB  BC  CD  ABD  AC  BD  ABC   BCD    ABCD    ACD   AD
                        CE            DE  AE    *E     BE
```

The following main effects plots indicate that no two-factor interactions are significant and factors B and C are significant.

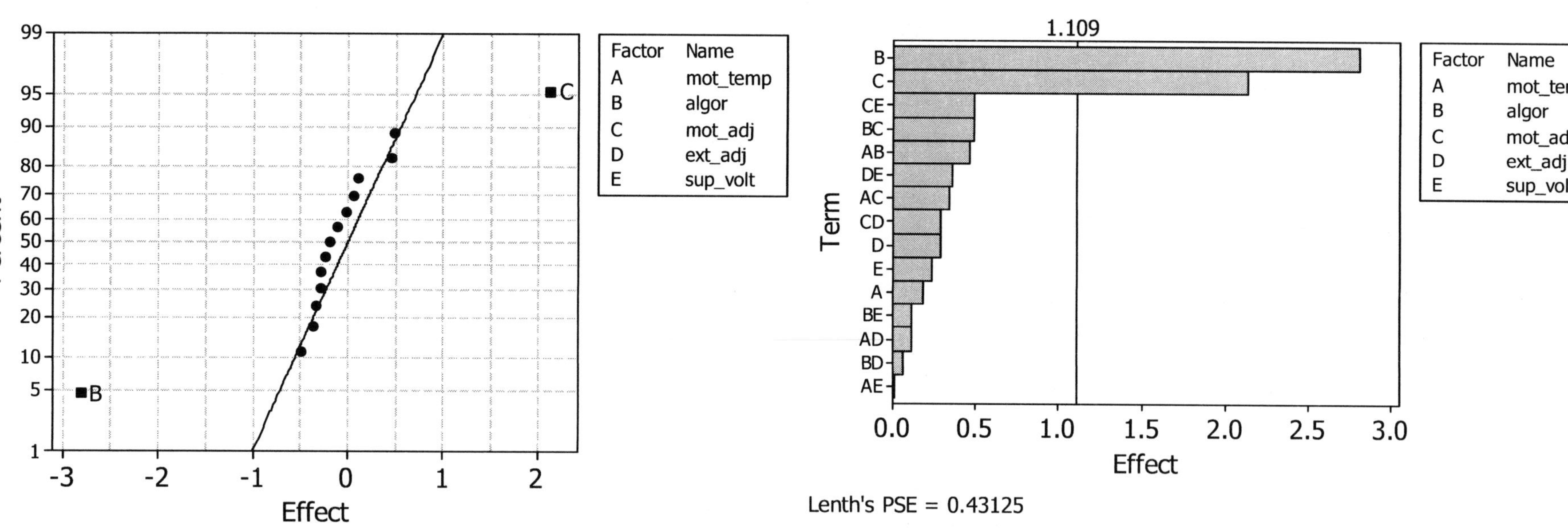

From Figure 32.1 *Integrated Enterprise Excellence, Volume III – Improvement Project Execution: A Management and Black Belt Guide for Going Beyond Lean Six Sigma and the Balanced Scorecard,* Forrest W. Breyfogle III, Bridgeway Books, 2008.

From Figure 32.2 *Integrated Enterprise Excellence, Volume III – Improvement Project Execution: A Management and Black Belt Guide for Going Beyond Lean Six Sigma and the Balanced Scorecard,* Forrest W. Breyfogle III, Bridgeway Books, 2008.

The following analysis indicates that algor (factor B) and mot-adj (factor C) are significant; however, one data point is considered an unusual event relative to the model which was built.

Fractional Factorial Fit

```
Estimated Effects and Coefficients for resp (coded units)

Term          Effect      Coef  StDev Coef       T      P
Constant                 4.844     0.1618    29.95  0.000
mot_temp     -0.187     -0.094     0.1618    -0.58  0.575
algor        -2.812     -1.406     0.1618    -8.69  0.000
mot_adj       2.138      1.069     0.1618     6.61  0.000
ext_adj      -0.288     -0.144     0.1618    -0.89  0.395
sup_volt     -0.238     -0.119     0.1618    -0.73  0.480


Analysis of Variance for resp (coded units)

Source             DF    Seq SS    Adj SS    Adj MS      F      P
Main Effects        5    50.613    50.613   10.1226  24.18  0.000
Residual Error     10     4.186     4.186    0.4186
Total              15    54.799


Unusual Observations for resp

Obs      resp      Fit  StDev Fit  Residual  St Resid
  6   5.60000  6.96250    0.39621  -1.36250    -2.66R
```

R denotes an observation with a large standardized residual

128

A main effects plot of the significant factors describes the factor effects and which factor levels yield the most desirable response, where lower numbers are the most desirable response for this situation.

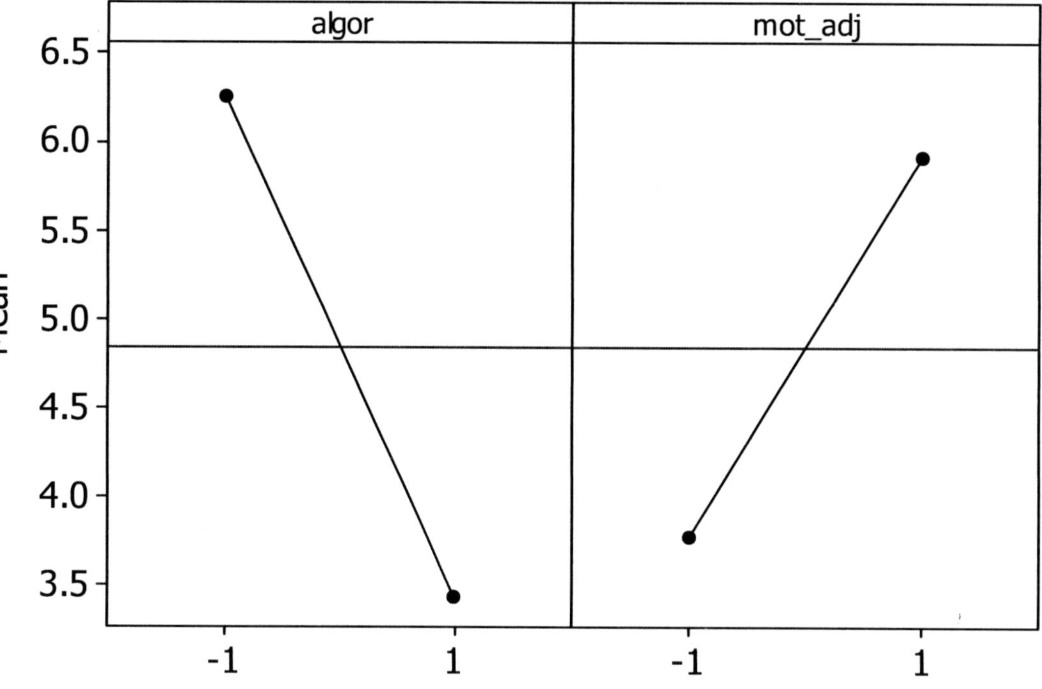

From Figure 32.3 *Integrated Enterprise Excellence, Volume III – Improvement Project Execution: A Management and Black Belt Guide for Going Beyond Lean Six Sigma and the Balanced Scorecard,* Forrest W. Breyfogle III, Bridgeway Books, 2008.

The following residual plot shows the outlier point, which was identified in the previous analysis.

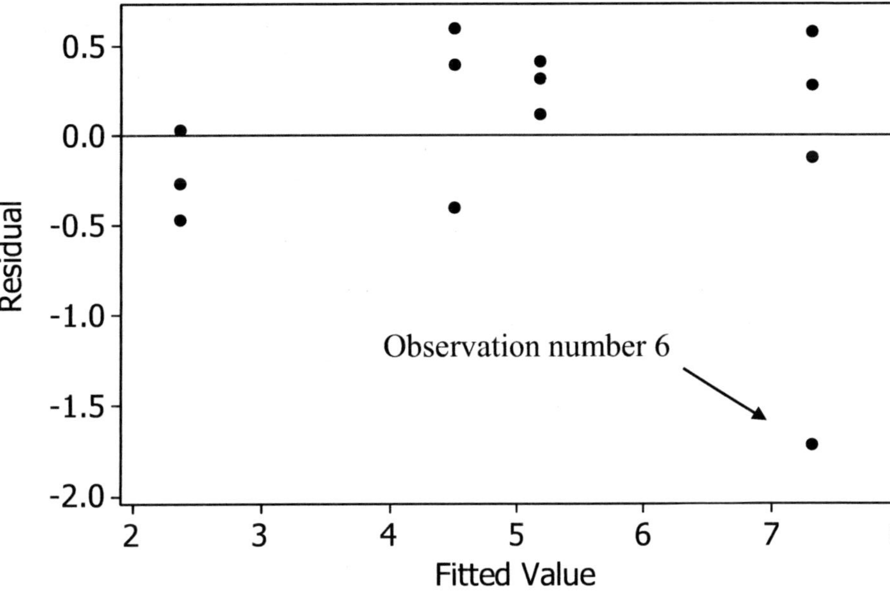

From Figure 32.4 *Integrated Enterprise Excellence, Volume III – Improvement Project Execution: A Management and Black Belt Guide for Going Beyond Lean Six Sigma and the Balanced Scorecard,* Forrest W. Breyfogle III, Bridgeway Books, 2008.

The following model, which contains only the two significant factors, still has the outlier.

```
Fractional Factorial Fit

Estimated Effects and Coefficients for resp (coded units)

Term            Effect      Coef  StDev Coef      T       P
Constant                   4.844     0.1532   31.61   0.000
algor           -2.812    -1.406     0.1532   -9.18   0.000
mot_adj          2.137     1.069     0.1532    6.98   0.000

Analysis of Variance for resp (coded units)

Source            DF      Seq SS     Adj SS     Adj MS      F       P
Main Effects       2     49.9163    49.9163    24.9581  66.44   0.000
Residual Error    13      4.8831     4.8831     0.3756
  Lack of Fit      1      0.9506     0.9506     0.9506   2.90   0.114
  Pure Error      12      3.9325     3.9325     0.3277
Total             15     54.7994

Unusual Observations for resp

Obs      resp       Fit  StDev Fit   Residual   St Resid
  6   5.60000   7.31875    0.26539   -1.71875     -3.11R

R denotes an observation with a large standardized residual
```

This outlier point should be further investigated. We will consider that a reason for the outlier point difference was identified; however, the trial could not be repeated. A re-analysis of the data without the outlier point yielded the following:

```
Fractional Factorial Fit

Estimated Effects and Coefficients for resp (coded units)

Term            Effect      Coef  StDev Coef       T       P
Constant                   4.976    0.08364    59.49   0.000
algor          -3.077     -1.538    0.08364   -18.39   0.000
mot_adj         2.402      1.201    0.08364    14.36   0.000

Analysis of Variance for resp (coded units)

Source             DF     Seq SS     Adj SS     Adj MS      F       P
Main Effects        2    52.9420    52.9420    26.4710 254.67   0.000
Residual Error     12     1.2473     1.2473     0.1039
  Lack of Fit       1     0.2156     0.2156     0.2156   2.30   0.158
  Pure Error       11     1.0317     1.0317     0.0938
Total              14    54.1893
```

A residual plot of this new model was well-behaved, as shown below.

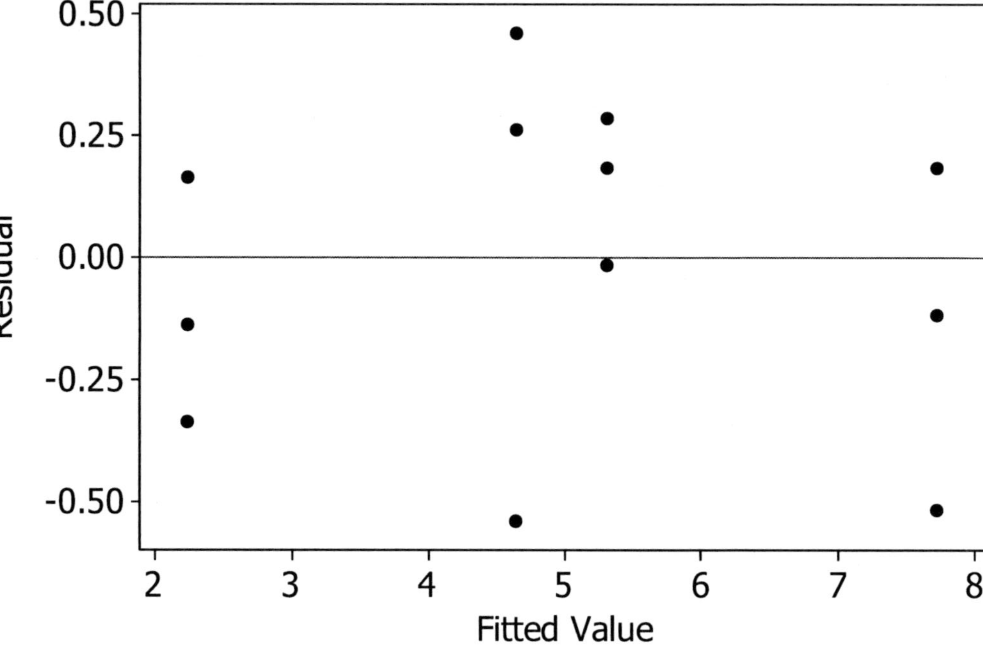

From Figure 32.6 *Integrated Enterprise Excellence, Volume III – Improvement Project Execution: A Management and Black Belt Guide for Going Beyond Lean Six Sigma and the Balanced Scorecard,* Forrest W. Breyfogle III, Bridgeway Books, 2008.

Roadmap step 8.2.28: A DCRCA of the four combinations of algorithm and motor adjustment from the original design is:

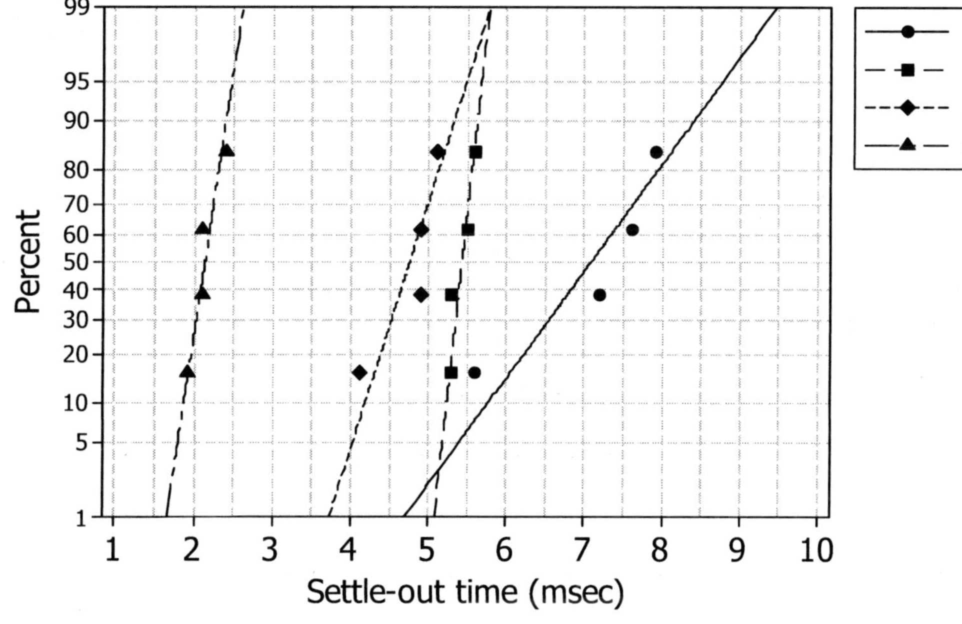

1: Algorithm = - (old)   motor adj = +

2: Algorithm = - (old)   motor adj = -

3: Algorithm = + (new) motor adj = +

4: Algorithm = + (new) motor adj = -

From Figure 32.9 *Integrated Enterprise Excellence, Volume III – Improvement Project Execution: A Management and Black Belt Guide for Going Beyond Lean Six Sigma and the Balanced Scorecard*, Forrest W. Breyfogle III, Bridgeway Books, 2008.

8.5 Creative Solution Development

Roadmap step: 8.10
Reference: *IEE Volume III*, Chapter 35

From a how-to create perspective, Jones (1999) states that to encourage creativity we need to put ourselves in the place of most potential which gives us insight to process improvement or breakthrough improvements. Jones lists nine points for creativity:

1. Creativity is the ability to look at the ordinary and see the extraordinary.
2. Every act can be a creative one.
3. Creativity is a matter of perspective.
4. There's always more than one right answer.
5. Re-frame problems into opportunities.
6. Don't be afraid to make mistakes.
7. Break the pattern.
8. Train your technique.
9. You've got to really care.

TRIZ (Russian: Theory of Problem Solving) states that some design problems may be modeled as technical contradiction. Creativity is required when attempts to improve some functional attributes lead to deterioration of other functional attributes. Design problems associated with a pair of functional contradiction can be solved by making trade-offs or by overcoming the obstacle. TRIZ stresses that an ideal design solution overcomes the conflict, as opposed to making a trade-off.

8.6 Learning by Doing

Roadmap step: 8.11
Reference: *IEE Volume III*, Section 36.2

Lean emphases the learning by doing approach, where process improvement team members consist of those who are most closely associated with adding value to the product. These improvement team activities are to be facilitated by an experienced teacher who uses the Socratic method of learning, where a dialog of questions leads to an agree-to solution. This is a very powerful methodology that should be strongly considered for every project, where implementation can take the form of a kaizen event. In IEE, it is suggested that other experts be included in this process improvement team.

Gemba is the workplace where value is added. A key Lean concept is using "try-storm," at the gemba, rather than conducting an improvement brainstorming session that is physically removed from the workplace. To illustrate this approach, consider the creation of a new work cell. At gemba, a trained facilitator might lead the team in modeling the new work cell using cardboard equipment mockups. Boxes would be moved around until the best layout is determined.

Before beginning this effort, it is important that all team members understand waste and its implication. Prior to redesigning a cell, teams can benefit from an identification-waste examination of other business areas. This experience can help teams create a cell redesigns that minimize waste.

8.7 Tool: Plan-Do-Check-Act (PDCA)

Roadmap step: 8.11
Reference: *IEE Volume III*, Section 36.3

The four-step process of PDCA is also known as the Deming cycle, Shewhart cycle, or plan-do-study-act (PDSA). Dr. Edwards Deming popularized PDCA, which he later modified to PDSA, since "study" better described his intended action than "check."

In an IEE project execution, passive data analyses and/or a DOE can directly lead to a long-lasting solution. However, there are situations when a solution is not obvious and knowledge needs to be gained through an over-time iterative fine-tuning process. For this type situation, a solution can be developed through reiteratively executing the PDCA cycle. When used in the improvement phase of P-DMAIC, assessment of change in the 30,000-foot-level project response can be considered part of the PDCA check step.

The PDCA execution model steps, which can be utilized in the improve phases of P-DMAIC or E-DMAIC and DIEE process development, are:

Plan: Plan a change and its test to determine if a process modification is beneficial.

Do: Implement the change and its test on a small scale.

Check or study: Assess the test results to determine what was learned. Describe what went right, what went wrong, and how well the change worked. A 30,000-foot-level control chart and a hypothesis test can provide a quantitative assessment of how the change impacted the process output.

Act: Determine whether to adopt the change, abandon the change, or repeat the PDCA cycle. A termination decision is appropriate when no significant value is anticipated through the execution of additional PDCA cycles. It can be appropriate either to abort or repeat the PDCA cycle when the evaluated change would create adherence issues or no/minimal improvements were observed. A repeat of the PDCA cycle would be appropriate when the amount of improvement was not as much as desired but additional change enhancement opportunities have been identified. When objectives are met, the process needs to be standardized. In IEE, agreed-to process enhancements are to be documented in the organization's E-DMAIC value chain.

The power of PDCA is in its apparent simplicity and inductive logic utilization. While being relative easy to understand, it can be difficult to accomplish on a on-going basis due to the analytical difficulty in judging tested hypotheses on the basis of measured results.

8.8   Tool: Poka-Yoke (Mistake proofing)

Roadmap step: 8.11-8.14
Reference: *IEE Volume III*, Section 36.6

A *poka-yoke* (pronounced POH-kah YOH-kay) either prevents a mistake from occurring or makes a mistake obvious at a glance. Shigeo Shingo, an industrial engineer at Toyota, is credited with creating and formalizing zero quality control (ZQC), an approach that relies heavily on poka-yoke, i.e., mistake-proofing or error-proofing.

Improvement focus should always be given to what can be done to mistake-proof the process, as opposed to inspecting quality into the produced product. Steps for poke-yoke execution are:

- Describe the potential defect.
- Identify where the defect is likely to occur.
- Analyze process steps.
- Identify errors that may contribute to the defect.
- Apply why-why or 5 Whys analysis to determine root causes.
- With the team, identify mistake-proofing strategies.
- Verify efficiency of the mistake-proofing actions.

8.9   Tool: Future State Value Stream Map

Roadmap step: 8.12
Reference: *IEE Volume III*, Section 14.17

If a Value Stream Map (VSM) was generated earlier in the project, an updated version should be created that documents the future state of the process after the improvements. Take time to fill it out with the best estimate of the future state so that the process owner can use it for a reference point that can be a baseline for future improvements.

8.10 Tool: Standard Work and Standard Operating Procedures

Roadmap step: 8.11-8.14
Reference: *IEE Volume III*, Section 36.4

A process' work combination is the blending of materials, process operations, people, and technology. In Lean, standard operations are the most efficient work combination created by the organization. Standards are not rigid. Standards should address the aspects of work time, operational sequence, and WIP. Standards are applicable in both repetitive and non-repetitive work such as design, maintenance, service, and management, where the development of the best and safest approach is a participative effort.

8.11 Tool: One-Piece Flow

Roadmap step: 8.11-8.14
Reference: *IEE Volume III*, Section 36.5

One-piece flow describes the sequence of activities through a process one unit at a time. For example, an insurance claim might be considered a single unit. In contrast, batch processing handles activities on a large number of transactions at one time – sending them together as a group through each operational step. A project process improvement could be a work flow change that reduces batch size or changes from batch processing to single-piece flow.

8.12 Tool: Visual Management

Roadmap step: 8.11-8.14
Reference: *IEE Volume III*, Section 36.7

Visual management can address both visual display and visual control. Visual displays present information, while visual control focuses on action needs. Information needs address items such as schedules, standard work, quality, and maintenance. Visual control can address whether a production line is running according to plan and highlights problems.
Visual management organizations can:
- improve quality through error prevention, detection, and resolution
- increase workplace efficiency
- improve workplace safety
- reduce total costs

8.13 Tool: 5S Method

Roadmap step: 8.13
Reference: *IEE Volume III*, Section 36.8

One primary reason for 5S is the creation of standardized work. 5S offers a basic housekeeping discipline for both the shop floor and office, which contains the following steps: sort, straighten, shine, standardize, and sustain. Activities for each of these steps are:

1. Sort: Clearly distinguish the needed from the unneeded tools, supplies, and material. Tag items (see Figure 36.3) if not used within a month, unnecessary to perform job, broken or not useable, or insufficient for intended purpose.

2. Straighten: All items in the work area have a marked place, and a place exists for everything to allow for easy and immediate retrieval.

3. Shine: The work area is cleaned and straightened regularly as you work.

4. Standardize: Work method, tools, and identification markings are standard and recognizable throughout the factory. 5S methods are applied consistently in a uniform and disciplined manner.

5. Sustain: 5S is a regular part of work, and continuous actions are taken to improve work. Established procedures are maintained by checklist. After cleaning an area, we can all identify with frustration after some period of time of not being able to find something

5S should be considered in two ways:

- As an everyday, continuous improvement activity for both individuals and small groups
- As a KPIV that should impact our 30,000-foot-level project/operational metrics

8.14 Tool: Kaizen Event

Roadmap step: 8.14
Reference: *IEE Volume III*, Section 36.9

- Purpose
  - The kaizen event is a team process that is used to make decisions and improvements.
  - In the IEE process, the kaizen method can be very useful in generating an improvement plan.
- What it is
  - The improvement should be determined through the improvement roadmap usage, not necessarily with a week-long kaizen event.
  - The kaizen event should include the improvement team and representatives of all process stakeholders.
  - The kaizen event should also include a senior manager or executive that is authorized to approve and fund any improvement plan actions derived from this meeting. If this senior person cannot attend, it is best to delay the event.
  - The output of the kaizen should be an approved improvement plan, not a proposal. Focus on doing, not planning.
  - As with other improvement efforts, benefits from a kaizen event need to be demonstrated as achievement of an improved state of 30,000-foot-level metric performance, as described later in this book.

Background:

The Japanese word kaizen literally means continuous improvement. The hallmark of a kaizen event is its empowerment of people fostering their creativity. Through the work of Taiichi Ohno, the Toyota production system (TPS) has become synonymous with the implementation of kaizen events, embodying the philosophy and applying the principles. Some companies use a kaizen event or kaizen blitz to fix specific problem or workflow issue within their organization. IEE integrates with this activity through 30,000-foot-level metrics, where a kaizen event is created when there is a need to improve a particular aspect of the business, as identified by this metric, and a kaizen event is a tool that can be used to accomplish this.

The generic steps when conducting a kaizen event follow. Appropriate modifications are made to these steps when executing an IEE project execution.

1. Prepare and train the team
2. Analyze present methods
3. Brainstorm, test, and evaluate ideas
4. Implement and evaluate improvements
5. Present results and follow-up

8.15 Tool: Kanban

Roadmap steps: 8.11-8.14
Reference: *IEE Volume III*, Section 36.10

Background:
A business system that creates work or a product before it is ordered or needed by the customer (could be the next step in a process) is called a push system. If there is no mechanism to keep the WIP below some level that is consistent with the customer demand, work output can become excessive, which can lead to many problems, including finished goods storage in the manufacturing case or excessive work and rework in a transactional case.

In *pull* systems, products and transactions are created at a pace that matches customer demand. Kanbans are used to buffer variations in customer or next process step demands. A most familiar form of kanban implementation is American-style supermarkets. In these supermarkets, each product has a short-term buffer, where its replenishment from a regional distribution facility is triggered when the item is scanned at checkout. When the distribution center receives the replenishment signal, an order to the supplier is triggered for a replenishment of the distribution center. The kanban is the signal that occurs when the product is scanned.

In supermarkets a customer can get (1) what is needed, (2) at the time needed, (3) in the amount needed (Ohno 1988). This is in contrast to Japan's traditional turn-of-the-century (i.e., 1900) merchandising methods, such as peddling medicines door to door, going around to customers to take orders, and hawking wares, America's supermarket system is more rational. From the seller's viewpoint, labor is not wasted carrying items that may not sell, while the buyer does not have to worry about whether to buy extra items.

The Japanese word kanban refers to the pulling of product through a production process, i.e., a pull system. The intent of kanban is to signal a preceding process that the next process needs parts/material. In the supermarket example, an order is placed with the originating supplier only after an item is sold to the final customer.

A bottleneck is a system constraint. In a pull system, the bottleneck should be used to set the pace for the entire production line. Buffers in high-volume manufacturing serve to balance the line. It's important that such operations receive the necessary supplies in a timely basis and that poorly sequenced work does not interfere with the process completion. Pull systems address what the external and internal customers need when they want it. Through this, WIP is reduced.

A simple kanban-managed transaction system is when the transactional process manager does not let any new work start until a transaction is completed and provided to the customer.

8.16 Tool: Continuous Flow and Cell Design

Roadmap steps: 8.11-8.14
Reference: *IEE Volume III*, Section 36.13

- Purpose
  - The team should include an assessment of the work area layout.
- What it is
  - This assessment is for more than just manufacturing.
  - Since changes are occurring in the process, every effort should be made to lay out the work area to obtain the advantages of continuous flow and cell work area designs.

Background;
The disadvantages of traditional batch production are large WIP, large conveyance time for parts, large lead time, and large liability for defect; e.g., all WIP if detected at last process step. Batching occurs in a transactional situation when groups of transactions collect in an in or out box and then are moved to the next process step in a group or they wait for an overnight computer update before processing further.

Small-lot production removes the walls from batch production, reduces WIP, lead times, and conveyance, if the product is allowed to move between steps in the same small groups. Small-lot production can be challenging in a transactional environment because the resource that does the work also moves the transaction, and they are probably rewarded for work time, not transportation time. Resistance to stopping batch process for this environment is usually high since it typically can take the same time to move one transaction as it would to move ten. It can be impossible, however, to balance task durations for machine operations with this push system, since one operator can spend a great deal of time waiting, and inventory can build up at a station.

A U-shaped cell offers balanced operator processing time to takt time.

8.17 Tool: Changeover Reduction

Roadmap steps: 8.11-8.14
Reference: *IEE Volume III*, Section 36.14

- Purpose
  - Evaluate the process for lost productive time when changing tasks, products, or transactions
- What it is
  - The manufacturing scenarios are easy to recognize; it is more difficult with transactional processes.
  - All reductions in the time to change tasks, products, or transactions improve the productivity and capacity.
  - Any interruption in a transactional process can be considered as a changeover in this assessment.
  - This issue addresses a problem that is pervasive but also unrecognized in the transactional work environment.
    - every interruption of a worker
    - every meeting
    - every change in tasking

The process:
  General steps in a changeover reduction effort
  1. Identify and classify changeover activities as either:
     - Internal: must be in the process critical path time
     - External: may be moved outside of the process critical path
  2. External or preparation activities should be maximized.
     - Cut or reduce waste activities such as movement, fetching tools, filling in forms.
  3. Try to convert internal activities to external.
     - Use additional resources or equipment to do pre-work.
  4. Apply process improvement (re-design) to the remaining internal activities.
  5. Minimize external activity time.
     - This is because in small-batch production there may be insufficient time to prepare for the changeover during a batch run.

Background:

Let's consider a 30,000-foot-level metric (Y variable or KPOV) that has a lead time reduction goal. For this situation, we would consider a Lean tool application, since one major objective of Lean is the reduction of lead time. To achieve this, the size of batches often needs reduction which creates a focus for reducing changeover times; i.e., time from the last piece of one batch to the first piece of the next batch.

Changeover time can have several components; e.g., internal when a machine is stopped and external which involves preparation. Other types of changeovers are manufacturing line changeover, maintenance operations, vehicle/aircraft loading/unloading, and office operations. The classic changeover is, of course, the grand prix pit stop! It's important not only to reduce the mean changeover time, but also reduce its variability using a standardized process.

Within Shingo's classic single-minute exchange of die (SMED), internal and external activities are classified within a flowchart of the changeover. It is desirable to move internal activities to external activities when possible. This permits more up time of the machine since the maximum amount of preparation is accomplished before the machine is stopped. Example applications for the improvement of external activities are placing tools on carts near the die and using color codes to avoid confusion. Example applications for the improvement of internal activities are quick-change nuts and the standardization of activities.

8.18 Tool: Total Productive Maintenance (TPM)

Roadmap step: 8.15
Reference: *IEE Volume III*, Section 36.15

- Purpose
  - Evaluate the process for efficiency and effectiveness.
- What it is
  - These methods were developed for a maintenance program, but the efficiency definitions are usable everywhere.
  - Inefficiencies exist in transactional processes as well as manufacturing processes.
    - Availability of people (resources)
    - Efficiency of people (time on task)
    - Quality of performance
  - Using these concepts to examine a transactional process may lead to true insight on where improvements can be achieved.

Background:
In implementing programs with a company, Lean and TPM have similarities. The TPM description within this section describes TPM and its linkage to an overall IEE implementation strategy. TPM is productive maintenance carried out by all employees through small group activities. Like TQC, which is company-wide total quality control, TPM is equipment maintenance performed on a company-wide basis.

Sources for the scheduled downtime of a machine are maintenance, breaks, and lunch. Sources for unscheduled downtime include machine breakdown, setup time, and part shortages. Equipment needs to be available and to function properly when needed. TPM emphasizes not only prevention but also improvement in productivity. To achieve these goals, we need the participation of both experts and operators with a feeling of ownership for this process.

Focus is given within TPM to eliminate the obstacles to the effectiveness of equipment. These *six big losses* can be broken down into three categories:
Downtime:
1. *Equipment failure* from breakdowns
2. *Setup and adjustment* from die changes, etc.

Speed losses:
1. *Idling and minor stoppages* due to abnormal sensor operation, etc.
2. *Reduced speed* due to discrepancies between the design and actual operational speed

Defect:
1. Process *defects in process* due to scrap and reworks
2. *Reduced yield* from machine startup to stable/predictable production

From an equipment point of view:
Load time and operating time are impacted by losses numbered 1 and 2.

Net operating time is impacted by losses numbered 3 and 4.
Valuable operating time is impacted by losses numbered 5 and 6.

Metrics within TPM could be tracked at the 30,000-foot-level, where improvement projects are initiated when the metrics are not satisfactory. The highest level TPM metric is overall equipment effectiveness (Nakajina 1988)

$$\text{Overall equipment effectiveness} = \text{Availability} \times \text{Performance efficiency} \times \text{Rate of quality products}$$

where the downtime loss metric (loss 1 from equipment failure and loss 2 from setup and adjustment) is

$$\text{Availability} = \frac{\text{operation time}}{\text{loading time}} = \frac{\text{loading time - downtime}}{\text{loading time}}$$

and the speed loss metric (loss 3 from idling and minor stoppages and loss 4 from reduced speed) is

$$\text{Performance efficiency} = \frac{\text{ideal cycle time} \times \text{processed amount}}{\text{operating time}} \times 100$$

and the defect loss metric (loss 5 from defects in process and loss 6 from reduced yield) is

$$\text{Rate of quality products} = \frac{\text{processed amount - defect amount}}{\text{processed amount}} \times 100$$

Based on experience (Nakajima 1998), the ideal conditions are
    Availability: greater than 90%
    Performance efficiency: greater than 95%
    Rate of quality products: greater than 99%.

Therefore, the ideal overall equipment effectiveness should be:

$$0.90 \times 0.95 \times 0.99 \times 100 = 85 + \%$$

Overall demands and constraints of the system need to be considered when selecting IEE projects that affect these metrics.

8.19 Tool: Process Modeling and Simulation in the Improve Phase

Roadmap step: 8.16-17
Reference: *IEE Volume III*, Section 37.2

- Purpose
  - Consider using simulation tools to verify or test the improvement plan.
- What it is
  - Many improvements cannot be verified to the organizational leadership without a permanent commitment to the change, which makes them very difficult to be approved.
  - Process simulation tools allow the team to evaluate the process improvements without actual implementation.
  - Use of process modeling in the improve phase can provide insight assessment for various what-if scenarios, which can be used to determine the effectiveness of these opportunities. A process model can provide:
    - Process performance animation
    - Quantified cycle and waiting times
    - Identified bottlenecks, capacity constraints, and costs
    - Effectiveness determination of various improvement options

8.20 Tools: Solution Selection and Pugh Matrices

Roadmap step: 8.16
Reference: *IEE Volume III*, Section 37.3

- Purpose
  - The use of an improvement selection matrix allows a fair ranking of many improvement options.
  - No team should settle on the first idea. Generate improvement ideas as in the wisdom of the organization phase effort to find causes.
- What it is
  - You should always compare your suggested improvements against no changes in order to ensure that it is a true benefit.
  - A best practice is to include two or more actions for every improvement area.
    - One that is permanent and effective although it may take some time to implement.
    - A second may be quick, but less effective. Why wait to start getting some gains?
  - A primary benefit is the ability to rank combinations of improvement ideas to gain optimal improvement.

Background:
The solution selection and Pugh matrices provide a systematic approach for selecting the best-thought approach.

Example:

Solution Selection Matrix						
	Effectivn ess of Solution to fix problem	**Benefits other areas**	**Short Time to implement**	**Low Cost of Solutio n**		<<<<Decision Criteria
	10	6	8	2		<<<<<<<<Importance
----- Process input -----	--------- Correlation of Input to Output ---------					--------- Total ---------
Lost time in transport						
Mechanical transport	6	1	3	1		92
Move work locations	9	1	6	6		156
Hire faster person	3	1	3	6		72
Current method/No change	1	1	9	9		106
Step 2 takes too long						
Training & SOP improvement	3	6	6	6		126
Re-distribute work load	9	6	9	9		216
Automate the step	9	1	3	1		122
Current method/No change	1	1	9	9		106
Low quality Product						
Training and SOP usage	3	6	6	6		126
Mistake proofing (template)	9	1	6	9		162
Increased quality feedback (operator self inspection)	6	3	6	3		132
Current method/No change	1	1	9	9		106

From Table 37.1 *Integrated Enterprise Excellence, Volume III – Improvement Project Execution: A Management and Black Belt Guide for Going Beyond Lean Six Sigma and the Balanced Scorecard,* Forrest W. Breyfogle III, Bridgeway Books, 2008.

Example:

Pugh Matrix Method				
	Current	Solution 1	Solution 2	Solution 3
Reduction in Defects (30,000-foot-level metric)	*	+	+	+
Lead time reduction	*	*	-	+
Reduce operating expenses	*	+	*	+
Resources required to implement	*	*	*	*
Cost to implement	*	+	-	-
Complete by due date	*	-	+	-
Number of (+)	0	3	2	3
Number of (-)	0	1	2	2
Total score	0	2	0	1

* = no benefit to current method

+ = beneficial to current method

- = not as beneficial as current method

Choose solution 1 because of higher total score

8.21 Tool: Walking the New Process and Value Chain Documentation

Roadmap step: 8.17
Reference: *IEE Volume III*, Section 37.4

If at all possible, the new process should undergo a step-by-step walk through. Often many optimization refinements can be uncovered using multiple quick plan-do-study-act cycles during this process refinement step. Upon completion of the detailed process, new procedure documentation can be made in the value chain utilizing swim lanes, drill downs, value stream maps, and/or attachment documents. This value chain procedural standardization should be an integral part of initial and on-going process-user training.

8.22 Tool: Pilot Testing

Roadmap step: 8.18
Reference: *IEE Volume III*, Section 37.5

As improvements are identified and evaluated, there may be some out-of-the-box ideas chosen. Many times the organization will then require more than a statistical estimation of the gain as enough evidence to approve the implementation. In these cases, it is beneficial to execute a pilot test of the solution recommendations.

Among other things, pilot testing provides the following benefits:
1. Allows the business to provide indisputable evidence of the identified cause-and-effect relationship and the solution effectiveness.
2. Allows the business to experience the solution without fully committing to the change.
3. Allows the business to better understand the impacts and to obtain feedback from customers and other downstream process participants.
.

8.23 Tool: Process Change Implementation Training and Project Validation

Roadmap step: 8.21
Reference: *IEE Volume III*, Section 37.6

When transitioning to the new process, there needs to be sufficient detailed planning so that implemented changes create as little disruption as possible to current work. Initial and futures users of the process need adequate training. When user training includes the organizational value chain with its associated procedures and metrics, process users gain insight to how their work integrates with the big picture. When appropriate, specific self-paced training can also be linked to value-chain-process steps.

Completed projects need to:

- Demonstrate their impact to a 30,000-foot-level metric.
- Show visually the estimated process capability/performance metric improvement.
- Describe statistically the magnitude of improvements.
- Describe project benefit, e.g., CODND.

The following examples illustrate this project-benefit-identification process. The next chapter will describe control mechanisms to maintain project gain.

8.24 Demonstrating and Quantifying Improvement

Roadmap steps: 8.3 – 8.6
Reference: *IEE Volume III*, Sections 37.7 – 37.9

Process improvements benefits can be demonstrated by showing baseline 30,000-foot-level metrics moving to an improved level of performance.

Example: Demonstrating improvement for continuous data, no specification

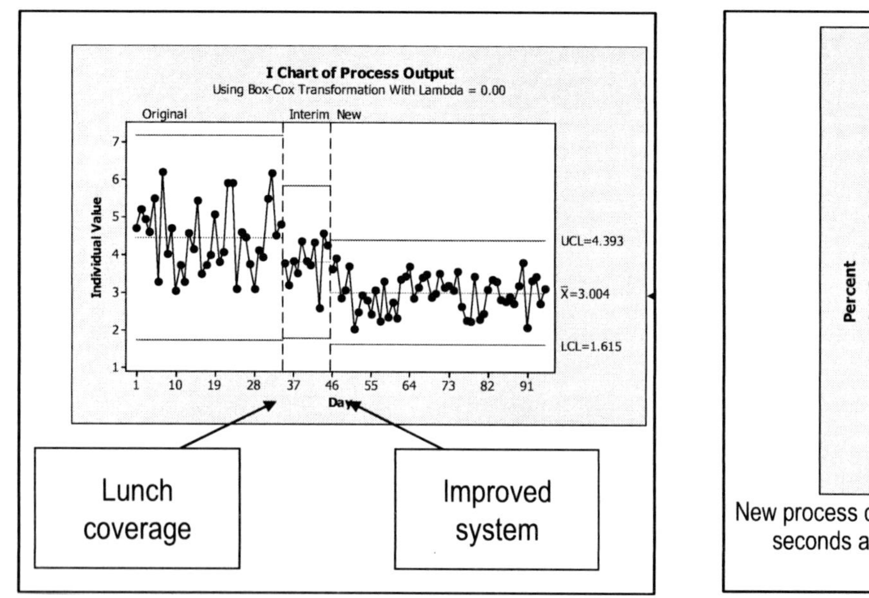

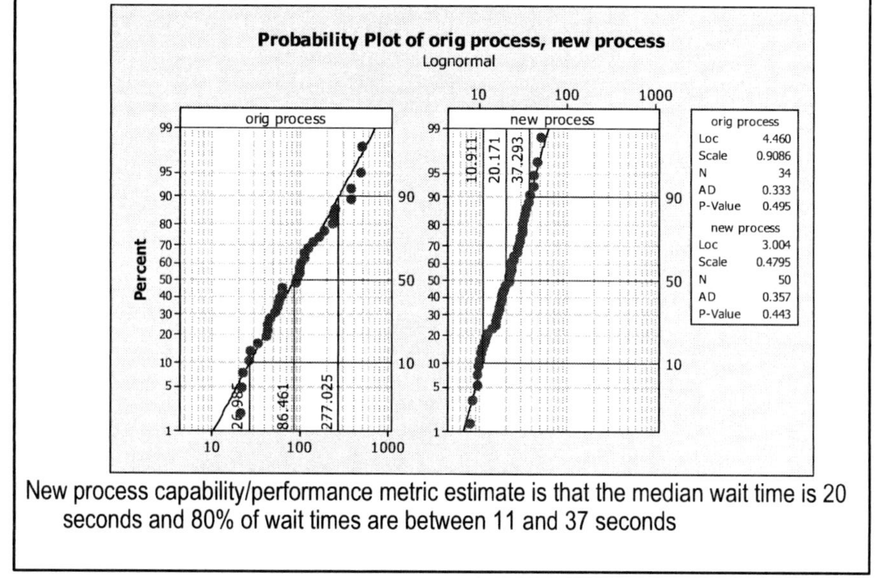

Example: Demonstrating improvement for an attribute situation

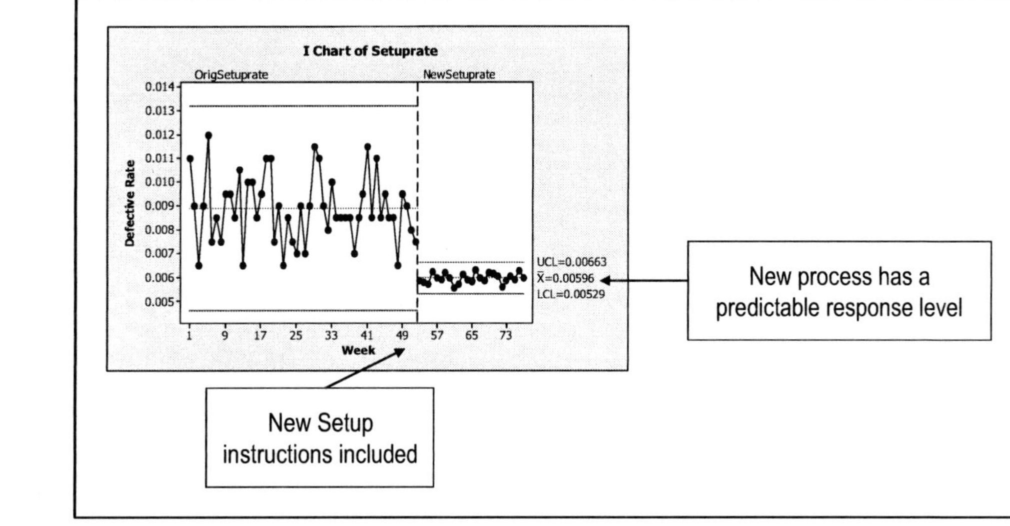

9 P-DMAIC: Control Phase

Purpose: To control variation sources and maintain the gains realized from improvement actions
Deliverables:
- Documentation of process changes
- Control plan with hand off to process owner
- Final report
- Communication of results and leveraging opportunities
- Financial audit of results

Reference: Chapter 38 – 39 of *Integrated Enterprise Excellence, Volume III* (Breyfogle 2008c)

9.1 *Roadmap*

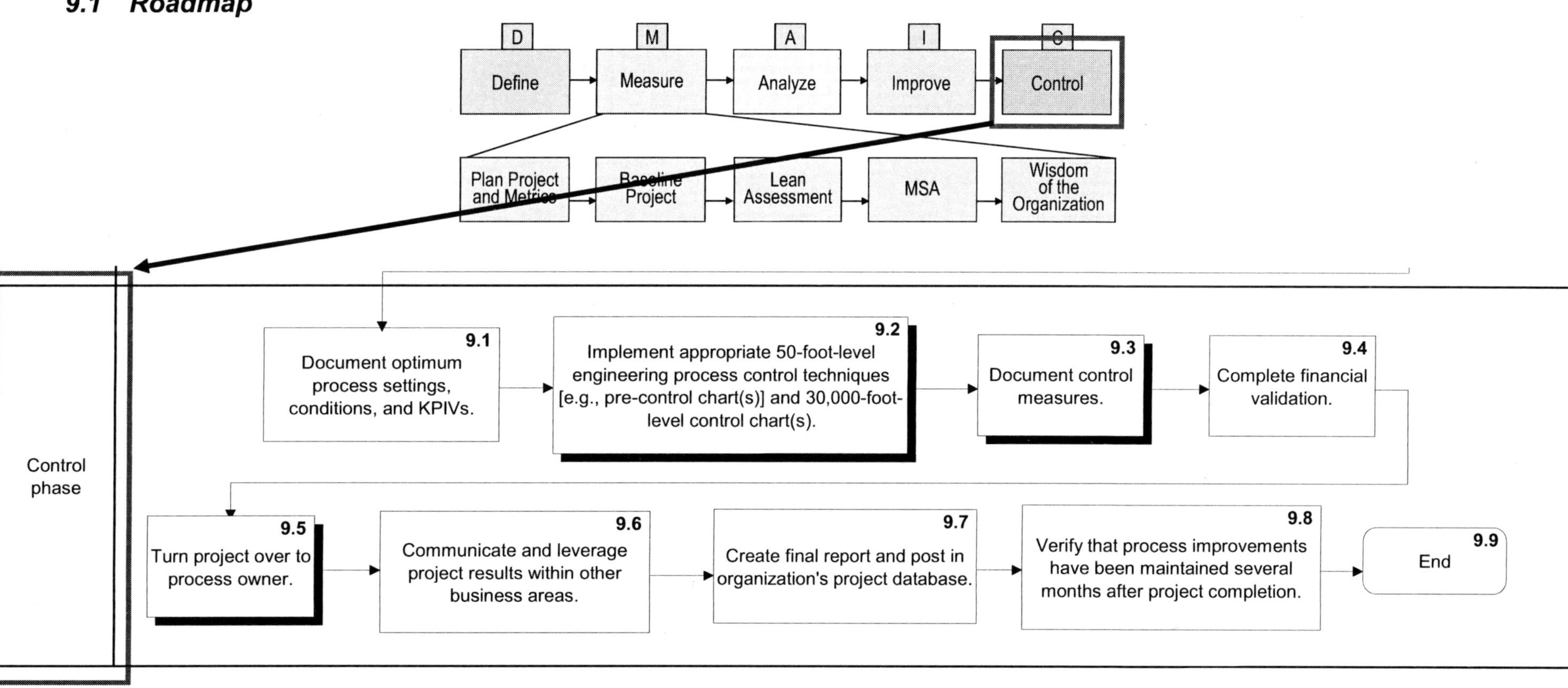

Step 9.2 drill down

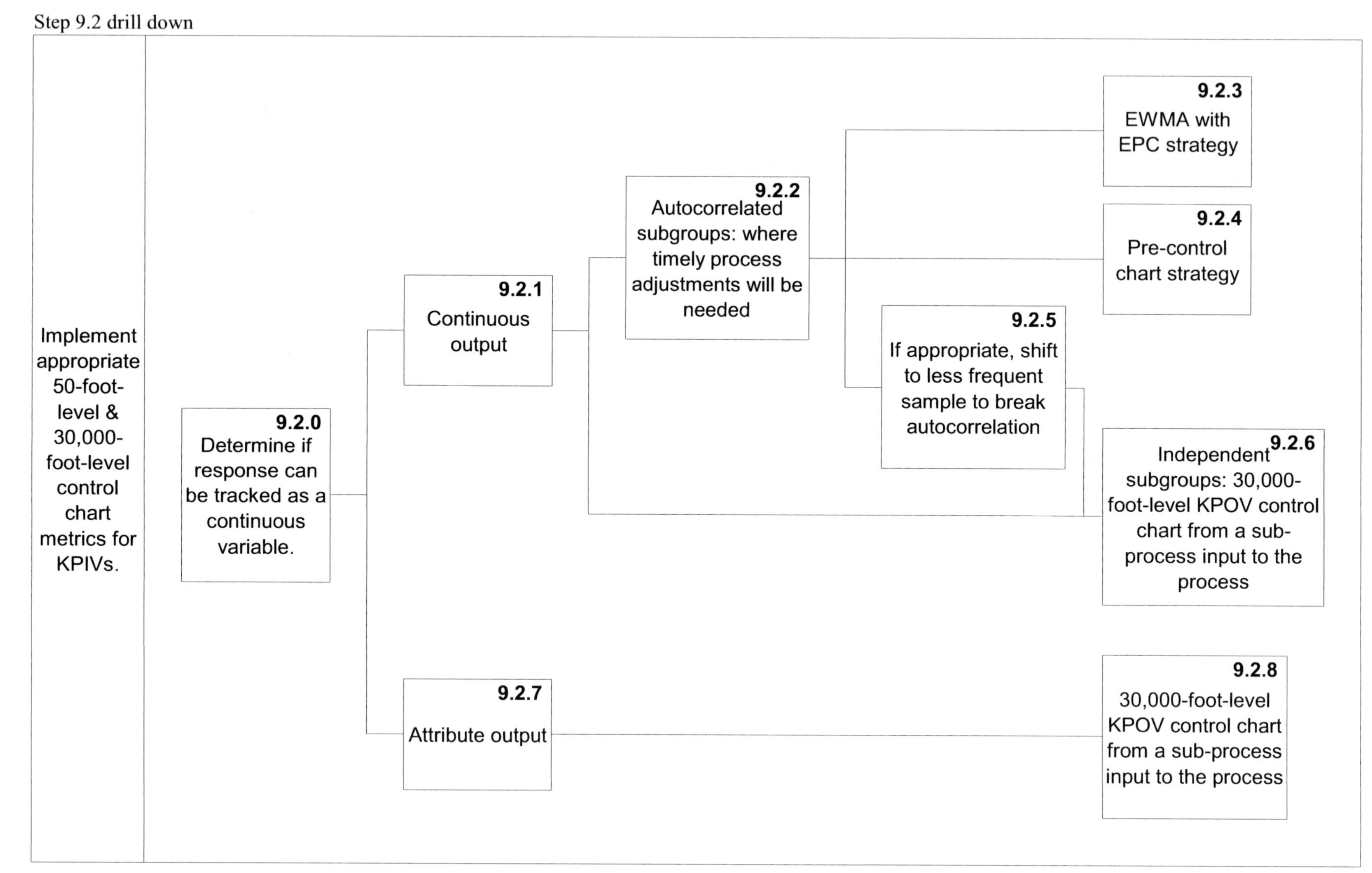

Step 9.3 drill down

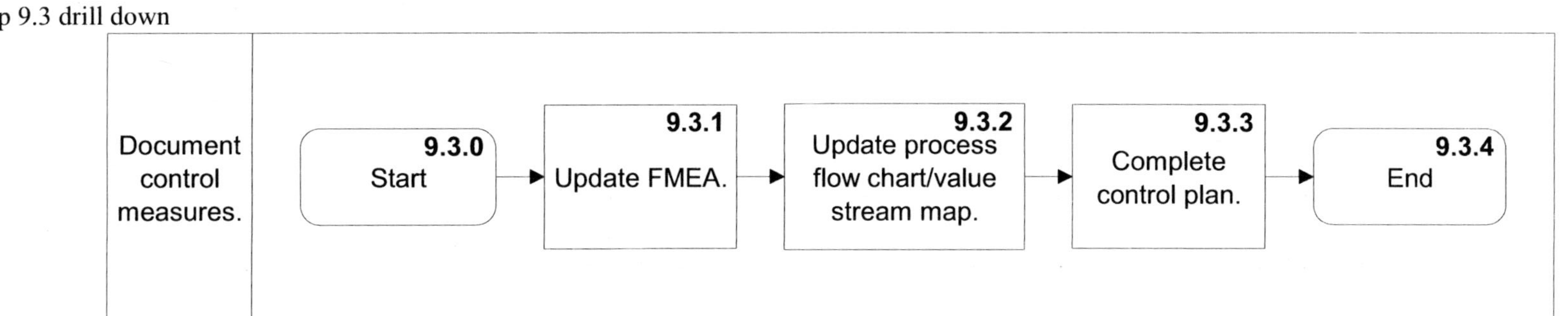

Step 9.5 drill down

9.2 Check Sheet

Control Phase Check Sheet		
Description	**Questions**	**Yes/No NA**
Tool/Methodology		
Process map /SOPs/FMEA	Were process changes and procedures documented with optimum process settings?	
Control charts	Were control charts created at the 50-foot-level or 30,000-foot-level appropriate?	
	Was the appropriate control chart used for the input variable data type?	
	Is the sampling plan sufficient?	
	Is a plan in place to maintain the 30,000-foot-level control chart using this metric and the process capability/performance metric as operational metrics?	
	Has the responsibility for process monitoring been assigned?	
	Is there a reaction plan for out-of-control conditions?	
	Have the 30,000-foot-level and 50-foot-level control metrics been assigned to the appropriate person's performance plan?	
Control plan	Are all items in the control plan sufficiently documented?	
Assessment	Were any process improvements made?	
	If so, were they statistically verified with the appropriate hypothesis test?	
	Did you describe the change over time on a 30,000-foot-level control chart?	
	Did you calculate and display the change in the process capability/performance metric?	
	Have you documented and communicated the improvements?	
	Have you summarized the benefits and annualized financial benefits?	
Communications plan	Has the project been handed off to the process owner?	
	Are the changes to the process and improvements being communicated appropriately throughout the organization?	
	Is there a plan to leverage project results to other areas of the business?	
Team		
Resources	Were all contributing members of the team acknowledged and thanked?	
	Has the project success been celebrated?	
	Is the process owner ready to take ownership of the project sustainment effort?	
Change management	Has the team considered obstacles to making this change last?	
Next Phase		
Final approval and closure	Is there a detailed plan to monitor KPIV and KPOV metrics over time to ensure that change is sustained?	
	Have all action items and project deliverables been completed?	
	Has a final project report been approved?	
	Was the project certified and the financial benefits validated?	
	Has the project database been updated?	

9.3   Document optimal settings

Roadmap step: 9.1
Reference: *IEE Volume III*, Chapter 36

- Purpose
  - All the knowledge gained during the course of the improvement project needs to be documented for the process owners.
- What it is
  - Include all possible process settings into the process documents, the training documents, and any support or maintenance documents.

9.4   Tool: Implement 50-foot-level process control

Roadmap step: 9.2
Reference: *IEE Volume III*, Sections 38.6 – 38.7

- Purpose
  - It is most desirable that processes are made robust so that input variability does not detrimentally impact the process response; however, that is not always possible because sometimes the nature of the process inputs require engineering process control. For example, adding or removing a help-desk attendant (process input variable) to compensate for demand fluctuations and to maintain an acceptable hold-time duration level (process output response).
- What it is
  - Process input controls can significantly improve the management of the process output levels.
  - The 30,000-foot-level methods are applicable to control input levels that do not require engineering process control, but other methods, such as pre-control, are also available when inputs need active control at the 50-foot-level.

9.5   Tool: Document Control Measures

Roadmap step: 9.3
Reference: *IEE Volume III*, Section 39.4

- Purpose
  - A published document that lists all the control methods, measurement systems, and reaction plans should be completed.

- What it is
  - The control plan is considered the document that transfers the solution from the team to the process owner.
  - This document transfers process knowledge to the process owner.

Background;
A control plan is a written document created to ensure that processes are run so that products or services meet or exceed customer requirements at all times. It should be a living document, which is updated with both additions and deletions of controls based on experience from the process. A control plan may need approval of the procuring organization(s).

A control plan check sheet is noted below [AIAG 1995a] where any negative comment is to have an associated comment and/or action required along with responsible part and due date.

- Was described control plan methods used in preparing the control plan?
- Have all known customer concerns been identified to facilitate the selection of special product/process characteristics?
- Are all special product/process characteristics included in the control plan?
- Were the appropriate FMEA techniques used to prepare the control plan?
- Are material specifications that require inspection identified?
- Are incoming material and component packaging issues addressed?
- Are engineering performance-testing requirements identified?
- Are required gages and test equipment available?
- If required, has there been customer approval?
- Are gage methods compatible between supplier and customer?

These guidelines are consistent with the basic IEE method. However, 30,000-foot-level controls should also be noted whenever appropriate. Obviously, IEE project results can have a major influence in the details of the control plan as it currently exists within an organization.

9.6   Complete Financial Validation

Roadmap step: 9.4
Reference: *IEE Volume III*, Sections 39.6

- Purpose
  - Estimate the true 30,000-foot-level and satellite level metric changes and the corresponding financial impact of the improvement.
- What it is
  - This should be based on actual changes in performance as compared to the CODND determined in the problem statement.
  - This estimate is generally signed off by a financial representative.

9.7 Turn Over Project to Process Owner

Roadmap step: 9.5
Reference: *IEE Volume III*, Sections 39.6

- Purpose
  - Transfer of responsibility for managing the improved process.
- What it is
  - This step is instrumental in the effort to make the changes permanent.
  - A written acknowledgement of the acceptance from the process owner is recommended.

9.8 Communication and Reporting

Roadmap step: 9.6 & 9.7
Reference: *IEE Volume III*, Sections 39.6

- Purpose
  - Provide a permanent record of the project activities, conclusions, data analysis, and knowledge for later review.
  - Provide a vehicle to leverage the benefits across the organization.
- What it is
  - There is usually a presentation created that covers the key points in the project
  - A written report that details the project activities should be generated that provides greater detail on the project. It may include;
    - All data collected during project
    - All hypotheses that were evaluated, no matter what was found.
    - All lessons learned
    - Recommended follow-up on actions.

9.9 Improvement Verification

Roadmap step: 9.8
Reference: *IEE Volume III*, Sections 39.6

- Purpose
  - Verify the improvement plan and control plan provided that there is a long-standing organizational gain.
- What it is
  - It is recommended to re-assess the gains between 2 and 6 months after implementation.
  - The entire improvement team generally re-convenes to audit the process.
  - If the improvements have not been sustained, the team may restart the improvement effort and develop a new improvement.

Appendix

10 Appendix A: Basic Concepts

This appendix describes basic concepts that are referenced in this book.

10.1 Data Types

Reference: *IEE Volume III*, Section 8.1

Continuous data can assume a range of numerical responses on a continuous scale, as opposed to data that can assume only discrete levels. Binary attribute data have the presence or absence of some characteristic in each device under test; e.g., proportion nonconforming in a pass/fail test.

Examples of continuous data are: micrometer dimensional readings from a production sample and the time it takes to complete a transaction. Examples of attribute data are: number of defects on a part recorded by inspectors and the failure rate in which parts are either passed or failed in an inspection process (as opposed to measuring and recording the dimension of the parts).

10.2 Tool: Time-Series Plot

Reference: *IEE Volume III*, Sections 8.2 – 8.3
Minitab Syntax: Graph>Time Series Plot

A run chart or time-series plot permits the study of data over time for trends or patterns, where the x-axis is time and the y-axis is the measured variable. Generally 20-25 points are needed to establish patterns and baselines.

Example (S&P 500 closing prices)

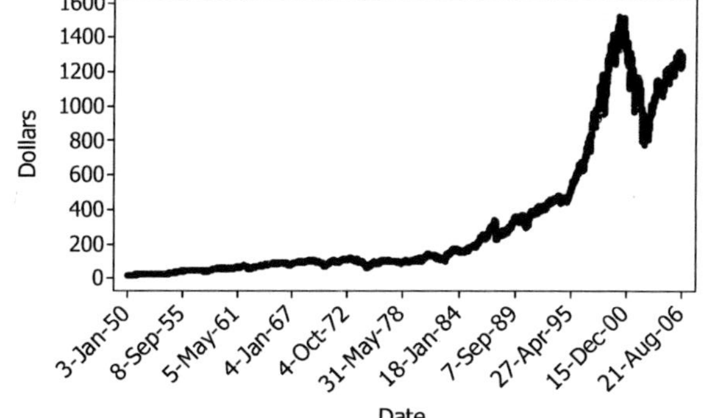

From Figure 8.1 *Integrated Enterprise Excellence, Volume III – Improvement Project Execution: A Management and Black Belt Guide for Going Beyond Lean Six Sigma and the Balanced Scorecard,* Forrest W. Breyfogle III, Bridgeway Books, 2008.

10.3 Mean, Standard Deviation, and Median

Reference: *IEE Volume III*, Sections 8.10 – 8.11
Minitab Syntax: Stat>Basic Statistics>Display Descriptive Statistics

A well-known statistic for a sample is the mean ($\bar{x}$). The mean is the arithmetic average of the data values (x_1, x_2, x_3, ..., x_i), which is mathematically expressed in the following equation using a summation sign Σ for sample size *(n)* as:

$$\bar{x} = \frac{\sum_{i=1}^{n} x_i}{n}$$

A sample yields an estimate $\bar{x}$ for the true mean of a population μ from which the sample is randomly drawn. Standard deviation is a statistic that quantifies the dispersion of data. A manager would be interested not only in the average duration of phone conversations but also in the variability of the length of conversation. One equation form for the standard deviation mean(s) of a sample is:

$$s = \left[\frac{\sum_{i=1}^{n} (x_i - \bar{x})^2}{n-1} \right]^{1/2}$$

A sample yields an estimate s for the true population standard deviation (σ). When data have a bell-shape distribution (i.e., are normally distributed), approximately 68.26% of the data is expected to be within a plus or minus one standard deviation range around the mean.

For a sample, median is the number that is in the middle when all observations are ranked in magnitude; i.e., 50% of the values are below and 50% above the median. When you have an even number of values, the median is the average of the two middle points.

10.4 Tool: Histogram

Reference: *IEE Volume III*, Sections 8.8 – 8.9
Minitab Syntax: Graph>Histogram

A histogram is a plot that frequently is used to describe both mean and variability (e.g., standard deviation). When creating a histogram of continuous response data, the data need to be placed into classes (i.e., groups or cells). For example, in a set of data, there might be six measurements that fall between the numbers of 0.501 and 1.500; these measurements can be grouped into a class that has a center value of 1. Many computer programs internally handle this grouping.

Example:

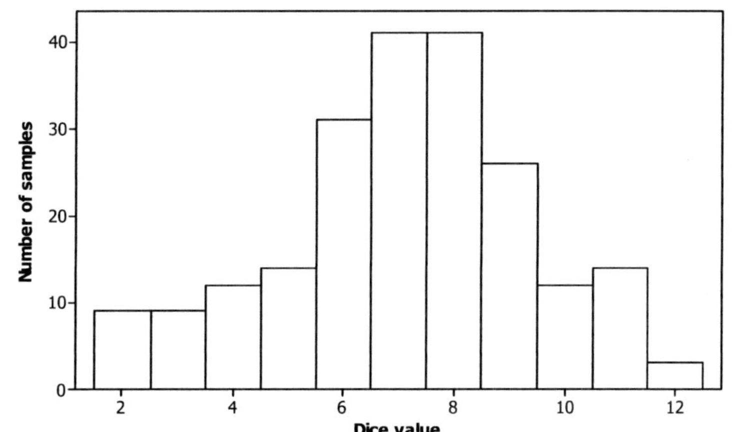

From Figure 8.8 *Integrated Enterprise Excellence, Volume III – Improvement Project Execution: A Management and Black Belt Guide for Going Beyond Lean Six Sigma and the Balanced Scorecard,* Forrest W. Breyfogle III, Bridgeway Books, 2008.

10.5 Tool: Dot Plot

Reference: *IEE Volume III*, Sections 8.8 – 8.9
Minitab Syntax: Graph>Dotplot

An alternative to a histogram is a dot plot, which presents symbols that represent individual observations from a batch of data, which are not placed into cells.

For example:

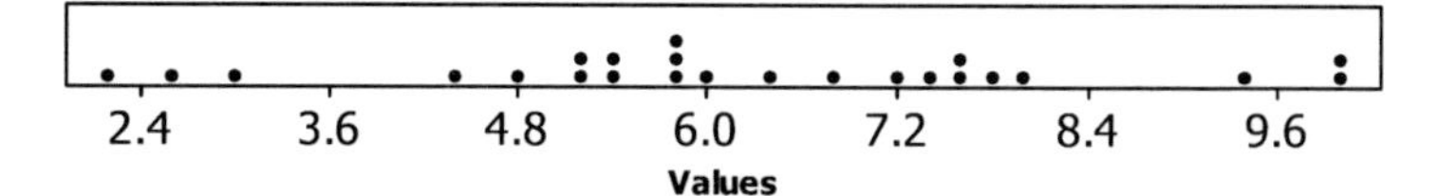

From Figure 8.6 *Integrated Enterprise Excellence, Volume III – Improvement Project Execution: A Management and Black Belt Guide for Going Beyond Lean Six Sigma and the Balanced Scorecard,* Forrest W. Breyfogle III, Bridgeway Books, 2008.

10.6 Distributions

Reference: *IEE Volume III*, Sections 8.14 – 8.16
Minitab Syntax: Graph>Probability Distribution Plot

The population of a continuous variable has an underlying distribution. This distribution might be represented as a normal, Weibull, or log-normal distribution. This distribution is sometimes called the parent distribution. From a population, samples can be taken with the objective of characterizing a population. A distribution that describes the characteristic of this sampling is called the sampling distribution or child distribution.

The shape of the distribution of a population does not usually need to be considered when making statements about the mean of a population because the sampling distribution of the mean tends to be normally distributed; i.e., the Central Limit Theorem. However, often a better understanding of the percentiles of the population yields more useful knowledge relative to the needs of the customer. To be able to get this information, knowledge is needed about the shape of the population distribution. Instead of representing continuous-response data using a normal distribution, the three-parameter Weibull distribution or log-normal distribution may, for example, better explain the general probability characteristics of the population.

10.7 Normal Distribution

Reference: *IEE Volume III*, Sections 8.15 – 8.16
Minitab Syntax: Graph>Probability Distribution Plot

The following two scenarios exemplify data that follow a normal distribution.

- A dimension on a part is critical. This critical dimension is measured daily on a random sample of parts from a large production process. The measurements on any given day are noted to follow a normal distribution.
- A customer orders a product. The time it takes to fill the order was noted to follow a normal distribution.

The normal distribution or normal probability density function (PDF) has a characteristic bell-shaped curve, while the normal cumulative distribution function (CDF) has an s-shape. The area shown under the PDF corresponds to the ordinate value of the CDF. Any normal X variable governed by $X{\sim}N(\mu\,;\,\sigma^2)$, a short-hand notation for a normally distributed random variable x with mean μ and variance σ^2, can be converted into variable $Z \sim N(0;1)$ using the relationship

$$Z = \frac{X - \mu}{\sigma}$$

The Z-statistic can be used to determine percent of population estimations.

Example:

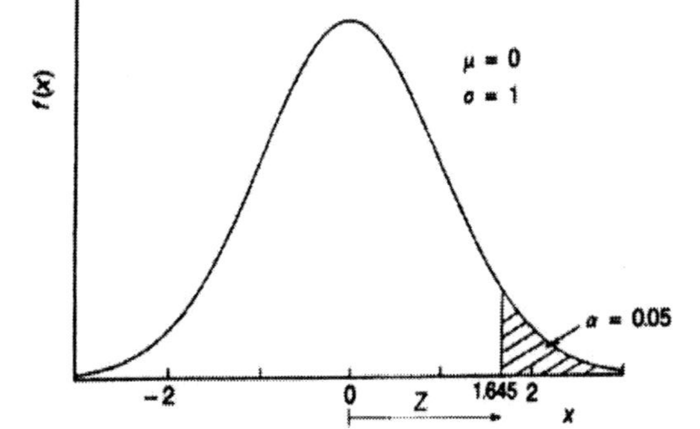

From Figure 8.13 *Integrated Enterprise Excellence, Volume III – Improvement Project Execution: A Management and Black Belt Guide for Going Beyond Lean Six Sigma and the Balanced Scorecard,* Forrest W. Breyfogle III, Bridgeway Books, 2008.

10.8 Tool: Probability Plotting

Reference: *IEE Volume III*, Sections 8.17 – 8.20
Minitab Syntax: Graph>Probability Plot

Percent characteristics of a population can be determined from the cumulative distribution function, CDF, which is the integration of the probability density function, PDF. Probability plots are useful in visually assessing how well data follow distributions and in estimating from data the unknown parameters of a PDF/CDF. These plots can also be used to estimate the percent less than, or greater than, characteristics of a population.

A basic concept behind probability plotting is that, if data plotted on a probability distribution scale follow a straight line, then the population from which the samples are drawn can be represented by that distribution. When the distribution of data is noted, statements can be made about percentage values of the population, which can often be more enlightening than the mean and standard deviation statistics. There are many different types of probability coordinate systems to address data from differing distributions; e.g., normal PDF or Weibull PDF.

Example:

- Percentage non-conformation when specification is 72-78
- 80% frequency of occurrence with median

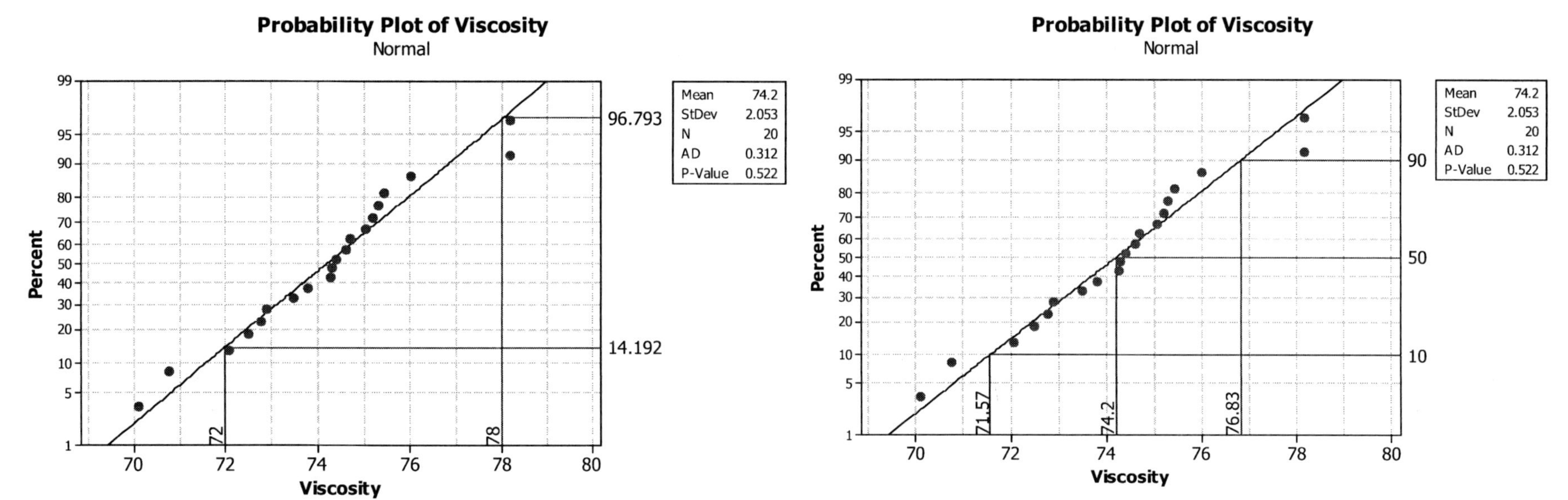

10.9 Tool: Pareto Chart

Reference: *IEE Volume III*, Sections 8.12 & 8.13
Minitab Syntax: Graph>Stat>Quality Tools>Pareto Chart

Application Examples:
- Transactional workflow metric (This metric could similarly apply to manufacturing; e.g., inventory or time to complete a manufacturing process): Random sample of last year's invoices; i.e., Days Sales Outstanding (DSO), where the number of days beyond the due date was measured and reported. If an invoice was beyond 30 days late, it was considered a failure or defective transaction. A Pareto chart showed the frequencies of delinquencies by company invoiced. Note that this procedure would not be the recommended strategy within IEE since much information is lost in the translation between continuous and attribute data.
- Transactional quality metric: Random sample of last year's invoices, where the invoices were examined to determine if there were any errors when filling out the invoice or within any other step of the process. Multiple errors or defects could occur when executing an invoice. The total number of defects when the invoice was executed was divided by the total number of opportunities for failure to estimate the defect per million opportunity rate of the process. A Pareto chart showed the frequencies of delinquencies by type of failure.
- Manufacturing quality metric: Random sample of printed circuit boards over the last year, where the boards were tested for failure. The number of defective boards was divided by the sample size to estimate the defective rate of the process. A Pareto chart showed the frequencies of defective units by printed circuit board type.
- Manufacturing quality metric: Random sample of printed circuit boards over the last year, where the boards were tested for failure. Multiple failures could occur on one board. The total number of defects on the boards was divided by the total number of opportunities for failure (sum of the number of components and solder joints from the samples) to estimate the defect per million opportunity rate of the process. A Pareto chart showed the frequencies of defects by failure type.

Pareto charts are a tool that can be helpful in identifying the source of chronic problems/common causes in a manufacturing process. The Pareto principle basically states that a vital few of the manufacturing process characteristics cause most of the quality problems on the line, while a trivial many of the manufacturing process characteristics cause only a small portion of the quality problems.

Example

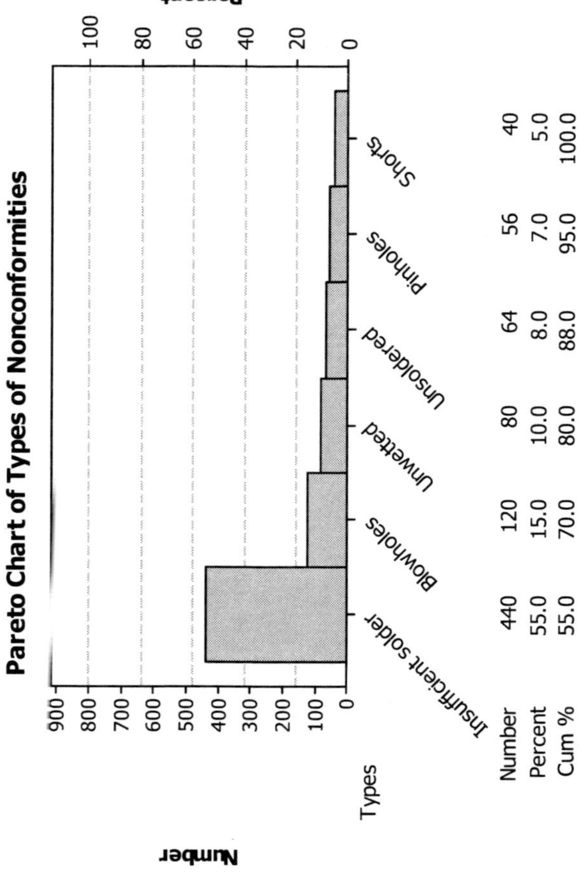

	Insufficient solder	Blowholes	Unwetted	Unsoldered	Pinholes	Shorts
Number	440	120	80	64	56	40
Percent	55.0	15.0	10.0	8.0	7.0	5.0
Cum %	55.0	70.0	80.0	88.0	95.0	100.0

From Figure 8.12 *Integrated Enterprise Excellence, Volume III – Improvement Project Execution: A Management and Black Belt Guide for Going Beyond Lean Six Sigma and the Balanced Scorecard,* Forrest W. Breyfogle III, Bridgeway Books, 2008.

10.10 Confidence Intervals and Hypothesis Tests

Reference: *IEE Volume III*, Sections 19.2 – 19.5

When executing the analyze and improve phases of both the P-DMAIC and E-DMAIC roadmaps, statistical tests are conducted for the purpose of making significance and confidence levels statements. Statistically, a population is a group of data from a single distribution. In a practical sense, a population could also be considered a segment or a group of data from a single source or category. In the process of explaining tools and techniques, multiple populations may be discussed as originating from different sources, locations, or machines.

Descriptive statistics help pull useful information from data, whereas probability provides, among other things, a basis for inferential statistics and sampling plans. In this chapter, focus will be given to inferential statistics where we will bridge from sample data to statements about the population. That is, properties of the population are inferred from the analysis of sample.

Samples can have random sampling with replacement and random sampling without replacement. In addition, there are more complex forms of sampling, such as stratified random sampling. For this form of sampling, a certain number of random samples are drawn and analyzed from divisions of the population space. We can also have systematic sampling where a sample might be taken after 20 parts are manufactured. We can also have subgroup sampling where 5 units might be drawn every hour.

From a random sample of a population, we can estimate characteristics of the population. The mean of a sample does not normally equate exactly to the mean of the population from which the sample is taken; i.e., the mean of a sample ($\bar{x}$) is a point estimate of the population mean (μ). A confidence interval provides probabilistic ranges of values for true population characteristics from sampled data. An experimenter has more confidence that a sample mean is close to the population mean when the sample size is large and less confidence when a sample size is small.

Statistical procedures quantify the uncertainty of a sample through a confidence interval statement. A confidence interval can be single-sided or double-sided and can also relate to other characteristics besides mean values; e.g., population variance. The following statements are examples of single- and double-sided confidence interval statements about the mean.

$$\mu \leq 8.0 \qquad \text{with 95\% confidence}$$
$$2.0 \leq \mu \leq 8.0 \qquad \text{with 90\% confidence}$$

These confidence intervals are determined from the equations, where the t tables (as opposed to the U tables) are used whenever the population standard deviation is not known. Because of the central limit theorem, the equations noted are robust even when data are not from a normal distribution.

	Single-Sided	Double-Sided
σ Known	$\mu \leq \bar{x} + \dfrac{U_\alpha \sigma}{\sqrt{n}}$ or $\mu \geq \bar{x} - \dfrac{U_\alpha \sigma}{\sqrt{n}}$	$\bar{x} - \dfrac{U_\alpha \sigma}{\sqrt{n}} \leq \mu \leq \bar{x} + \dfrac{U_\alpha \sigma}{\sqrt{n}}$
σ Unknown	$\mu \leq \bar{x} + \dfrac{t_\alpha s}{\sqrt{n}}$ or $\mu \geq \bar{x} - \dfrac{t_\alpha s}{\sqrt{n}}$	$\bar{x} - \dfrac{t_\alpha s}{\sqrt{n}} \leq \mu \leq \bar{x} + \dfrac{t_\alpha s}{\sqrt{n}}$
Using reference tables	U_α: Table B t_α: Table D[a]	U_α: Table C t_α: Table E[a]

[a] $\nu = n - 1$ (i.e., the number of degrees of freedom used in the t table is equal to one less than the sample size).

From Table 20.1 *Integrated Enterprise Excellence, Volume III – Improvement Project Execution: A Management and Black Belt Guide for Going Beyond Lean Six Sigma and the Balanced Scorecard*, Forrest W. Breyfogle III, Bridgeway Books, 2008.

Similar statements can be made about standard deviation and other population characteristics.

Hypothesis tests address the situation of making a selection between two choices from sampled data (or information). Because we are dealing with sampled data, there is always the possibility that our sample was not an accurate representation of the population. Hypothesis tests address this risk. The statistical analysis techniques described later in this book provide the basis for statistical significance tests of stratifications that were thought important by teams (e.g., through brainstorming) when executing IEE projects.

10.11 Hypothesis Testing

Reference: *IEE Volume III*, Sections 19.4 – 19.6

In industrial situations, we frequently want to decide whether the parameters of a distribution have particular values or relationships. That is, we may wish to test a hypothesis that the mean or standard deviation of a distribution has a certain value or that the difference between two means is zero. Hypothesis testing procedures are used for these tests. Here are some practical examples:

1. A manufacturer wishes to introduce a new product. In order to make a profit, he needs to be able to manufacture 1200 items during the 200 work hours available for the workforce in the next five weeks. The product can be successfully manufactured if the mean time that is required to manufacture an item is no more than six labor hours per part. The manufacturer can evaluate manufacturability by testing the hypothesis that the mean time for manufacture is equal to six hours.
2. The same manufacturer is planning to modify the process to decrease the mean time required to manufacture another type of product. The manufacturer can evaluate the effectiveness of the change by testing the hypothesis that the mean manufacturing time is the same before and after the process change.

Both of these situations involve tests on the mean values of populations. Hypothesis tests may also involve the standard deviations or other parameters.

A statistical hypothesis has the following elements:
- A null hypothesis (H_0) that describes the value or relationship being tested
- An alternative hypothesis (H_a)
- A test statistic, or rule, used to decide whether to reject the null hypothesis
- A specified probability value (noted as α) that defines the maximum allowable probability that the null hypothesis will be rejected when it is true
- The power of the test, which is the probability (noted as $[1-\beta]$) that a null hypothesis will be rejected when it is false
- A sample of observations to be used for testing the hypothesis

The result of a hypothesis test is a decision either to reject or not reject the null hypothesis; that is, the hypothesis is either rejected or we reserve judgment about it. In practice, we may act as though the null hypothesis is accepted if it is not rejected. Because we do not know the truth, we can make one of the following two possible errors when running a hypothesis test:

1. We can reject a null hypothesis that is in fact true.
2. We can fail to reject a null hypothesis that is false.

The first error is called a type I error, and the second is called a type II error. Hypothesis tests are designed to control the probabilities of making either of these errors; we do not know that the result is correct, but we can be assured that the probability of making an error is within acceptable limits. The probability of making a type I error is controlled by establishing a maximum allowable value of the probability, called the level of the test, usually noted as α. The specific rule used to govern the decision reject or fail to reject the null hypothesis (H_o) is determined by selecting a particular value for α. A statistical analysis provides a calculated probability value or P value. This P value is compare to the α criterion value. When the P value is lower than the α criterion, the null hypothesis is rejected. An often quoted statement for this condition is: if P is low, ho (i.e., H_o) must go.

11 Appendix B: List of Symbols

The following symbols are referenced in this manual.

AIAG	Automotive industry action group
ANOM	Analysis of means
ANOVA	Analysis of variance
CDF	Cumulative distribution function
CI	Confidence interval
CTQ	Critical to quality
CODND	Cost of doing nothing differently
COPQ	Cost of poor quality
C_p	A traditional process capability index metric
C_{pk}	A traditional process capability index metric
DCP	Data collection plan
DCRCA	DOE collective response capability assessment
DF	Degrees of freedom
DFMEA	Design failure mode and effects analysis
DMADV	Define-measure-analyze-design-verify
DMAIC	Define-measure-analyze-improve-control
DOE	Design of experiments
dpmo	Defects per million opportunities
DSO	Days sales outstanding
$E=MC^2$	Organization's existence/excellence = more customers and cash
EFHM	Enterprise functional hand-off metrics
EIP	Enterprise improvement process
EPC	Engineering process control
EWMA	Exponentially weighted moving average
F	F distribution value
FMEA	Failure mode and effects analysis
H_A	Alternative hypothesis
H_0	Null hypothesis
I-chart	Individuals chart (also X-chart)
I-mR chart	Individuals and moving range chart (also X-MR chart)
IEE	Integrated enterprise excellence

IT	Information technology
KPIV	Key process input variable
KPOV	Key process output variable
LCL	Lower control limit
$\overline{MR}$	Mean moving range
MSA	Measurement systems analysis
MS	Mean square
NID	Normally and independently distributed
NVA	Non-value-added time
PDF	Probability density function
PI	Prediction interval
P	Probability
PFMEA	Process failure mode and effects analysis
P_p	A traditional process performance index metric
P_{pk}	A traditional process performance index metric
s	Sample standard deviation
S^4	Smarter six sigma solutions
SIPOC	Supplier-input-process-output-customer
SMED	Single-minute exchange of die
SS	Sum of squares
TOC	Theory of constraints
UCL	Upper control limit
VA	Value-added time
X-chart	Individuals chart (also I-chart)
X-mR chart	Individuals and moving range chart (also I-MR chart)
$\overline{x}$	Sample mean
μ	population mean
σ	population standard deviation

12 Appendix C: Statistical Tables

TABLE A Area Under the Standardized Normal Curve

Z♦	0	0.01	0.02	0.03	0.04	0.05	0.06	0.07	0.08	0.09
0	0.5000	0.4960	0.4920	0.4880	0.4840	0.4801	0.4761	0.4721	0.4681	0.4641
0.1	0.4602	0.4562	0.4522	0.4483	0.4443	0.4404	0.4364	0.4325	0.4286	0.4247
0.2	0.4207	0.4168	0.4129	0.4090	0.4052	0.4013	0.3974	0.3936	0.3897	0.3859
0.3	0.3821	0.3783	0.3745	0.3707	0.3669	0.3632	0.3594	0.3557	0.3520	0.3483
0.4	0.3446	0.3409	0.3372	0.3336	0.3300	0.3264	0.3228	0.3192	0.3156	0.3121
0.5	0.3085	0.3050	0.3015	0.2981	0.2946	0.2912	0.2877	0.2843	0.2810	0.2776
0.6	0.2743	0.2709	0.2676	0.2643	0.2611	0.2578	0.2546	0.2514	0.2483	0.2451
0.7	0.2420	0.2389	0.2358	0.2327	0.2296	0.2266	0.2236	0.2206	0.2177	0.2148
0.8	0.2119	0.2090	0.2061	0.2033	0.2005	0.1977	0.1949	0.1922	0.1894	0.1867
0.9	0.1841	0.1814	0.1788	0.1762	0.1736	0.1711	0.1685	0.1660	0.1635	0.1611
1	0.1587	0.1562	0.1539	0.1515	0.1492	0.1469	0.1446	0.1423	0.1401	0.1379
1.1	0.1357	0.1335	0.1314	0.1292	0.1271	0.1251	0.1230	0.1210	0.1190	0.1170
1.2	0.1151	0.1131	0.1112	0.1093	0.1075	0.1056	0.1038	0.1020	0.1003	0.0985
1.3	0.0968	0.0951	0.0934	0.0918	0.0901	0.0885	0.0869	0.0853	0.0838	0.0823
1.4	0.0808	0.0793	0.0778	0.0764	0.0749	0.0735	0.0721	0.0708	0.0694	0.0681
1.5	0.0668	0.0655	0.0643	0.0630	0.0618	0.0606	0.0594	0.0582	0.0571	0.0559
1.6	0.0548	0.0537	0.0526	0.0516	0.0505	0.0495	0.0485	0.0475	0.0465	0.0455
1.7	0.0446	0.0436	0.0427	0.0418	0.0409	0.0401	0.0392	0.0384	0.0375	0.0367
1.8	0.0359	0.0351	0.0344	0.0336	0.0329	0.0322	0.0314	0.0307	0.0301	0.0294
1.9	0.0287	0.0281	0.0274	0.0268	0.0262	0.0256	0.0250	0.0244	0.0239	0.0233
2	0.0228	0.0222	0.0217	0.0212	0.0207	0.0202	0.0197	0.0192	0.0188	0.0183
2.1	0.0179	0.0174	0.0170	0.0166	0.0162	0.0158	0.0154	0.0150	0.0146	0.0143
2.2	0.0139	0.0136	0.0132	0.0129	0.0125	0.0122	0.0119	0.0116	0.0113	0.0110
2.3	0.01072	0.01044	0.01017	0.00990	0.00964	0.00939	0.00914	0.00889	0.00866	0.00842
2.4	0.00820	0.00798	0.00776	0.00755	0.00734	0.00714	0.00695	0.00676	0.00657	0.00639
2.5	0.00621	0.00604	0.00587	0.00570	0.00554	0.00539	0.00523	0.00508	0.00494	0.00480
2.6	0.00466	0.00453	0.00440	0.00427	0.00415	0.00402	0.00391	0.00379	0.00368	0.00357
2.7	0.00347	0.00336	0.00326	0.00317	0.00307	0.00298	0.00289	0.00280	0.00272	0.00264
2.8	0.00256	0.00248	0.00240	0.00233	0.00226	0.00219	0.00212	0.00205	0.00199	0.00193
2.9	0.00187	0.00181	0.00175	0.00169	0.00164	0.00159	0.00154	0.00149	0.00144	0.00139

Z♦	0	0.1	0.2	0.3	0.4	0.5	0.6	0.7	0.8	0.9
3	1.350E-03	9.676E-04	6.871E-04	4.834E-04	3.369E-04	2.326E-04	1.591E-04	1.078E-04	7.235E-05	4.810E-05
4	3.167E-05	2.066E-05	1.335E-05	8.540E-06	5.413E-06	3.398E-06	2.112E-06	1.301E-06	7.933E-07	4.792E-07
5	2.867E-07	1.698E-07	9.964E-08	5.790E-08	3.332E-08	1.899E-08	1.072E-08	5.990E-09	3.316E-09	1.818E-09
6	9.866E-10	5.303E-10	2.823E-10	1.488E-10	7.769E-11	4.016E-11	2.056E-11	1.042E-11	5.231E-12	2.600E-12

TABLE B Probability Points of the t Distribution: Single Sided

Probability of a larger value, Sign Ignored

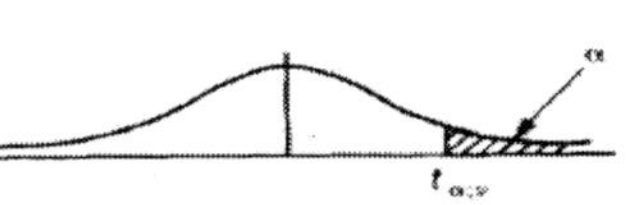

Degrees of Freedom	0.4	0.3	0.2	0.1	0.05	0.025	0.01	0.005	0.001	0.0005
1	0.325	0.727	1.376	3.078	6.314	12.706	31.821	63.657	318.309	636.619
2	0.289	0.617	1.061	1.886	2.920	4.303	6.965	9.925	22.327	31.599
3	0.277	0.584	0.978	1.638	2.353	3.182	4.541	5.841	10.215	12.924
4	0.271	0.569	0.941	1.533	2.132	2.776	3.747	4.604	7.173	8.610
5	0.267	0.559	0.920	1.476	2.015	2.571	3.365	4.032	5.893	6.869
6	0.265	0.553	0.906	1.440	1.943	2.447	3.143	3.707	5.208	5.959
7	0.263	0.549	0.896	1.415	1.895	2.365	2.998	3.499	4.785	5.408
8	0.262	0.546	0.889	1.397	1.860	2.306	2.896	3.355	4.501	5.041
9	0.261	0.543	0.883	1.383	1.833	2.262	2.821	3.250	4.297	4.781
10	0.260	0.542	0.879	1.372	1.812	2.228	2.764	3.169	4.144	4.587
11	0.260	0.540	0.876	1.363	1.796	2.201	2.718	3.106	4.025	4.437
12	0.259	0.539	0.873	1.356	1.782	2.179	2.681	3.055	3.930	4.318
13	0.259	0.538	0.870	1.350	1.771	2.160	2.650	3.012	3.852	4.221
14	0.258	0.537	0.868	1.345	1.761	2.145	2.624	2.977	3.787	4.140
15	0.258	0.536	0.866	1.341	1.753	2.131	2.602	2.947	3.733	4.073
16	0.258	0.535	0.865	1.337	1.746	2.120	2.583	2.921	3.686	4.015
17	0.257	0.534	0.863	1.333	1.740	2.110	2.567	2.898	3.646	3.965
18	0.257	0.534	0.862	1.330	1.734	2.101	2.552	2.878	3.610	3.922
19	0.257	0.533	0.861	1.328	1.729	2.093	2.539	2.861	3.579	3.883
20	0.257	0.533	0.860	1.325	1.725	2.086	2.528	2.845	3.552	3.850
21	0.257	0.532	0.859	1.323	1.721	2.080	2.518	2.831	3.527	3.819
22	0.256	0.532	0.858	1.321	1.717	2.074	2.508	2.819	3.505	3.792
23	0.256	0.532	0.858	1.319	1.714	2.069	2.500	2.807	3.485	3.768
24	0.256	0.531	0.857	1.318	1.711	2.064	2.492	2.797	3.467	3.745
25	0.256	0.531	0.856	1.316	1.708	2.060	2.485	2.787	3.450	3.725
26	0.256	0.531	0.856	1.315	1.706	2.056	2.479	2.779	3.435	3.707
27	0.256	0.531	0.855	1.314	1.703	2.052	2.473	2.771	3.421	3.690
28	0.256	0.530	0.855	1.313	1.701	2.048	2.467	2.763	3.408	3.674
29	0.256	0.530	0.854	1.311	1.699	2.045	2.462	2.756	3.396	3.659
30	0.256	0.530	0.854	1.310	1.697	2.042	2.457	2.750	3.385	3.646
40	0.255	0.529	0.851	1.303	1.684	2.021	2.423	2.704	3.307	3.551
50	0.255	0.528	0.849	1.299	1.676	2.009	2.403	2.678	3.261	3.496
60	0.254	0.527	0.848	1.296	1.671	2.000	2.390	2.660	3.232	3.460
80	0.254	0.526	0.846	1.292	1.664	1.990	2.374	2.639	3.195	3.416
100	0.254	0.526	0.845	1.290	1.660	1.984	2.364	2.626	3.174	3.390
200	0.254	0.525	0.843	1.286	1.653	1.972	2.345	2.601	3.131	3.340
500	0.253	0.525	0.842	1.283	1.648	1.965	2.334	2.586	3.107	3.310
∞	0.253	0.524	0.842	1.282	1.645	1.960	2.326	2.576	3.090	3.291

TABLE C Probability Points of the t Distribution: Two Sided

Degrees of Freedom	0.4	0.3	0.2	0.1	0.05	0.025	0.01	0.005	0.001	0.0005
1	1.376	1.963	3.078	6.314	12.706	25.452	63.657	127.321	636.619	1273.239
2	1.061	1.386	1.886	2.920	4.303	6.205	9.925	14.089	31.599	44.705
3	0.978	1.250	1.638	2.353	3.182	4.177	5.841	7.453	12.924	16.326
4	0.941	1.190	1.533	2.132	2.776	3.495	4.604	5.598	8.610	10.306
5	0.920	1.156	1.476	2.015	2.571	3.163	4.032	4.773	6.869	7.976
6	0.906	1.134	1.440	1.943	2.447	2.969	3.707	4.317	5.959	6.788
7	0.896	1.119	1.415	1.895	2.365	2.841	3.499	4.029	5.408	6.082
8	0.889	1.108	1.397	1.860	2.306	2.752	3.355	3.833	5.041	5.617
9	0.883	1.100	1.383	1.833	2.262	2.685	3.250	3.690	4.781	5.291
10	0.879	1.093	1.372	1.812	2.228	2.634	3.169	3.581	4.587	5.049
11	0.876	1.088	1.363	1.796	2.201	2.593	3.106	3.497	4.437	4.863
12	0.873	1.083	1.356	1.782	2.179	2.560	3.055	3.428	4.318	4.716
13	0.870	1.079	1.350	1.771	2.160	2.533	3.012	3.372	4.221	4.597
14	0.868	1.076	1.345	1.761	2.145	2.510	2.977	3.326	4.140	4.499
15	0.866	1.074	1.341	1.753	2.131	2.490	2.947	3.286	4.073	4.417
16	0.865	1.071	1.337	1.746	2.120	2.473	2.921	3.252	4.015	4.346
17	0.863	1.069	1.333	1.740	2.110	2.458	2.898	3.222	3.965	4.286
18	0.862	1.067	1.330	1.734	2.101	2.445	2.878	3.197	3.922	4.233
19	0.861	1.066	1.328	1.729	2.093	2.433	2.861	3.174	3.883	4.187
20	0.860	1.064	1.325	1.725	2.086	2.423	2.845	3.153	3.850	4.146
21	0.859	1.063	1.323	1.721	2.080	2.414	2.831	3.135	3.819	4.110
22	0.858	1.061	1.321	1.717	2.074	2.405	2.819	3.119	3.792	4.077
23	0.858	1.060	1.319	1.714	2.069	2.398	2.807	3.104	3.768	4.047
24	0.857	1.059	1.318	1.711	2.064	2.391	2.797	3.091	3.745	4.021
25	0.856	1.058	1.316	1.708	2.060	2.385	2.787	3.078	3.725	3.996
26	0.856	1.058	1.315	1.706	2.056	2.379	2.779	3.067	3.707	3.974
27	0.855	1.057	1.314	1.703	2.052	2.373	2.771	3.057	3.690	3.954
28	0.855	1.056	1.313	1.701	2.048	2.368	2.763	3.047	3.674	3.935
29	0.854	1.055	1.311	1.699	2.045	2.364	2.756	3.038	3.659	3.918
30	0.854	1.055	1.310	1.697	2.042	2.360	2.750	3.030	3.646	3.902
40	0.851	1.050	1.303	1.684	2.021	2.329	2.704	2.971	3.551	3.788
50	0.849	1.047	1.299	1.676	2.009	2.311	2.678	2.937	3.496	3.723
60	0.848	1.045	1.296	1.671	2.000	2.299	2.660	2.915	3.460	3.681
80	0.846	1.043	1.292	1.664	1.990	2.284	2.639	2.887	3.416	3.629
100	0.845	1.042	1.290	1.660	1.984	2.276	2.626	2.871	3.390	3.598
200	0.843	1.039	1.286	1.653	1.972	2.258	2.601	2.839	3.340	3.539
500	0.842	1.038	1.283	1.648	1.965	2.248	2.586	2.820	3.310	3.504
∞	0.253	0.524	0.842	1.282	1.645	1.960	2.326	2.576	3.090	3.291

TABLE D Probability Points of the Variance Ratios (F Distribution)

Probability								Numerator										
Point	♦.	1	2	3	4	5	6	7	8	9	10	12	15	20	24	30	40
0.1	1	39.9	49.5	53.6	55.8	57.2	58.2	58.9	59.4	59.9	60.2	60.7	61.2	61.7	62.0	62.3	62.5
0.05		161	199	216	225	230	234	237	239	241	242	244	246	248	249	250	251
0.01		4052	4999	5403	5625	5764	5859	5928	5981	6022	6056	6106	6157	6209	6235	6261	6287
0.1	2	8.53	9.00	9.16	9.24	9.29	9.33	9.35	9.37	9.38	9.39	9.41	9.42	9.44	9.45	9.46	9.47
0.05		18.5	19.0	19.2	19.2	19.3	19.3	19.4	19.4	19.4	19.4	19.4	19.4	19.4	19.5	19.5	19.5
0.01		98.5	99.0	99.2	99.2	99.3	99.3	99.4	99.4	99.4	99.4	99.4	99.4	99.4	99.5	99.5	99.5
0.1	3	5.54	5.46	5.39	5.34	5.31	5.28	5.27	5.25	5.24	5.23	5.22	5.20	5.18	5.18	5.17	5.16
0.05		10.1	9.6	9.3	9.1	9.0	8.9	8.9	8.8	8.8	8.8	8.7	8.7	8.7	8.6	8.6	8.6
0.01		34.1	30.8	29.5	28.7	28.2	27.9	27.7	27.5	27.3	27.2	27.1	26.9	26.7	26.6	26.5	26.4
0.1	4	4.54	4.32	4.19	4.11	4.05	4.01	3.98	3.95	3.94	3.92	3.90	3.87	3.84	3.83	3.82	3.80
0.05		7.7	6.9	6.6	6.4	6.3	6.2	6.1	6.0	6.0	6.0	5.9	5.9	5.8	5.8	5.7	5.7
0.01		21.2	18.0	16.7	16.0	15.5	15.2	15.0	14.8	14.7	14.5	14.4	14.2	14.0	13.9	13.8	13.7
0.1	5	4.06	3.78	3.62	3.52	3.45	3.40	3.37	3.34	3.32	3.30	3.27	3.24	3.21	3.19	3.17	3.16
0.05		6.61	5.79	5.41	5.19	5.05	4.95	4.88	4.82	4.77	4.74	4.68	4.62	4.56	4.53	4.50	4.46
0.01		16.3	13.3	12.1	11.4	11.0	10.7	10.5	10.3	10.2	10.1	9.89	9.72	9.55	9.47	9.38	9.29
0.1	6	3.78	3.46	3.29	3.18	3.11	3.05	3.01	2.98	2.96	2.94	2.90	2.87	2.84	2.82	2.80	2.78
0.05		5.99	5.14	4.76	4.53	4.39	4.28	4.21	4.15	4.10	4.06	4.00	3.94	3.87	3.84	3.81	3.77
0.01		13.7	10.9	9.8	9.1	8.7	8.5	8.3	8.1	8.0	7.9	7.7	7.6	7.4	7.3	7.2	7.1
0.1	7	3.59	3.26	3.07	2.96	2.88	2.83	2.78	2.75	2.72	2.70	2.67	2.63	2.59	2.58	2.56	2.54
0.05		5.59	4.74	4.35	4.12	3.97	3.87	3.79	3.73	3.68	3.64	3.57	3.51	3.44	3.41	3.38	3.34
0.01		12.25	9.55	8.45	7.85	7.46	7.19	6.99	6.84	6.72	6.62	6.47	6.31	6.16	6.07	5.99	5.91
0.1	8	3.46	3.11	2.92	2.81	2.73	2.67	2.62	2.59	2.56	2.54	2.50	2.46	2.42	2.40	2.38	2.36
0.05		5.32	4.46	4.07	3.84	3.69	3.58	3.50	3.44	3.39	3.35	3.28	3.22	3.15	3.12	3.08	3.04
0.01		11.26	8.65	7.59	7.01	6.63	6.37	6.18	6.03	5.91	5.81	5.67	5.52	5.36	5.28	5.20	5.12
0.1	9	3.36	3.01	2.81	2.69	2.61	2.55	2.51	2.47	2.44	2.42	2.38	2.34	2.30	2.28	2.25	2.23
0.05		5.12	4.26	3.86	3.63	3.48	3.37	3.29	3.23	3.18	3.14	3.07	3.01	2.94	2.90	2.86	2.83
0.01		10.56	8.02	6.99	6.42	6.06	5.80	5.61	5.47	5.35	5.26	5.11	4.96	4.81	4.73	4.65	4.57
0.1	10	3.29	2.92	2.73	2.61	2.52	2.46	2.41	2.38	2.35	2.32	2.28	2.24	2.20	2.18	2.16	2.13
0.05		4.96	4.10	3.71	3.48	3.33	3.22	3.14	3.07	3.02	2.98	2.91	2.85	2.77	2.74	2.70	2.66
0.01		10.04	7.56	6.55	5.99	5.64	5.39	5.20	5.06	4.94	4.85	4.71	4.56	4.41	4.33	4.25	4.17
0.1	11	3.23	2.86	2.66	2.54	2.45	2.39	2.34	2.30	2.27	2.25	2.21	2.17	2.12	2.10	2.08	2.05
0.05		4.84	3.98	3.59	3.36	3.20	3.09	3.01	2.95	2.90	2.85	2.79	2.72	2.65	2.61	2.57	2.53
0.01		9.65	7.21	6.22	5.67	5.32	5.07	4.89	4.74	4.63	4.54	4.40	4.25	4.10	4.02	3.94	3.86
0.1	12	3.18	2.81	2.61	2.48	2.39	2.33	2.28	2.24	2.21	2.19	2.15	2.10	2.06	2.04	2.01	1.99
0.05		4.75	3.89	3.49	3.26	3.11	3.00	2.91	2.85	2.80	2.75	2.69	2.62	2.54	2.51	2.47	2.43
0.01		9.33	6.93	5.95	5.41	5.06	4.82	4.64	4.50	4.39	4.30	4.16	4.01	3.86	3.78	3.70	3.62
0.1	13	3.14	2.76	2.56	2.43	2.35	2.28	2.23	2.20	2.16	2.14	2.10	2.05	2.01	1.98	1.96	1.93
0.05		4.67	3.81	3.41	3.18	3.03	2.92	2.83	2.77	2.71	2.67	2.60	2.53	2.46	2.42	2.38	2.34
0.01		9.07	6.70	5.74	5.21	4.86	4.62	4.44	4.30	4.19	4.10	3.96	3.82	3.66	3.59	3.51	3.43
0.1	14	3.10	2.73	2.52	2.39	2.31	2.24	2.19	2.15	2.12	2.10	2.05	2.01	1.96	1.94	1.91	1.89
0.05		4.60	3.74	3.34	3.11	2.96	2.85	2.76	2.70	2.65	2.60	2.53	2.46	2.39	2.35	2.31	2.27
0.01		8.86	6.51	5.56	5.04	4.69	4.46	4.28	4.14	4.03	3.94	3.80	3.66	3.51	3.43	3.35	3.27
0.1	15	3.07	2.70	2.49	2.36	2.27	2.21	2.16	2.12	2.09	2.06	2.02	1.97	1.92	1.90	1.87	1.85
0.05		4.54	3.68	3.29	3.06	2.90	2.79	2.71	2.64	2.59	2.54	2.48	2.40	2.33	2.29	2.25	2.20
0.01		8.68	6.36	5.42	4.89	4.56	4.32	4.14	4.00	3.89	3.80	3.67	3.52	3.37	3.29	3.21	3.13

TABLE D Probability Points of the Variance Ratios (F Distribution) continued

Probability Point	ϕ_2	Numerator 1	2	3	4	5	6	7	8	9	10	12	15	20	24	30	40
0.1	16	3.05	2.67	2.46	2.33	2.24	2.18	2.13	2.09	2.06	2.03	1.99	1.94	1.89	1.87	1.84	1.81
0.05		4.49	3.63	3.24	3.01	2.85	2.74	2.66	2.59	2.54	2.49	2.42	2.35	2.28	2.24	2.19	2.15
0.01		8.53	6.23	5.29	4.77	4.44	4.20	4.03	3.89	3.78	3.69	3.55	3.41	3.26	3.18	3.10	3.02
0.1	17	3.03	2.64	2.44	2.31	2.22	2.15	2.10	2.06	2.03	2.00	1.96	1.91	1.86	1.84	1.81	1.78
0.05		4.45	3.59	3.20	2.96	2.81	2.70	2.61	2.55	2.49	2.45	2.38	2.31	2.23	2.19	2.15	2.10
0.01		8.40	6.11	5.18	4.67	4.34	4.10	3.93	3.79	3.68	3.59	3.46	3.31	3.16	3.08	3.00	2.92
0.1	18	3.01	2.62	2.42	2.29	2.20	2.13	2.08	2.04	2.00	1.98	1.93	1.89	1.84	1.81	1.78	1.75
0.05		4.41	3.55	3.16	2.93	2.77	2.66	2.58	2.51	2.46	2.41	2.34	2.27	2.19	2.15	2.11	2.06
0.01		8.29	6.01	5.09	4.58	4.25	4.01	3.84	3.71	3.60	3.51	3.37	3.23	3.08	3.00	2.92	2.84
0.1	19	2.99	2.61	2.40	2.27	2.18	2.11	2.06	2.02	1.98	1.96	1.91	1.86	1.81	1.79	1.76	1.73
0.05		4.38	3.52	3.13	2.90	2.74	2.63	2.54	2.48	2.42	2.38	2.31	2.23	2.16	2.11	2.07	2.03
0.01		8.18	5.93	5.01	4.50	4.17	3.94	3.77	3.63	3.52	3.43	3.30	3.15	3.00	2.92	2.84	2.76
0.1	20	2.97	2.59	2.38	2.25	2.16	2.09	2.04	2.00	1.96	1.94	1.89	1.84	1.79	1.77	1.74	1.71
0.05		4.35	3.49	3.10	2.87	2.71	2.60	2.51	2.45	2.39	2.35	2.28	2.20	2.12	2.08	2.04	1.99
0.01		8.10	5.85	4.94	4.43	4.10	3.87	3.70	3.56	3.46	3.37	3.23	3.09	2.94	2.86	2.78	2.69
0.1	21	2.96	2.57	2.36	2.23	2.14	2.08	2.02	1.98	1.95	1.92	1.87	1.83	1.78	1.75	1.72	1.69
0.05		4.32	3.47	3.07	2.84	2.68	2.57	2.49	2.42	2.37	2.32	2.25	2.18	2.10	2.05	2.01	1.96
0.01		8.02	5.78	4.87	4.37	4.04	3.81	3.64	3.51	3.40	3.31	3.17	3.03	2.88	2.80	2.72	2.64
0.1	22	2.95	2.56	2.35	2.22	2.13	2.06	2.01	1.97	1.93	1.90	1.86	1.81	1.76	1.73	1.70	1.67
0.05		4.30	3.44	3.05	2.82	2.66	2.55	2.46	2.40	2.34	2.30	2.23	2.15	2.07	2.03	1.98	1.94
0.01		7.95	5.72	4.82	4.31	3.99	3.76	3.59	3.45	3.35	3.26	3.12	2.98	2.83	2.75	2.67	2.58
0.1	23	2.94	2.55	2.34	2.21	2.11	2.05	1.99	1.95	1.92	1.89	1.84	1.80	1.74	1.72	1.69	1.66
0.05		4.28	3.42	3.03	2.80	2.64	2.53	2.44	2.37	2.32	2.27	2.20	2.13	2.05	2.01	1.96	1.91
0.01		7.88	5.66	4.76	4.26	3.94	3.71	3.54	3.41	3.30	3.21	3.07	2.93	2.78	2.70	2.62	2.54
0.1	24	2.93	2.54	2.33	2.19	2.10	2.04	1.98	1.94	1.91	1.88	1.83	1.78	1.73	1.70	1.67	1.64
0.05		4.26	3.40	3.01	2.78	2.62	2.51	2.42	2.36	2.30	2.25	2.18	2.11	2.03	1.98	1.94	1.89
0.01		7.82	5.61	4.72	4.22	3.90	3.67	3.50	3.36	3.26	3.17	3.03	2.89	2.74	2.66	2.58	2.49
0.1	25	2.92	2.53	2.32	2.18	2.09	2.02	1.97	1.93	1.89	1.87	1.82	1.77	1.72	1.69	1.66	1.63
0.05		4.24	3.39	2.99	2.76	2.60	2.49	2.40	2.34	2.28	2.24	2.16	2.09	2.01	1.96	1.92	1.87
0.01		7.77	5.57	4.68	4.18	3.85	3.63	3.46	3.32	3.22	3.13	2.99	2.85	2.70	2.62	2.54	2.45
0.1	26	2.91	2.52	2.31	2.17	2.08	2.01	1.96	1.92	1.88	1.86	1.81	1.76	1.71	1.68	1.65	1.61
0.05		4.23	3.37	2.98	2.74	2.59	2.47	2.39	2.32	2.27	2.22	2.15	2.07	1.99	1.95	1.90	1.85
0.01		7.72	5.53	4.64	4.14	3.82	3.59	3.42	3.29	3.18	3.09	2.96	2.81	2.66	2.58	2.50	2.42
0.1	27	2.90	2.51	2.30	2.17	2.07	2.00	1.95	1.91	1.87	1.85	1.80	1.75	1.70	1.67	1.64	1.60
0.05		4.21	3.35	2.96	2.73	2.57	2.46	2.37	2.31	2.25	2.20	2.13	2.06	1.97	1.93	1.88	1.84
0.01		7.68	5.49	4.60	4.11	3.78	3.56	3.39	3.26	3.15	3.06	2.93	2.78	2.63	2.55	2.47	2.38
0.1	28	2.89	2.50	2.29	2.16	2.06	2.00	1.94	1.90	1.87	1.84	1.79	1.74	1.69	1.66	1.63	1.59
0.05		4.20	3.34	2.95	2.71	2.56	2.45	2.36	2.29	2.24	2.19	2.12	2.04	1.96	1.91	1.87	1.82
0.01		7.64	5.45	4.57	4.07	3.75	3.53	3.36	3.23	3.12	3.03	2.90	2.75	2.60	2.52	2.44	2.35
0.1	29	2.89	2.50	2.28	2.15	2.06	1.99	1.93	1.89	1.86	1.83	1.78	1.73	1.68	1.65	1.62	1.58
0.05		4.18	3.33	2.93	2.70	2.55	2.43	2.35	2.28	2.22	2.18	2.10	2.03	1.94	1.90	1.85	1.81
0.01		7.60	5.42	4.54	4.04	3.73	3.50	3.33	3.20	3.09	3.00	2.87	2.73	2.57	2.49	2.41	2.33
0.1	30	2.88	2.49	2.28	2.14	2.05	1.98	1.93	1.88	1.85	1.82	1.77	1.72	1.67	1.64	1.61	1.57
0.05		4.17	3.32	2.92	2.69	2.53	2.42	2.33	2.27	2.21	2.16	2.09	2.01	1.93	1.89	1.84	1.79
0.01		7.56	5.39	4.51	4.02	3.70	3.47	3.30	3.17	3.07	2.98	2.84	2.70	2.55	2.47	2.39	2.30

TABLE D Probability Points of the Variance Ratios (F Distribution) continued

Probability Point	ν_2	Numerator ν_1															
		1	2	3	4	5	6	7	8	9	10	12	15	20	24	30	40
0.1	40	2.84	2.44	2.23	2.09	2.00	1.93	1.87	1.83	1.79	1.76	1.71	1.66	1.61	1.57	1.54	1.51
0.05		4.08	3.23	2.84	2.61	2.45	2.34	2.25	2.18	2.12	2.08	2.00	1.92	1.84	1.79	1.74	1.69
0.01		7.31	5.18	4.31	3.83	3.51	3.29	3.12	2.99	2.89	2.80	2.66	2.52	2.37	2.29	2.20	2.11
0.1	60	2.79	2.39	2.18	2.04	1.95	1.87	1.82	1.77	1.74	1.71	1.66	1.60	1.54	1.51	1.48	1.44
0.05		4.00	3.15	2.76	2.53	2.37	2.25	2.17	2.10	2.04	1.99	1.92	1.84	1.75	1.70	1.65	1.59
0.01		7.08	4.98	4.13	3.65	3.34	3.12	2.95	2.82	2.72	2.63	2.50	2.35	2.20	2.12	2.03	1.94
0.1	120	2.75	2.35	2.13	1.99	1.90	1.82	1.77	1.72	1.68	1.65	1.60	1.55	1.48	1.45	1.41	1.37
0.05		3.92	3.07	2.68	2.45	2.29	2.18	2.09	2.02	1.96	1.91	1.83	1.75	1.66	1.61	1.55	1.50
0.01		6.85	4.79	3.95	3.48	3.17	2.96	2.79	2.66	2.56	2.47	2.34	2.19	2.03	1.95	1.86	1.76
0.1	121	2.71	2.30	2.08	1.94	1.85	1.77	1.72	1.67	1.63	1.60	1.55	1.49	1.42	1.38	1.34	1.30
0.05		3.84	3.00	2.60	2.37	2.21	2.10	2.01	1.94	1.88	1.83	1.75	1.67	1.57	1.52	1.46	1.39
0.01		6.63	4.61	3.78	3.32	3.02	2.80	2.64	2.51	2.41	2.32	2.18	2.04	1.88	1.79	1.70	1.59

13 Appendix D: Glossary

Accuracy: The closeness of agreement between an observed value and the accepted reference value (AIAG 2002).

Alias: *See* Confounded.

Affinity diagram: A methodology by which a team can organize and summarize the natural grouping from a large number of ideas and issues.

Alpha (α) risk: Risk of rejecting the null hypothesis erroneously. Also called type I error or producer's risk.

Alternative hypothesis (H_a): *See* Hypothesis testing.

Analysis of means (ANOM): A statistical procedure to compare the means of individual groups to the grand mean.

Analysis of variance (ANOVA): A statistical procedure for analyzing the differences in the means of two or more groups.

Attribute data (Discrete data): The presence or absence of some characteristic in each device under test, e.g., proportion nonconforming in a pass/fail test.

Autocorrelation: In time series analyses, correlation between values and previous values of the same series.

Average: A location parameter; frequently the arithmetic mean.

Baseline: Beginning information from which a response change is assessed.

Benchmarking: A discovery process for determining what is the best practice or performance within your company, a competitor, or another industry.

Beta (β) risk: Chance of not rejecting the false null hypothesis; also called type II error or consumer's risk.

Bias: The difference between the observed average of measurements (trials under repeatability conditions) and a reference value; historically referred to as accuracy. Bias is evaluated and expressed at a single point with the operating range of the measurement system. (AIAG 2002)

Bimodal distribution: A distribution that is a combination of two different distributions resulting in two distinct peaks.

Binomial distribution: A distribution that is useful to describe discrete variables or attributes that have two possible outcomes: e.g., a pass/fail proportion test, heads/tails outcome from flipping a coin, defect/no defect present.

Black belts (BBs): Process improvement Six Sigma and IEE practitioners who typically receive four weeks of training over four months. It is most desirable that black belts are dedicated resources; however, many organizations utilize part-time resources. During training, black belt trainees lead the execution of a project that has in-class report-outs and critiques. Between training sessions black belt trainees should receive project coaching, which is a very important key to their success. They are expected to deliver high quality report-outs to peers, champions, and executives. Upon course completion, black belts are expected to continue delivering financial beneficial projects; e.g., 4 – 6 projects per year with financial benefits of $500,000 - $1,000,000. Black belts can mentor green belts.

Bottleneck: The slowest operation in a chain of operations; it will pace the output of the entire line.

Box-Cox transformation: A general approach for transforming data to a normal distribution, where values (Y) are transformed to the power of λ; i.e., Y^{λ}.

Brainstorming: Consensus-building among experts about a problem or issue using group discussion.

Capability/performance metric: *See* Process capability/performance metric.

Capability, Process: See Process capability.

Categorical variables: Represent types of data which may be divided into groups. Examples of categorical variables are race, gender, age group, and educational level. While the latter two variables may also be considered in a numerical manner by using exact values for age and highest grade completed, it is often more informative to categorize such variables into a relatively small number of groups.

Cause-and-effect diagram (C&E diagram): This technique, sometimes called an Ishikawa diagram or fishbone diagram, is useful in problem solving using brainstorming sessions. With this technique, possible causes from such sources as materials, equipment, methods, and personnel are typically identified as a starting point to begin discussion.

Central limit theorem: The means of samples from a population will tend to be normally distributed around the population mean.

Champions: Executive-level managers who are responsible for managing and guiding the Lean Six Sigma or IEE deployment and its projects.

Checks sheets: Sheets used to systematically record and compile data from historical or current observations.

Chi-square test: The proper statistical name is the chi-square test of independence. This is different from the chi-square goodness-of-fit test, which has a different purpose. The only similarity is that the chi-square statistic is used for estimating significance. This volume uses the term chi-square test to describe a chi-square test of independence.

Coefficient: *See* Regression analysis.

Coefficient of determination (R^2): The correlation coefficient squared, where values for R^2 describe the percentage of variability accounted for by the model. For example, $R^2 = 0.8$ indicates that 80% of the variability in the data is accounted for by the model.

Coefficient of variation: A measure of dispersion where standard deviation is divided by the mean and is expressed as a percentage.

Common cause: Natural or random variation that is inherent in a process over time, affecting every outcome of the process. If a process is in-control, it has only common-cause variation and can be said to be predictable. When a process experiences common-cause variability but does not meet customer needs, it can be said that the process is not capable. Process or input variable change is needed to improve this situation; i.e., this metric is creating a pull for project creation.

Confidence interval: The region containing the limits or band of a parameter with an associated confidence level that the bounds are large enough to contain the true parameter value. The bands can be single-sided to describe an upper/lower limit or double-sided to describe both upper and lower limits.

Confounded: Two factor effects that are represented by the same comparison are aliases of one another, i.e., different names for the same computed effect. Two effects that are aliases of one another are confounded, or confused, with one another. Although the word *confounded* is commonly used to describe aliases between factorial effects and block effects, it can more generally be used to describe any effects that are aliases of one another.

Consumer's risk: *See* Beta (β) risk.

Continuous data (Variables data): Data that can assume a range of numerical responses on a continuous scale, as opposed to data that can assume only discrete levels.

Continuous distribution: A distribution used in describing the probability of a response when the output is continuous (see Response).

Contrast column effects: The effect in a contrast column, which might have considerations that are confounded.

Control chart: A procedure used to track a process with time for the purpose of determining if common or special causes exist.

Control: *In control* or predictable is used in process control charting to indicate when the chart shows that there are no indicators that the process is not predictable.

Correlation coefficient (r): A statistic that describes the strength of a relationship between two variables is the sample correlation coefficient. A correlation coefficient can take values between -1 and +1. A -1 indicates perfect negative correlation, while a +1 indicates perfect positive correlation. A zero indicates no correlation.

Cost of doing nothing differently (CODND): To keep IEE from appearing as a quality initiative, I prefer to reference the Six Sigma metric COPQ as the cost of doing nothing differently (CODND), which has even broader costing implications than COPQ. In this volume, I make reference to the CODND.

Cost of poor quality (COPQ): Traditionally, cost of quality issues have been given the broad categories of internal failure costs, external failure costs, appraisal costs, and prevention costs. See Glossary description for cost of doing nothing differently. Within Six Sigma, COPQ addresses the cost of not performing work correctly the first time or of not meeting customer's expectations.

Cumulative distribution function (CDF) [$F(x)$]: The calculated integral of the PDF from minus infinity to x. This integration takes on a characteristic "percentage less than or percentile" when plotted against x.

Customer: Someone for whom work or a service is performed. The end user of a product is a customer of the employees within a company that manufactures the product. There are also internal customers in a company. When an employee does work or performs a service for someone else in the company, the person who receives this work is a customer of this employee.

Cycle Time: Frequency that a part/product is completed by process. Also, time it takes for operator to go through work activities before repeating the activities. In addition, cycle time can be used to quantify customer order to delivery time.

DCP: Data Collection Plan

Discrete data: Discrete data are based on counts. Only a finite number of values are possible, and the values cannot be subdivided meaningfully; e.g., the number of parts damaged in shipment.

Defect: A nonconformity or departure of a quality characteristic from its intended level or state.

Defective: A nonconforming item that contains at least one defect or has a combination of several imperfections, causing the unit not to satisfy intended requirements.

Descriptive statistics: Descriptive statistics help pull useful information from data, whereas probability provides among other things a basis for inferential statistics and sampling plans.

Degrees of freedom (df or v): Number of measurements that are independently available for estimating a population parameter. For a random sample from a population, the number of degrees of freedom is equal to the sample size minus one.

Design of experiments (DOE): A structured experiment where the response effects of several factors are studied at one time.

Discrete data (Attribute data): The presence or absence of some characteristic in each device under test; e.g., proportion nonconforming in a pass/fail test.

Discrete distribution: A distribution function that describes the probability for a random discrete variable.

Discrimination (of a measurement system): Alias smallest readable unit, discrimination is the measurement resolution, scale limit, or smallest detectable unit of the measurement device and standard. It is an inherent property of gage design and reported as a unit of measurement or classification. The number of data categories is often referred to as the discrimination ratio (not to be confused with the discrimination ratio used in Poisson sequential testing) since it describes how many classifications can be reliably distinguished given the observed process variation (AIAG 2002).

Distinct data categories: The number of data classifications (ndc) or categories that can be reliably distinguished, determined by the effective resolution of the measurement system and part variation from the observed process for a given application. (AIAG 2002)

Distribution: A pattern that is followed from a random sample from a population. Described normal, Weibull, Poisson, binomial, and lognormal distributions are applicable to the modeling of various industrial situations.

DMAIC: Define-measure-analyze-improve-control Six Sigma roadmap.
DMADV: Define-measure-analyze-design-verify DFSS and DFIEE roadmap.

Dot plot: A plot of symbols that represent individual observations from a batch of data.

Double-sided test: A statistical consideration whereby, for example, an alternative hypothesis is that the mean of a population is not equal to a criterion value. *See* single-sided test.

DPMO: When using the non-conformance rate calculation of defects per million opportunities (DPMO), one needs first to describe what the opportunities for defects are in the process; e.g., the number of components and solder joints when manufacturing printed circuit boards. Next, the number of defects is periodically divided by the number of opportunities to determine the DMPO rate.

E-DMAIC (Roadmap): An IEE enterprise define-measure-analyze-improve-control roadmap, which contains among other things a value chain measurement and analysis system where metric improvement needs can pull for project creation.

Effect: The main effect of a factor in a two-level factorial experiment is the mean difference in responses between the two levels of the factor, which is averaged over all levels of the other factors.

Enterprise improvement plan (EIP): A project drill-down strategy that follows: goal—strategies—high potential area—projects.
Error (experimental): Ambiguities during data analysis caused from such sources as measurement bias, random measurement error, and mistake.

Error proofing: See Mistake proofing.

Experimental error: Variations in the experimental response under identical test conditions; also called residual error.

Factorial experiment: *See* Full factorial experiment and Fractional factorial experiment.

Factors: Variables that are studied at different levels in a designed experiment.

Failure: A device is said to fail when it no longer performs its intended function satisfactorily.

Failure mode and effects analysis (FMEA): Analytical approach directed toward problem prevention through the prioritization of potential problems and their resolution. Term is opposite of fault tree analysis.

Failure rate: Failures/unit time or failures/units of usage, i.e., l/MTBF. Sample failure rates are: 0.002 failures/hour, 0.0003 failures/auto miles traveled, 0.01 failures/1000 parts manufactured. Failure rate criterion (ρ_a) is a failure rate value that is not to be exceeded in a product. Tests to determine if a failure rate criterion is met can be fixed or sequential in duration. With fixed-length test plans, the test design failure rate (ρ_t) is the sample failure rate that cannot be exceeded in order to certify the criterion (ρ_a) at the boundary of the desired confidence level. With sequential test plans, failure rates ρ_1 and ρ_0 are used to determine the test plans.

50-foot-level: Low-level tracking of a key process input variable; e.g., process temperature when manufacturing plastic parts or daily salesperson activity. This type of chart can involve frequent sampling to make sure that the desired input level is maintained over time. Tracking at the 50-foot-level can lead to the timely detection and resolution of problems or undesirable drifts in input levels so that the 30,000-foot-level metric for product/service quality, timeliness, and other metrics is not jeopardized.

Fractional factorial experiment: A designed experiment strategy that assesses several factors/variables simultaneously in one test, where only a partial set of all possible combinations of factor levels is tested to identify important factors more efficiently. This type of test is much more efficient than a traditional one-at-a-time test strategy.

Full factorial experiment: Factorial experiment where all combinations of factor levels are tested.

Gage repeatability and reproducibility (R&R) study: The evaluation of measuring instruments to determine capability to yield a precise response. Gage repeatability is the variation in measurements, considering one part and one operator. Gage reproducibility is the variation between operators measuring one part.

Gantt chart: A bar chart that shows activities as blocks over time. A block's beginning and end correspond to the beginning and end date of the activity.

Green belts (GBs): Part-time practitioners who typically receive two weeks of training over two months. Their primary focus is on projects that are in their functional area. The inference that someone becomes a green belt before a black belt should not be made. Business and personal needs/requirements should influence the decision whether someone becomes a black belt or green belt. If someone's job requires a more in-depth skill set, such as the use of DOE, then the person should be trained as a black belt. Also, at deployment initiation black belt training should be conducted first so that this additional skill set can be used when coaching others.

Histogram: A frequency diagram in which bars proportionally in area to the class frequencies are erected on the horizontal axis. The width of each section corresponds to the class interval of the variate.

Hoshin kanri: Japanese name for policy deployment. Used by some Lean companies to guide their operations strategy.

Hypothesis: A tentative statement, which has a possible explanation to some event or phenomenon. Hypotheses are not a theoretical statement. Instead, hypotheses are to have a testable statement, which might include a prediction.

Hypothesis testing: Consists of a null hypothesis (H_0) and alternative hypothesis (H_a) where, for example, a null hypothesis indicates equality between two process outputs and an alternative hypothesis indicates non-equality. Through a hypothesis test, a decision is made whether to reject a null hypothesis or not.

When a null hypothesis is rejected, there is α risk of error. Most typically, there is no risk assignment when we fail to reject the null hypothesis. However, an appropriate sample size could be determined so that failure to reject the null hypothesis is made with β risk of error.

IEE: *See* Integrated enterprise excellence.

IEE scorecard/dashboard metric reporting process:
1. Assess process predictability.
2. When the process is considered predictable, formulate a prediction statement for the latest region of stability. The usual reporting format for this statement is:
   a. When there is a specification requirement: nonconformance percentage or defects per million opportunities (DPMO)
   b. When there are no specification requirements: median response and 80% frequency of occurrence rate

IEE Workout: See Workout (IEE).

Individuals control chart: A control chart of individual values where between-subgroup variability affects the calculated upper and lower control limits; i.e., the width between the upper and lower control limits increases when there is more between-subgroup variability. When plotted individuals chart data are within the upper and lower control limits and there are no patterns, the process is said to be stable/predictable and typically referenced as an in-control process. In IEE, this common-cause state is referenced as a predictable process. Control limits are independent of specification limits or targets.

In control: The description of a process where variation is consistent over time; i.e., only common causes exist. The process is predictable.

Infrequent subgrouping/sampling: Traditionally, rational subgrouping issues involve the selection of samples that yield relatively homogeneous conditions within the subgroup for a small region of time or space, perhaps five in a row. For an $\bar{x}$ and R chart, the within-subgroup variation defines the limits of the control chart on how much variation should exist between the subgroups. For a given situation, a differing subgrouping/sampling methodology can dramatically affect the measured variation within subgroups, which in turn affects the width of the control limits. For the high-level metrics of IEE, we want infrequent subgrouping/sampling so that short-term variations caused by KPIV perturbations are viewed as common-cause variability; i.e., typical process variability is to occur between subgroups in an individuals control chart. This type of control chart can reduce the amount of firefighting in an organization. However, this does not mean that a problem does not exist within the process. When process capability/performance metric improvements are needed for these metrics, we can initiate an IEE project; i.e., IEE projects are pulled into the system, as they are needed by the metrics.

Integrated Enterprise (process) Excellence (IEE, I double E): A roadmap for the creation of an enterprise process system in which organizations can significantly improve both customer satisfaction and their bottom line. IEE is a structured approach that guides organizations through the tracking and attainment of organizational goals. IEE goes well beyond traditional Lean Six Sigma and the balanced scorecard methods. IEE integrates enterprise process measures and improvement methodologies with tools such as Lean and Theory of constraints (TOC) in a never-ending pursuit of excellence. IEE becomes an enabling framework, which integrates, improves, and aligns with other initiatives such as Total Quality Management (TQM), ISO 9000, Malcolm Baldrige Assessments, and the Shingo Prize. IEE is the organizational orchestration that moves toward the achievement goal of the three Rs of Business; i.e., everyone is doing the Right things and doing them Right at the Right time.

Interaction: A description for the measure of the differential comparison of response for each level of a factor at each of the several levels of one or more other factors.

Inventory turns: The number of times that a company's inventory cycles or turns over per year.

Kaizen: Continuous incremental improvement.

Kaizen event or blitz: An intense short-term project that gives focus to improve a process. Substantial resources are committed during this event; e.g., Operators, Engineering, Maintenance, and others are available for immediate action. A facilitator directs the event, which usually includes training followed by analysis, design, and area rearrangement.

KPIV (Key Process Input Variable): Factors within a process correlated to an output characteristic(s) important to the internal or external customer. Optimizing and controlling these is vital to the improvement of the KPOV.

KPOV (Key Process Output Variable): Characteristic(s) of the output of a process that are important to the customer. Understanding what is important to the internal and external customer is essential to identifying KPOVs.

Lambda plot: A technique to determine a normalizing transformation for data.

Lean: Improving operations and the supply chain with an emphasis on the reduction of wasteful activities such as waiting, transportation, material hand-offs, inventory, and overproduction.

Lead time: Time for one piece to move through a process or a value stream. Lead time can also describe the setup time to start a process.

Levels: The settings of factors in a factorial experiment (e.g., high and low levels of temperature).

Location parameter (x_0): A parameter in the three-parameter Weibull distribution that equates to the minimum value for the distribution.

Main effect: An estimate of the effect of a factor measured independently of other factors.

Master black belts (MBBs): Black belts who have undertaken two weeks of advanced training and have a proven track record delivering results through various projects and project teams. They should be a dedicated resource to the deployment. Before they train, master black belts need to be certified in the material that they are to deliver. Their responsibilities include coaching black belts, monitoring team progress, and assisting teams when needed.

Maximum likelihood estimator (MLE): Maximum likelihood estimates are calculated through maximizing the likelihood function. For each set of distribution parameters, the likelihood function describes the chance that the true distribution has the parameters based on the sample.

Mean: The mean of a sample ($\bar{x}$) is the sum of all the responses divided by the sample size. The mean of a population (μ) is the sum of all responses of the population divided by the population size. In a random sample of a population, $\bar{x}$ is an estimate of the μ of the population.

Measurement systems: The complete process of obtaining measurements. This includes the collection of equipment, operations, procedures, software, and personnel that affects the assignment of a number to a measurement characteristic.

Measurement systems analysis: *See* Gage repeatability and reproducibility (R&R).

Measurement system error: The combined variation due to gage bias, repeatability, reproducibility, stability, and linearity (AIAG 2000).

Median: For a sample, the number that is in the middle when all observations are ranked in magnitude. For a population, the value at which the cumulative distribution function is 0.5.

Metric: a measurement that quantifies a particular characteristic.

Mistake-proofing: A structured approach for process or design creation so that specific mistakes will not occur or which makes a mistake obvious at a glance; i.e., error-proofing or poke-yoke.

Multimodal distribution: A combination of more than one distribution that has more than one distinct peak.

Multi-vari chart: A chart that is constructed to display the variation within units, between units, between samples, and between lots.

Nonconformance: Failure to meet specification requirement.

Nominal group technique (NGT): A voting procedure to expedite team consensus on relative importance of problems, issues, or solutions.

Normal distribution: A bell-shaped distribution that is often useful to describe various physical, mechanical, electrical, and chemical properties.

Null hypothesis (H_0): *See* Hypothesis testing.

One-at-a-time experiment: An individual tries to fix a problem by making a change and then executing a test. Depending on the findings, something else may need to be tried. This cycle is repeated indefinitely.

One-sided test: *See* Single-sided test.

One-way analysis of variance: *See* single-factor analysis of variance.

Outlier: A data point that does not fit a model because of an erroneous reading or some other abnormal situation.

Out of control: Control charts exhibit special-cause conditions. The process is not predictable.

Pareto chart: A graphical technique used to quantify problems so that effort can be expended in fixing the "vital few" causes, as opposed to the "trivial many." Named after Vilfredo Pareto (born 1848), an Italian economist.

Pareto principle: Eighty percent of the trouble comes from 20% of the problems, i.e., the vital few problems.

Part variation (PV): Related to measurement systems analysis, PV represents the expected part-to-part and time-to-time variation for a stable process (AIAG 2002).

Passive analysis: In IEE and a traditional DMAIC, most Six Sigma tools are applied in the same phase. However, the term passive analysis is often used in IEE to describe the analyze phase, where process data are observed passively, i.e., with no process adjustments, in an attempt to find a causal relationship between input and output variables. It should be noted that improvements can be made in any of the phases. If there is "low-hanging fruit" identified during a brainstorming session in the measure phase, this improvement can be made immediately, yielding a dramatic improvement to the 30,000-foot-level output metric.

P-DMAIC (Roadmap): An IEE project define-measure-analyze-improve-control roadmap for improvement project execution, which contains a true integration of Six Sigma and Lean tools.

Percent (%) R&R: The percentage of process variation related to the measurement system for repeatability and reproducibility.

Performance, Process: *See* Process performance.

Plan-do-check-act (PDCA) or Plan-do-study-act (PDSA): PDCA is frequently referred to as the Deming cycle or Shewhart cycle. The check step can be replaced by a study step; i.e., PDSA. PDCA has the following components: Plan – Recognize a need for change and then establish objectives and process for delivering desired results; Do – Implement change that is to be assessed; Check – study results and identify lessons learned; Act – Use lessons learned to take appropriate action. If change was not satisfactory, repeat the process.

Point estimate: An estimate calculated from sample data without a confidence interval.

Population: Statistically, a population is a group of data from a single distribution. In a practical sense, a population could also be considered to be a segment or a group of data from a single source or category. In the process of explaining tools and techniques, multiple populations may be discussed as originating from different sources, locations, or machines.

Predictable: The control limits in a control chart are calculated from the data. Specifications in no way affect the control limits. This chart is a statement of the voice of the process (VOP) relative to whether the process is considered in statistical control or not; i.e., stable or not. Since people often have difficulty in understanding what *in control* means, I prefer to use the term *predictable* instead of *in control*.

Predictable process: A stable, controlled process where variation in outputs is caused only by natural or random variation in the inputs or in the process itself.

Probability (*P*): A numerical expression for the likelihood of an occurrence.

Probability density function (PDF) [*f*(*x*)]: A mathematical function that can model the probability density reflected in a histogram.

Probability plot: Data are plotted on a selected probability plot coordinate system to determine if a particular distribution is appropriate (i.e., the data plot as a straight line) and to make statements about percentiles of the population. The plot can be used to make prediction statements about stable/predictable processes.

Process capability/performance metric: IEE uses the term process capability/performance metric to describe a process's predictive output in terms that everyone can understand. The process to determine this metric is: 1. An infrequent subgrouping/sampling plan is determined so that the typical variability from process input factors occurs between subgroups, e.g., subgroup by day, week, or month. 2. The process is analyzed for predictability using control charts. 3. For the region of predictability, the non-compliant proportion or parts per million (ppm) are estimated and reported. If there are no specifications, the estimated median response and 80% frequency of occurrence are reported.

Producer's risk: *See* Alpha (α) risk.

Pull: A Lean term that results in an activity when a customer or down-stream process step requests the activity. A homebuilder that builds houses only when an agreement is reached on the sale of the house is using a pull system. *See* push.

Push: A Lean term that results in an activity that a customer or down-stream process step has not specifically requested. This activity can create excessive waste and/or inventory. A homebuilder that builds houses on the speculation of sale is using a push system. If the house does not sell promptly upon completion, the homebuilder has created excess inventory for his company, which can be very costly. *See* pull.

***P* value or *P*:** The significance level for a term in a model.

Regression analysis: Data collected from an experiment are used to quantify empirically through a mathematical model the relationship that exists between the response variable and influencing factors. In a simple linear regression model, $y = b_0 + b_1 x + \varepsilon$, x is the regressor, y is the expected response, b_0 and b_1 are coefficients, and ε is random error.

Regressor: *See* Regression analysis.

Repeatability: The variability resulting from successive trials under defined conditions of measurement. Often referred to as equipment variation (EV); however, this can be a misleading term. The best term for repeatability is *within*-system variation when the conditions of measurement are fixed and defined, i.e., fixed part, instrument, standard, method, operator, environment, and assumptions. In addition to within-equipment variation, repeatability will include all within variation from the conditions in the measurement error model. (AAIG 2002)

Replication: Test trials that are made under identical conditions.

Reproducibility: The variation in the average of measurements caused by a normal condition(s) of change in the measurement process. Typically, it has been defined as the variation in average measurements of the same part between different appraisers (operators) using the same measurement instrument and method in a stable environment. This is often true for manual instruments influenced by the skill of the operator. It is not true, however, for measurement processes, i.e., automated systems, where the operator is not a major source of variation. For this reason, reproducibility is referred to as the average variation *between*-systems or *between*-conditions of measurement. (AIAG 2002)

Residuals: In an experiment, the differences between experimental responses and predicted values that are determined from a model.

Residual error: Also called experimental error. An ANOVA output can list residual error as having a pure error and lack-of-fit component. Pure error is represented by replicates since the differences between observed responses are caused by random variation. During model term reduction when a resulting lack-of-fit P value is less than the selected α level, the term that was removed from the model should be retained.

Resolution III: A DOE where main effects and two-factor interaction effects are confounded.

Resolution IV: A DOE where the main effects and two-factor interaction effects are not confounded; however, two-factor interaction effects are confounded with each other.

Resolution V: A DOE where all main effects and two-factor interaction effects are not confounded with other main effects or two-factor interaction effects.

Resolution V+: Full factorial designed experiment.

Response: Three described outputs are continuous (variables), attribute (discrete), and logic pass/fail. A response is said to be continuous if any value can be taken between limits (e.g., 2, 2.0001, and 3.00005). A response is said to be attribute if the evaluation takes on a pass/fail proportion output; e.g., 999 out of 1000 sheets of paper on the average can be fed through a copier without a jam. In this series of volumes, a response is considered to be logic pass/fail if combinational considerations are involved that are said always to cause an event either to pass or fail; e.g., a computer display design will not work in combination with a particular keyboard design and software package.

Risk priority number (RPN): Product of severity, occurrence, and detection rankings within an FMEA. The ranking of RPN prioritizes design concerns; however, issues with a low RPN still deserve special attention if the severity ranking is high.

Rolled throughput yield (RTY): For a process that has a series of steps, RTY is the product of yields for each step.

Run (control chart): A consecutive number of points, for example, that are consistently decreasing, increasing, or on one side of the central line in a control chart.

Run chart: A time series plot permits the study of observed data for trends or patterns over time, where the x-axis is time and the y axis is the measured variable.

Sample size: The number of observations made or the number of items taken from a population.

Sarbanes-Oxley (SOX): This legislation act was created in 2002 partly in response to the Enron and WorldCom financial scandals. SOX protects shareholders and the public from enterprise process accounting errors and from fraudulent practices. In addition, it also ensures a degree of consistency in access to and reporting of information that could impact the value of a company's stock.

Satellite-level: Used to describe a high-level IEE business metric that has infrequent subgrouping/sampling so that short-term variations, which are caused by typical variation from key process input variables, will result in control charts that view these as common-cause variability. This metric has no calendar boundaries and the latest region of stability can be used to provide a predictive statement for the future.

Scatter plot: A plot to assess the relationship between two variables. A scatter plot is sometimes called a scatterplot or a scatter diagram.

Sigma: The Greek letter (σ) that is often used to describe the standard deviation of a population.

Sigma level or sigma quality level: A quality that is calculated by some to describe the capability of a process to meet specification. A six sigma quality level is said to have a 3.4 ppm rate.

Significance: A statistical statement indicating that the level of a factor causes a difference in a response with a certain degree of risk of being in error.

Single-factor analysis of variance ANOVA: One-way analysis of variance with two levels (or treatments) that is to determine if there is a statistically significant difference between level effects.

Single-sided test: A statistical consideration where, for example, an alternative hypothesis is that the mean of a population is less than a criterion value. *See* double-sided test.

SIPOC (supplier-input-process-output-customer): A tool that describes the events from trigger to delivery at the targeted process. Provides a snapshot of workflow, where the process aspect of the diagram consists of only 4-7 blocks.

Six Sigma: This is a term coined by Motorola that emphasizes the improvement of processes for the purpose of reducing variability and making general improvements. GE in the mid 1990s expanded the scope of Six Sigma so that it became a project-based selection and execution system with a support infrastructure, where projects were to have organizational benefits.

SMART goals: Not everyone uses the same letter descriptors for SMART. My preferred descriptors are italicized in the following list: S - *specific*, significant, stretching; M - *measurable*, meaningful, motivational; A - agreed upon, attainable, achievable, acceptable, action-oriented, *actionable*; R - realistic, *relevant*, reasonable, rewarding, results-oriented; T - *time-based*, timely, tangible, trackable.

Special cause: Variation in a process from a cause that is not an inherent part of that process. That is, it's not a common cause.

Stability: Refers to both statistical stability of measurement process and measurement stability over time. Both are vital for a measurement system to be adequate for its intended purpose. Statistical stability implies a predictable, underlying measurement process operating within common-cause variation.

Stakeholders: Those people or organizations who are not directly involved with project work but are affected its success or can influence its results. Examples of stakeholders are process owners, managers affected by the project, and people who work in the studied process. Stakeholders also include internal departments, which support the process, finance, suppliers, and customers.

Standard deviation (σ, s): A mathematical quantity that describes the variability of a response. It equals the square root of variance. The standard deviation of a sample (s) is used to estimate the standard deviation of a population (σ).

Standard error: The square root of the variance of the sampling distribution of a statistic.

Statistical process control (SPC): The application of statistical techniques in the control of processes. SPC is often considered a subset of SQC, where the emphasis in SPC is on the tools associated with the process but not on product acceptance techniques.

Statistical quality control (SQC): The application of statistical techniques in the control of quality. SQC includes the use of regression analysis, tests of significance, acceptance sampling, control charts, distributions, and so on.

Stratified random sampling: Samples can be either from random sampling with replacement or random sampling without replacement. In addition, there are more complex forms of sampling such as stratified random sampling. For this form of sampling, a certain number of random samples are drawn and analyzed from divisions to the population space.

Subgrouping: Traditionally, rational subgrouping issues involve the selection of samples that yield relatively homogeneous conditions within the subgroup for a small region of time or space, perhaps five in a row. Hence, the within-subgroup variation defines the limits of the control chart on how much variation should exist between the subgroups. For a given situation, differing subgrouping/sampling methodologies can dramatically affect the measured variation within subgroups, which in turn affect the width of the control limits. For the high-level metrics of IEE, we want infrequent subgrouping/sampling so that typical short-term KPIV perturbations are viewed as common-cause variabiltiy. A 30,000-foot-level individuals control chart, which is created with infrequent subgrouping/sampling, can reduce the amount of firefighting in an organization. However, this does not mean that a problem does not exist within the process. IEE describes approaches to view the process capability/performance metric, or how well the process meets customer specifications or overall business needs. When improvements are needed to a process capability/performance metric, we can create an IEE project that focuses on this need; i.e., IEE projects are pulled for creation when metric improvements are needed.

Sum of squares (*SS*): The summation of the squared deviations relative to zero, to level means, or the grand mean of an experiment.

Theory of constraints (TOC): Constraints can be broadly classified as being internal resource, market, or policy. The outputs of a system are a function of the whole system, not just individual processes. System performance is a function of how well constraints are identified and managed. When we view our system as a whole, we realize that the output is a function of the weakest link. The weakest link of the system is the constraint. If care is not exercised, we can be focusing on a subsystem that, even though improved, does not impact the overall system output. We need to focus on the orchestration of efforts so that we optimize the overall system, not individual pieces. Unfortunately, organization charts lead to workflow by function, which can result in competing forces within the organization. With TOC, systems are viewed as a whole and work activities are directed so that the whole system performance measures are improved.

Three Rs of business: Everyone doing the Right things and doing them Right at the Right time.

30,000-foot-level: A Six Sigma KPOV, CTQ, or Y variable response that is used in IEE to describe a high-level project or operation metric that has infrequent subgrouping/sampling so that short-term variations, which might be caused by typical KPIV swings, will result in charts that view these perturbations as common-cause variability. It is not the intent of the 30,000-foot-level control chart to provide timely feedback for process intervention and correction, as traditional control charts do. Examples of 30,000-foot-level metrics are lead time, inventory, defective rates, and a critical part dimension. There can be a drill down to a 20,000-foot-level metric if there is an alignment; e.g., the largest product defect type. A 30,000-foot-level individuals control chart can reduce the amount of firefighting in an organization when used to report operational metrics. As a business metric, 30,000-foot-level reporting can lead to more efficient resource utilization and less playing games with the numbers.

TOC: *See* Theory of constraints.

Toyota production system (TPS): Toyota developed techniques that focus on adding value and reducing waste through setup, lead time, and lot size reduction. The term has become synonymous with Lean manufacturing.

TQM: *See* Total quality management.

Trial: One of the factor combinations in an experiment.

t test: A statistical test that utilizes tabular values from the t distribution to assess, for example, whether two population means are different.

20,000-foot-level: A cascading of a 30,000-foot-level metric, which still has infrequent subgrouping/sampling. A 20,000-foot-level metric could be the tracking of the largest defect from a 30,000-foot-level metric. Another 20,000-foot-level metric could be the cascading of a corporate on-time delivery 30,000-foot-level metric to one site's on-time delivery performance.

Type I error: *See* Alpha (α) risk.

Type II error: *See* Beta (β) risk.

Type III error: Answering the wrong question.

Two-sided test: *See* Double-sided test.

Value chain: Describes in flowchart fashion both primary and support organizational activities and their accompanying 30,000-foot-level or satellite-level metrics. An example primary activity flow is develop product—market product—sell product—produce product—invoice/collect payments—report satellite-level metrics. Examples of support activities include IT, finance, HR, labor relations, safety & environment, and legal.

Value stream mapping: At Toyota, value stream mapping is known as "material and information flow mapping." In the Toyota production system, current and future states/ideal states are depicted by practitioners when they are developing plans to install Lean systems. Attention is given to establishing flow, eliminating waste, and adding value. Toyota views manufacturing flows as material, information, and people/process. The described value-stream mapping covers the first two of these three items (Rother and Shook 1999).

Variables data (Continuous data): Data that can assume a range of numerical responses on a continuous scale, as opposed to data that can assume only discrete levels.

Variance (Statistical) [σ^2, s^2]: A measure of dispersion of observations based upon the mean of the squared deviations from the arithmetic mean.

Validation: Proof after implementation of an action over time and that the action does what is intended. *See* verification.

Verification: The act of establishing and documenting whether processes, items, services, or documents conform to a specified requirement. Verification is proof before implementation that an action does what is intended. *See* validation.

Voice of the customer (VOC): The identification and prioritization of true customer needs and requirements, which can be accomplished through focus groups, interviews, data analyses, and other methods.

Voice of the process (VOP): A quantification of what the process delivers. A voice of the process to voice of the customer needs assessment can identify process improvement focus areas; e.g., a 30,000-foot-level assessment indicates an 11% delivery-time non-conformance rate.

Waste: Seven elements to consider for the elimination of muda, a Japanese term for waste, are correction, overproduction, processing, conveyance, inventory, motion, and waiting.

WIP: A general description for inventory that is being processed within an operation or is awaiting another operation.

Work in process (WIP): *See* WIP.

Work in progress (WIP): *See* WIP.

Workout (IEE): An IEE workout is a week-long concentrated effort to build the E-DMAIC framework; i.e., a kaizen event to create the E-DMAIC framework. Typically on Monday and Tuesday there is an executive workshop, which among other things describes IEE and its structure. On Wednesday through Thursday the facilitator works with an IEE in-house technical team and others to build the E-DMAIC framework with its process drilldowns. On Friday, a two-hour report out of the customization of the E-DMAIC system, as described on Monday, is presented to the executive team that attended the Monday session. This presentation will include, among other things, a comparison of a sample of their 30,000-foot-level metric report outs with their current reporting methods. After the week-long session, the workout facilitator will continue work with the IEE in-house technical team to continually refine their E-DMAIC system.

WOTO: Wisdom of the Organization

Yellow belts (YBs): Process improvement team members who typically receive three-days of training, which helps them in the effectiveness of their participation in project execution such as data collection, identifying voice of the customer, and team meetings.

14 Appendix E: References

- AIAG (1995a), *Advanced Product Quality Planning (APQP) and Control Plan Reference Manual*, Chrysler Corporation, Ford Motor Company, General Motors Corporation.
- Breyfogle, F. W. (2008a), *Integrated Enterprise Excellence Volume I - The Basics: Four Golfing Buddies Going Beyond Lean Six Sigma and the Balanced Scorecard*, Bridgeway Books, Austin, TX.
- Breyfogle, F. W. (2008b), *Integrated Enterprise Excellence Volume II - Business Deployment: A Leaders' Guide for Going Beyond Lean Six Sigma and the Balanced Scorecard*, Bridgeway Books, Austin, TX.
- Breyfogle, F. W. (2008c), *Integrated Enterprise Excellence Volume III - Improvement Project Execution: A Management and Black Belt Guide for Going Beyond Lean Six Sigma and the Balanced Scorecard*, Bridgeway Books, Austin, TX.
- Breyfogle, F. W. (2008d), *The Integrated Enterprise Excellence System: An Enhanced Approach to Balanced Scorecards, Strategic Planning and Business Improvement*, Bridgeway Books, Austin, TX.
- Breyfogle, F. W. (2003), *Implementing Six Sigma*, 2nd edition, Wiley, NJ.
- Goldratt, E. M. (1992), *The Goal*, 2nd ed., North River Press, New York.
- Jones, D. (1999), *Everyday Creativity*, Star Thrower Distribution Corp., St. Paul, MN.
- Nakajima, S. (1988), *Introduction to TPM: Total Productive Maintenance*, Productivity Press, Portland, OR.
- Snee, R. D., and Hoerl, R. W. (2003), *Leading Six Sigma*, Prentice Hall, New York.